GLIMPSES OF A SOUL

ON PEACE: "I've no doubt war will come. Nor do I doubt that we will win. But for how long? Until when? We can't wipe out the Arab people. Hence the sadness, the sadness of young men destined for endless war."

ON YOUTH: "In another week I'll be twenty-three, and I do not regret what I have done and what I'm about to do. I'm convinced that what I'm doing is right. I believe in myself, in my country, and in my future. I also believe in my family. That's a great deal for a man of my age who has already managed to feel very young and very old."

ON ZIONISM: "I belong to Israel, Father, the way Israel belongs to me and to you and to every other Jew."

ON LIFE IN ISRAEL: "The gap between our daily life and our political life is astounding. We are facing a series of wars (which we shall win), yet we spend our time on arguments about religious laws in the Knesset, on airline strikes, on buying fabrics and antique furniture, and on 'when shall we get married.' Maybe it's just as well, but there is something comic and pathetic about it. There are also some crumbs of what is eternally human."

SCULPTURE BY MIRI MARGOLIN, 1978. PHOTOGRAPH BY I. ZAFRIR.

SELF-PORTRAIT
OF A
HERO

FROM THE LETTERS OF
JONATHAN NETANYAHU, 1963-1976

JONATHAN NETANYAHU

With Notes and an Afterword by his brother
Iddo Netanyahu

WARNER BOOKS

A Time Warner Company

Grateful acknowledgment is made to Doris-Jeanne Gourévitch for permission to use her translation of a poem by Paul Verlaine, from *Selected Verse*, entitled "Autumn Song."

WARNER BOOKS EDITION

This Warner Books edition is published by arrangement with Random House, New York, NY

Warner Books, Inc., 1271 Avenue of the Americas, New York, NY 10020

Visit our Web site at http://warnerbooks.com

A Time Warner Company

Printed in the United States of America

First Warner Books Printing: May 1998

10 9 8 7 6 5 4 3 2 1

Library of Congress Cataloging-in-Publication Data

Netanyahu, Yonatan, 1946-1976.
 [Mikhteve Yoni. English]
 Self-portrait of a hero : from the letters of Jonathan Netanyahu, 1963-1976 / Jonathan Netanyahu ; with notes and an afterword by his brothers Benjamin and Iddo Netanyahu.
    p. cm.
 Originally published: New York : Random House, c1980.
 ISBN 0-446-67461-3
 1. Netanyahu, Yonatan, 1946-1976--Correspondence. 2. Israel. Tseva haganah le-Yisra 'el--Officers--Correspondence. I. Netanyahu, Binyamin. II. Netanyahu, 'Ido. III. Title.
U55.N46A313 1998
356'.166'092--dc21
 [B]   98-10170
                                                   CIP

Cover design by Rachel McClain

Contents

Foreword

THE GATHERING OF YONI'S LETTERS began shortly after his death. Within a few weeks, we managed to get hold of more than three hundred and thirty, written to his family, friends and fellow soldiers. They stretch across a period of thirteen years: from March 28, 1963, when he had just turned seventeen, to a few days before he fell in Uganda on July 4, 1976.

Not all of Yoni's letters were incorporated in this volume, nor were all the letters it contains reproduced in their entirety. We included, however, the greater part of the material, and we consistently retained every passage that throws light on Yoni's life.

The bulk of the translation from the Hebrew into English was done by Shoshana Perla; the last section was translated by Miriam Arad. Both did their work skillfully and conscientiously. Ruth Rigbi, who checked part of the translation, and Edward Grossman, who went over the whole of it, made a number of fine revisions and suggestions. Our own part was primarily to see to it that the translation was faithful to the original throughout—in style as well as in content. Lastly, Anne Freedgood of Random House added her final touches.

The six chapters of the book correspond to the periods into which Yoni's life from 1963 to 1976 may be divided. We have preceded each chapter with some background data pertinent to the period in which the letters were written. We have also added an Afterword on some aspects of Yoni's thinking which may offer a fuller understanding of his views in the latter years of his life.

Finally, we wish to express our gratitude to all those who provided us with Yoni's letters, and to those who were helpful in producing the English version presented in these pages.

— BENJAMIN AND IDDO NETANYAHU

Ode to Yoni

SHORTLY AFTER YONI FELL AT
Entebbe, I met with a British television producer who wanted to discuss
a dramatization of my brother's life. After reviewing the events of Yoni's
life and death, the producer said to me: "Leave it alone. A great biog-
raphy or play of a great life needs the perspective of decades."

Two decades have passed since that day, and each year I am reminded
of the wisdom of that advice. For Yoni's image grows with the passage of
time, as does the appreciation of his unique character. That spirit, that
willingness to throw himself into the maelstrom of Israel's struggle to sur-
vive, was captured best by Yoni himself. Unknowingly, he was his own
biographer. The letters he wrote to the members of his family, to his
friends, and to the women in his life offer a compelling record of not only
the turbulent events in the life of a warrior but the passionate inner soul
of a noble spirit.

Perhaps before I die a great work of art will be made about Yoni. But
I will take with me to my last days, as I experienced from my earliest ones,
the imprint of his fortitude and courage, his belief in the justice of our
cause, his steadfastness in the face of the greatest adversity, and, above all,
his humor and humanity.

The death of a brother cut down in his prime is traumatic in every
way; it changed my life and directed it to its present course. But the
impact on a brother is a distant second to the greatest agony of all, the
death of a son. Over the years, as I have visited agonizing parents who
have lost their children in battle or to bouts of savage terrorism, I have

grieved for them as I grieved for my parents. And it is to all the parents of Israel who have borne the ultimate sacrifice that I dedicate this book. They can find comfort in the fact that in Yoni's testament there resonates the private heroism of so many of Israel's fallen sons.

—BENJAMIN NETANYAHU

THE
UNITED STATES
(1963–1964)

Counselor in Young Judea Camp in New Hampshire, 1962

Iₙ JANUARY 1963, YONI AND HIS TWO younger brothers went to the United States with their parents, Benzion and Cela Netanyahu. The family, long-time residents of Jerusalem, was to live for some years in America while Benzion, then editor-in-chief of the *Encyclopedia Judaica,* pursued his researches in Jewish history. For Yoni, seventeen years old, this move constituted a profound change.

President of the student body at his high school in Jerusalem, an outstanding student in the eleventh grade and head of his Scout troop, Yoni now faced a world he barely knew. Entering an American high school in mid-term, he had to cope with problems stemming from the social, linguistic and educational differences between Israel and the United States. But what distressed him most was his separation from Israel, from the life he led there and from his friends, even though he knew that this separation would last only a year and a half, until his enlistment in the Israeli army.

March 28, 1963

Koshe,*

It's almost three months since I came to America. I go to a very nice school. Half the people know me as "the boy from Israel," but the truth is I haven't got a single friend here. Not because they don't welcome foreigners (quite the contrary, they want to befriend us), but because *I* keep aloof. And I do so not because I dislike them, but because I feel I belong to a different world. I'm remote from them, and as time goes by, the distance doesn't diminish, but quite the reverse—it increases continually.

There's not a moment here—even the most precious and beautiful one —that I wouldn't trade for my immediate return to Israel. My friends in Israel, my social life there, and above all the land itself—I miss very much.

Longing is difficult to describe. I always used to laugh at the word; I

*Yosi Karpeles, one of Yoni's schoolmates in Jerusalem.

always thought that you could forget, but I was wrong; believe me you can't. To adapt oneself to a new life—yes, that's possible; but to forget the old—that's impossible.

And I want to return, return, return . . . the word keeps floating up to the surface . . . without purpose, without hope . . . yet always gnawing, stabbing, hurting.

April 7, 1963

Rina,*

I'm here, I live here, yet I'm not really here. I'm far from here, yet far from Israel too . . . Sometimes I think I'm caught in a dream. Not the kind of dream that when you awake from it, you return to reality, but a dream which *is* reality . . . the only reality there is. I feel as if I'm wrapped in smoke. Alone in a crowd.

If you've ever sat in a bar in a dark corner with distant voices in the background and people moving round and round, seemingly close to you yet you don't belong to them, you don't belong to anyone, you're *far away* from them—if you've ever experienced this feeling, you might understand the reality in which I find myself.

I look outside the window and see a pale moon shrouded in a misty sky. The moonlight is faint, illuminating nothing. I look at the sky and there are no stars—it's all darkness. Between the sky and the window I see the tips of the bare branches of two huge trees and through them the stain of light from above.

I don't know why I described the moon. Maybe so you could understand the feeling that has taken hold of me at this moment, past one o'clock in the morning; a feeling that isn't fleeting or unique to this night, but constant, always reappearing.

I live in a certain reality, but it's a reality that doesn't touch me.

April 8, 1963

Dear Koshe,

How did you manage to appear out of the blue, like the morning star? Your letter brightened my spirits, brought them out of the darkness into

*A fellow Scout leader with Yoni in Jerusalem.

the light, if only foɪ a moment. Go to Ephraim Kishon* and ask him to recommend you as a writer of a study on humor in Israel. Your wretched jokes almost made me laugh.

Listen, it's not worth your while to send time-bombs by mail because I'm bursting anyway, waiting for the moment when I'll be able to go back. Besides, a bomb costs money; and besides—I want to live.

"A wide and spacious country," said Yoni. All this space that surrounds me leaves me without any air to breathe. I yearn for a place that's narrow, hot, rotten, filthy—a place that's more than 60 percent desert and that one can scarcely find on a map of the world; a place full of special problems, where not to be a party member is practically a crime; a place just right for dumb killers, who don't know that if you want to bump someone off, you don't inform him ahead of time (bombs, my friend, bombs!).

My friend—I'm a very good student; I've overcome the language problem and the rest of my difficulties in school. I've found that if I want to learn something, I can do it very well. All it takes is a little work and effort.

Now I feel good; I'm on vacation and have just come back from Naomi's in Washington,† and I received a letter from Israel (that is, from Koshe). Write soon, or else I'll sink into a depression and perhaps not live to see the beloved Land, its dear people, fathers and sons, etc.

April 10, 1963

Koshe,

I'm in a letter-writing mood.

Your last letter moved me to renew the ties between me and those I left behind. Why haven't I written until now? I don't know. But I know that from now on I will write.

I've taken on a new role here in the U.S.—making propaganda for Israel. A month ago I was interviewed in the student newspaper. Apparently the interview was quite successful; I'm being invited to homes, parties, etc., because "the parents want to meet me." Last night I stayed up until one in the morning with four girls and a boy and preached Zionism and such. I'm glad to note that I've discovered a number of

*Israeli satirical writer.
†Naomi Harman, daughter of Abraham Harman, at that time Israel's ambassador to the United States.

human beings here with a high level of wisdom and intelligence. The trouble with the youth here is that their lives are meager in content, drifting as though in a dream or a game.

April 20, 1963

Rina,

A long time ago, nearly a year now, when I took on the leadership of the troop,* the first thing I had to do was to form a team, to find counselors, and then—even before I really knew you—when I asked you to leave the *Ein Gedi* troop to become a group leader in *Arazim,* and you began to talk, I thought suddenly, "I'm sorry for her, she thinks too much!"

I'm sorry for you and for everyone who grapples with the life about him, with life as we see it, in all its frailty and ugliness. It's clear to me that there are people who find their lives complete, altogether flawless, although they lack a purpose and a future. Countless times I have envied a child's existence and gone back into my past, to the perfect world of an infant hidden in the grass, gazing at the world with eyes full of wonder and love, for whom all is his and he is all.

Someone once told me, "Learn to love man as he is; don't try to find in him what is in yourself." I haven't learned that yet. I come in contact with people, but I'm not one of them. I live, but in a world that's shattered and ruined. I study, but I don't learn a thing. Why am I like this and not different? I'm sorry that I'm not like the others. I've thought more than once: I'm born, I live, even create—and in the end I die. I'll turn to dust and my grave will be trodden on by others who in their turn will die too to preserve the endless cycle of life and death. It can't be that I live in order to create—if that were so, why should death overtake me? And if I live in order to die—why do I live at all? Why was I born? In that case, it would have been better not to have been born at all.

The instinctive life-force drives me to go on. Perhaps the only reason for my existence is to try to find answers to the questions that plague me.

Write me more about everyone in *Arazim,* write about them in the greatest detail—what are they doing? What are the problems of the troop? Write about each and every group leader. How do they get on together? When I was a part of *Arazim* and *Arazim* a part of me, I considered it most important for me to be aware of these matters so that

*The Jerusalem Scout troop called *Arazim* ("The Cedars").

all of you could function as a team. I know I took an interest in each person, in his problems and aspirations. I'm writing about *Arazim* and myself in the past tense. Perhaps I'll never return to it, but I feel that its successes and failures are mine, even when I cannot influence the course of events.

How do I live in America? I get up in the morning, go to school, come home and study. Read a great deal and walk. Go to bed. Another day gone. A day without content or meaning. A day that will dawn again tomorrow only to die out too.

Two things can happen to an Israeli in America—either he becomes a full-fledged American (something that, I'm sorry to say, I have seen happen many times), or he becomes, in blood and spirit, more of an Israeli than he has ever been. I'm waiting for the moment I can go back—and begin to live again.

See you,
Yoni

April 21, 1963

(To Rina)
"There is no limit and no end to man's understanding." I live in this moment; I die in another. Is there any difference between the two? Are they not one and the same? There are times it is better to die than to live, and sometimes it is better not to feel than to suffer. Then there are times it is also good to feel that there's a purpose to your actions, that you're not helpless but strong, that you are great and mighty. Sometimes it is good to believe that man is a giant, a force before whom nothing can stand.

"Where there's a will, there's a way." Is that really so? Can man really overcome everything?

Null and void, all is vanity, concept veiled within concept, a dense fog concealing everything, a breath on the mirror clouding the image. . . .

I am consumed from within. I live without purpose, aching and crying out. I despair.

At this moment I'm going to sleep. It's still early. Too early. Why don't I want to stay awake? Because I've nothing to do while awake. Study? What for? I see no point in it. Read? Read what? What will I gain from the writings of others? They write of their own concerns, ideas, lives. That will not do to solve the problems of my life.

Well then, fall asleep? What for? So I can get up tomorrow and repeat the process again. Do I need sleep? Why, I'm not tired at all. This is a moment of emptiness. A moment that holds nothing. A moment of eternity. . . .

> Smoke, curling and spreading, covers everything;
> Rising, ascending in heavy columns.
> The land, enraged, can find no peace;
> Fearful, atremble, it struggles in secret,
> Waging a soundless bitter battle.
> All is in vain, all is over,
> A black cloud enveloped the world . . .

Rina,

All that I wrote on the preceding pages was not intended as a letter, but since it's been written, I've decided to send it to you.

Yoni

May 4, 1963

Rina,

Once, when I was a small child, I used to sign certain letters like this: "Your friend who is longing to see you, Yoni." Today I see no sense in even signing a letter. For me a letter is the continuation of a conversation which for some reason was not concluded. In a letter you don't say everything, and everything is disjointed. But when one letter follows another, the tie is not broken—the chain seems endless.

You are all so far away, beyond my sphere of influence. I want to intervene, correct what's wrong, put things straight, create new things— but I can't. It's all so remote, and yet—how strange!—so clear, so lucid, that I can see it all—but only see, and no more.

When four work together, they can do everything—remember that. A kingdom can be turned into one of two things—either into a minor state or a great power. If you and the others are truly serious about *Arazim*, as I hope you are, and work for it with complete dedication, then you are already more than halfway to victory.

When I was in *Arazim* I wanted to bring a troop into the eighth grades, a real troop, and not just a group about to disintegrate; a troop in which each individual would feel himself an integral part, without which the entire machinery would somehow suffer. Little by little, as the months passed, I saw how twenty children turned into forty, and then into sixty, eighty, and finally into more than a hundred. I saw how near-infants were transformed into a force which had to be treated seriously and respectfully. I saw a child turning into an adult and a troop taking shape.

Should you continue to serve as a counselor next year? I can't answer that; that's a matter for you alone to decide. If you feel that you're creating something, that not a day slips by without your making some contribution, if you feel you're needed—then I'm sure you'll continue. If not, then finish your work on a high note, so that no bitter taste remains when you leave.

Actually, since you're the Rina I knew, I'm sure you'll do the right thing. You've never disappointed me. Whether or not you continue as counselor, I'm sure you've made the most of your time in the troops.

How do I feel? Recently I read a poem translated into Hebrew by Jabotinsky: "Autumn Song" by Paul Verlaine.

The sobbing winds
Of violins
    Of autumn drone,
Wound my heart,
Languors start
    In monotone.

                    Choked up inside
                    As something died
                        The hour tolls deep,
                    My thoughts dwell on
                    Those days bygone
                    And I weep;

                                        And so I go
                                        Where ill winds blow
                                            Broken and brief
                                        Here and there
                                        As in the air
                                            The dying leaf.

                                                    May 20, 1963

Dear Koshe (dear since the last inflation),
    As I returned home in the biting cold, the sun smiling in its blurred color and the heavens weeping bitterly for some incomprehensible reason, my eyes fell—without any advance notice—upon a letter from Israel, and

from Koshe no less, and what's more—it was even open. I was beside myself with happiness!

My friend, I realize that the glue on the envelopes in Israel tastes like eggplant, but just the same do try to seal the envelope. *Mine,* in any case, taste of peppermint, so it's pleasant to lick the flap; that's why I don't use post-cards.

By the way, you might save yourself the effort of telling me what's happening in the Middle East. I really know what's going on (so it turns out), and it's a pity to waste Israeli ink.

About school—

In mathematics I'm the best in the class, as well as the youngest; and in literature, as far as analyzing poetry is concerned, you can compare my fellow classmates to what we were in our glorious days back in the seventh and eighth grades. Maybe.

Aside from that, I'm tops in history. I also spend a sixth of the time studying that the average student here does; also, I'm friends with all the teachers; also, I'm doing well in other subjects, and also—well, there's really nothing else.

I'm longing to return.

About my surroundings—

I live outside Philadelphia. My school has about 1,500 students who don't know what they're doing there. It looks more like the Tel-Aviv Sheraton than a school (beautiful even by American standards, brand new, and it cost 6.5 *million* dollars to build). My house is "terribly" nice, surrounded by lawns and trees and empty, meaningless life.

The only thing people talk about is cars and girls. Life revolves around one subject—sex; I think Freud would have found very fertile soil here. Bit by bit I'm becoming convinced I'm living among apes and not human beings.

May 23, 1963

Rina,

You're almost sixteen. Do you realize you've lived nearly a quarter of your life? An insect, which lives only a few days, probably feels that its life span is enormous. Perhaps that's why we believe that we still have an eternity ahead of us. But man does not live forever, and he should put the days of his life to the best possible use. He should try to live life to its fullest. How to do this I can't tell you. If I had a clear answer, I'd have

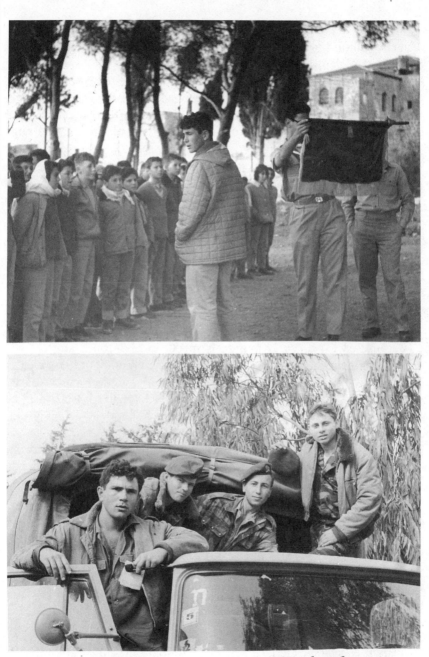

(top) *Yoni with his Scout troop in Israel, 1961*
(bottom) *As platoon commander, 1966*

half the solution to the puzzle called life. I only know that I don't want to reach a certain age, look around me and suddenly discover that I've created nothing, that I'm like all the other human beings who dash about like so many insects, back and forth, never accomplishing anything, endlessly repeating the routine of their existence only to descend to their graves, leaving behind them progeny that will merely repeat the same "nothingness."

Why am I writing all this to you? Perhaps to protest against your failure to realize that with every passing day you acquire a complete world. Now, this very moment, you've gained something. From every mistake you make you gain a little. Every single moment of your life is a whole epoch.

Do you remember Rudyard Kipling's poem "If"? In one of the stanzas, he says:

> If you can fill the unforgiven minute
> With sixty seconds worth of distance run,
> Yours is the earth . . .

Because each and every minute is made up of seconds and of even briefer fragments of time, and every tiny fragment ought not to be allowed to pass in vain. I must feel certain that not only at the moment of my death shall I be able to account for the time I have lived; I ought to be ready at every moment of my life to confront myself and say—This is what I've done.

Regrettably, Rina, we can't go back to where we were. To this very day I swear that the best and most beautiful days I ever had were those when I was a little child, living in Talpiot,* hiding in huge fields, covered almost completely by grass, looking for lady-bugs, seeing the world as the most marvellous place, and grown-ups—as veritable giants. But this period, too, is over, and now I'm facing the coming years of my life. I can remember the past, but I cannot return to it. It has *passed*, it's gone, finished. I gaze at the future and dream of the life yet to come, with one year chasing another . . .

In Israel, I lived in *one* world (a person can't live in two worlds), but that world of mine was divided into many parts. A world with aims (one of them, for example, was common to us both—to set up a troop). Life consists of countless experiences and is measured from innumerable points of view. But the things I did, I did with utter sincerity, and devoted all my strength to their accomplishment. All this did not prevent me from

*A suburb of Jerusalem.

living with myself, from contemplating things that no one beside me knew anything about.

Here—I have little contact with people my age, I have no interest in them, and I don't need them. I am not part of them. They're too frivolous. I've come across many like them in Israel and I must admit that those in Israel didn't interest me any more than the ones here. That I'm alone (and believe me, in Israel too I was alone) does not detract from the fact that I, as an individual, as a single unit, constitute an entire world. My life will be complete not because of others, but because of myself. If I err and make mistakes, I'll start again and build anew. There's no reason why the tower I build around myself, around my person, whatever it may be, should not stand forever.

Death—that's the only thing that disturbs me. It doesn't frighten me; it arouses my curiosity. It is a puzzle that I, like many others, have tried to solve without success. I do not fear it because I attribute little value to a life without a purpose. And if I should have to sacrifice my life t~ attain its goal, I'll do so willingly.

Generally, my mood hasn't changed. I can't stand America and I'm dying to return.

Miss you,
Yoni

May 26, 1963

(To his former classmates)
My beloved friends,

I'm writing this letter with an attractive red Parker pen which I think used to belong to Bella. At least the ink will return to its owner.

How are you, my dear ones? How are the exams going? These questions, which on the surface appear inconsequential, cannot be appreciated by the twisted brains of my wretched classmates. They should open an entire world before you, reveal to you the stormy background of my life here, lay bare my heart with its anguished cry, and give you an opportunity to chatter a bit in reply—and heaven help you if you don't!

Dedicated to the Following:

Batya, I understand you. So what? It happens to everyone. Try to overcome the bitter blow. Muster your strength and try to concentrate a little more on your studies instead of wasting your precious time on a world that is gone.

Yes, yes, I know there's a good chance you'll have to repeat the year. I know you "barely" got through last year, that half-an-hour before you took the exam you had "already" flunked, and that you don't know "anything." Yes, I know all that, nothing escapes me. "Big Brother is watching . . ."

Friends, I don't mean to be a tell-tale but . . . Batya is terribly in love with me, I swear! She told me so herself. And I quote: "This sentence (on a private matter) hurts my aching soul more than anything in the world! Although I knew from the start that your heart did not belong to me, I never dreamed of so much cruelty!

"With a broken heart, great anger and torrents of tears, your former love" (I know this is not in earnest).

The name need not be mentioned
"B.B." (mentioned just the same)

Rivka, cutie-pie, how are the braids? Now there's no one to play "cowboys" with, right? I want you to know from now on that it was all Koshe's fault because it was he who persuaded me to gallop away to the dreamworld of America. It wasn't my fault, believe me! I'll stop here because I don't want you to take too much time from sociology class (or perhaps it's Bible? or history? or God knows what).

Shimshon—regards from what's-her-name. She too is anxious to see you, but the trouble is she's got a husband. She claims that if you can take care of him, everything will be okay. If you can . . . ! Needless to say, it's not all smooth sailing in America and sometimes I miss Israel. Let this be a consolation to you and all you lucky ones who "got a raw deal" and had to stay in Israel: Israeli girls are a thousand times better looking. In America there's nothing to them but make-up.

Ehud—I salute you! "Be strong and of good courage!" Don't give up! Encourage the others and maybe together you'll manage to turn the classes that are still interesting into even wilder circuses than those described in your marvellous letter. Comrade—there is no purpose and no hope without battle. I'm depending on you to do your best.

My friends—what's it like in America? How can it be anything without Rachel's almonds, without paper darts, cast-off shoes and fist fights during recesses, without turning the school upside down and without breaking the piano? How can anything be interesting without my boring classmates from *Massada**—who can I quarrel with here? So tell me, friends, how can it be fun?

---

*The Scout organization that competed with Yoni's.

How can I keep from crying every time I think of you?

Less than a month left to the end of the year and its sorrows, but first I've got to pass final exams in five subjects. Since I missed more than half of the school year, this is quite depressing.

Look, I understand you and realize you'll all have to repeat the year. Don't despair! If you'll all promise faithfully that you'll make every effort, I pledge to repeat the year too, and then we'll have lots to write about.

Miss you,
Yoni

June 3, 1963

To Koshe,

To stop work on your paper in literature, or more accurately, not to begin it at all, is like committing suicide. Don't be crazy, you little deserter. Are you fed up with life? Really, Koshe, don't be a fool! Rouse yourself from the darkness that surrounds you and look at the world with sober eyes.

I always knew the Scouts would not let you go just like that without "fixing" you in some way. To take a fellow who's prepared to pay . . . (how much did you say?) and send him far away for months and months, knowing that he's likely to desert and remain there for good (this must be the reason they chose you; they still have hopes!)—well, only the leaders of the Jerusalem Scouts are capable of doing such a thing, and only to Koshe. Be that as it may, congratulations; I wish you great success! Next time, my friend, while you wander in the world, try to roll around to my doorstep in the "land of beautiful sunshine,"* and tell me in your melodious voice, which I've been longing to hear since the winter I left your abode, about all the hardships, wonders and marvels you experienced in your travels.

Since I last left your threshold my soul has known no peace. I don't intend to tell you all that's befallen me since that painful moment, but to avoid causing you undue worry let me assure you, Sire, that I am well, and as to the soundness of my reasoning and my strong desire to return to my homeland, may your mind rest at peace, my lord.

*This and the following paragraph are written in the style of a famous poem by the Hebrew poet Bialik.

At this point it would be better to stop writing like a moron and return to the world of reality. Well—as you see, I've gotten stuck on the word "well"—well, I haven't heard anything from Young Judea* yet, but Michal, who has also joined our delegation, hasn't heard from them either, so I'm still hoping. School will end in sixteen days. I've got eight school days and five final exams to go.

Say, have you lost your mind? Thoughts of heresy and sin may creep into the mind of any mischievous boy! Nevertheless, when you grow up it would make sense for you to decide to go to Nahal.† What will I do there without you? Besides, ultimately you'll have to join the army; and there's always time to become an egghead. In fact, it's better to become one when you're older and more capable of understanding what you are learning and what you want to be.

New Hampshire
Summer 1963

Dear Mother and Father, Iddo and Bibi,‡

I've been here§ more than ten days. Our task is to provide American youth with a more solid knowledge of Israel, to serve as a living testimony of Israel's independence and to represent its youth. The impression that Israel makes here is tremendous. They're constantly talking about the Israelis who've been here, discussing their virtues and weaknesses as if they were saints. The camp is simply in love with me; all of them, young and old, know me, and I believe I'm doing my job properly. There are also two girls with me from the delegation, and we're all making a good impression.

I'm counselor to campers aged nine to sixteen. Everyone's convinced I'm about nineteen, and they don't believe I'm only seventeen. All the other counselors here are nineteen to twenty-three, and I'm good friends with all of them. The fact that I'm an Israeli gives me an enormous advantage. Besides, I don't feel younger than any of them; often it's just the opposite.

*"Young Judea"—a Zionist youth organization in the United States, which brought Scout delegations from Israel to serve as counselors in Jewish summer camps. Yoni had been approached about joining such a delegation.
†"Nahal"—a branch of Israel's army which combines military service with work on agricultural settlements.
‡Nickname of Benjamin, Yoni's brother.
§In the Young Judea summer camp.

New Hampshire
Summer 1963

Dear Bibi,

After the sensational "opening" of your letter I'm giving up any attempt to match it. So I'll go straight to the point.

The sun rose behind an ominous cloud, when an ear-splitting shout was heard: "Yoni!" Not wasting a moment, I leapt from my cot and swiftly dashed to collect your epistle.

Your fascinating letter brought me indescribable happiness. After all, your long silence led me to fear that you'd decided to commit suicide without warning me, or at least that you'd run away from home.

I want you to know that for hours on end I had been sitting in the treetops, picking nuts, yawning away and weaving a noose, intending to hang myself if you or Iddo continued to remain silent.

The rest of this letter will be scrawled because I am now riding in a pickup truck which is taking me and my campers to dine at a restaurant as a prize for being selected the "honor bunk." I'm not the only one who thinks that this is *the* bunk; everyone else thinks so too.

To tell you that I enjoy being here would be superfluous, since you've read all about it in every letter I've written so far. The truth is I'm longing to see you all.

How tall are you? How do you look? Send me a color photo. By the way, why didn't you tell me which records you were planning to buy? They had a sale here at Zayre's and I bought "West Side Story" and "South Pacific." Try to buy "Porgy and Bess."

Don't fritter away your vacation, Bibi. Try to make good use of it; read something or work on something. Don't let the days just slip by. I do a lot of reading.

Conclusion:

As twilight falls, the heavens are coated by fluffy light clouds. Zephyrs play on our flaming faces, perspiring with the day's exhausting labors. Our breasts swell as we breathe in the moist, refreshing air. The universe awakens. The air is resonant with the songs of birds. Men and women with babes in their arms stroll in the streets, dressed in their Sunday best, celebrating their victory over the day's hard toil. The whole world is joyous and full of song. All this, of course, has nothing to do with this letter. So what? I can write anything I wish, can't I?

A few friends are sitting around me, asking whom I'm writing to. They refuse to believe the letter is to my dear brother. They're certain I'm writing a platonic missive to a sweetheart in a distant land.

New Hampshire
Summer 1963

Dear Mother, Father, and brothers,

I don't know whether you're aware of it, but the Scouts are returning to Israel on September 2nd and not on the 9th, so our final trip will be cut short, and we probably won't make it to Philadelphia and Washington. At any rate, we'll visit many places, including Niagara Falls. According to what we've been told, the trip should be great.

But I have a serious problem, namely I find it difficult to study here, as it's always hard to study in a camp, despite one's good intentions. I can only concentrate at home, in libraries, and places like that. So I think I may have to give up the trip (I've already visited most of the places anyway), and reconcile myself to coming home earlier. There's an added advantage in this—we'll be together earlier. The main job I came to do, I've done; I've worked and am still working as hard as I can, and I have no reason to regret the marvellous vacation I had here. What do you think?

I'm happy to hear that Mother's condition has improved; the mere fact that you can go away for a vacation shows she's recovering—I really hope you're enjoying yourselves. I can hardly wait to see Father's book come out. I'm sure I'll enjoy reading it and learning from it, since I can learn more from Father than from any other man.

August 1963

Dear Mother, Father, and brothers,

I'm overjoyed to learn about all that's happening at home. I'm certain that I'll come home to find giants instead of the brothers I left behind.

As regards physics, try to find out what paper I have to prepare. Also, try to obtain a list of subjects for that paper and write me about it. This really worries me.

I was glad to get my report card. It seems that despite the excitement of leaving for camp, I did well in all my finals. I think I'm one of the very few at school who received an A in mathematics at the end of the school year. I'm really glad.

Let me describe my daily schedule to you. Yesterday morning, after finishing the work in the bunk, I taught Hebrew for two hours. Later, I took about thirty boys aged fourteen–fifteen to "nature" (i.e., outdoors exercises). In the late afternoon I led a discussion on Israel as part of a series of talks called "The Jewish People's Struggle for Freedom." After supper I took a canoe and we paddled downstream on the Snake River which winds through a jungle of trees and shrubs and at times becomes so narrow that we barely got the canoe through.

Right now I'm on "guard duty" and as soon as I finish this letter I'll start reading *King of Flesh and Blood.** I read a lot here, because—as Grandma says—"Thank God," I brought lots of reading material: Max Nordau's *Writings*, *The Apology* of Socrates, Plato's *The State*, a few books of short stories, some textbooks, and more.

Philadelphia
September 28, 1963

Koshe,

Believe it or not, about two weeks ago I might almost have appeared suddenly at 14 King George Street† and said "Hi," but for various reasons I'm still stuck here. In any case, the chances were so good that when the thing fell through, I sank into such a depression that I didn't budge from my corner or do anything. Luckily for me, the knowledge that I'd return to Israel in eight months brought me back to normal; so this wretched creature continues to live, i.e., to eat, drink, study and sleep.

At school, the only subject that saves the day is math. During the summer I met (in the delegation from Israel) some students from the "Reali"‡ and discovered that I was somewhat ahead of them. This year I'm studying advanced math with twenty other students—the sun is shining and the whole universe is aglow. After this class, darkness descends as I enter the other classes (which contain a large number of "blockheads"). I say this in all seriousness. My relations with the teachers are excellent—they're the only ones I can talk to.

I've turned into an anti-social creature, cynical and scornful. If I wanted to laugh all day, there's enough comic material here to make me laugh

*An historical novel by Moshe Shamir about Alexander Yannai, a Jewish king of the Hasmonean dynasty.
†Koshe's home in Jerusalem.
‡High school in Haifa, which emphasizes mathematics and science.

myself to death. And if I wanted to shed tears, I could hardly escape drowning. The only option I'm left with is to become indifferent and ignore my surroundings. Two days ago, in English class, I got so fed up with it all that for forty-five minutes I told those forty poor souls what I thought of them, of America, of the ideals they don't have, of their world. Since then, every time they see me, they bow down to the ground and begin every sentence they address to me with the words, "This will probably sound stupid to you . . . "

You can't conceive the meaning of longing. You can't imagine how badly I want to see you all.

Give my regards to everyone.

December 20, 1963

Dear Koshe,

I'm now at the post office near my school. I can hardly write because my hands are numb. It's snowing outside and so cold that my breath all but freezes! The temperature is below −8°C, Christmas vacation begins tomorrow. Since this is the last day before the start of a pretty long vacation, I decided there was no point in going to school. So I "played hookey," and here I am.

Two weeks ago we got our report cards. Mine was one of the best. I'm beginning to imagine the moment, some five or six months from now, when I'll return to Israel. It's not so long to go. I feel as if I've been writing a telegram, trying to save words, so I'll stop using such brief sentences and go into greater detail.

You once asked me to describe the place I live in. Well, Elkins Park is one of the suburbs of Philadelphia, about three-quarters of an hour's drive from downtown. In America big cities are encircled by suburbs; some of the largest suburbs may have more than 100,000 inhabitants. There are hardly any apartment blocks here, rather scores of palatial private homes that were built over a hundred years ago. Every house is surrounded by a spacious garden, particularly by lawns. There are lots of trees and lakes—now frozen solid—and a world full of movement and life, judging by the number of cars on the roads.

Now that I've lived here a considerable length of time, I can tell you without any hesitation: this is an awful world, there is nothing to do here, everything is decaying. There's no real life here.

I have a girl friend who's really an exception among American girls: A.

she's intelligent; B. she's really good-looking; C. you should meet her.

Tell me when you're all joining the army. Since I'm coming back soon, I want to know, I must know what's going on. Write me anything that's on your mind—who's going where, when, etc.

January 23, 1964

Dear Koshe,

This letter will be very short (as far as I can predict), since tomorrow I have two semi-final exams: Spanish and math; the math teacher explicitly told us that anyone who doesn't study at least forty to fifty hours had better not show up, and I've yet to open a book. You'll forgive me for having to find out whether

$$\frac{dy}{dx} = y = \int \frac{750\,(x-76)}{(x+y)^2\,(x^2-y^2)^3}$$

Now I want you to know that I finished *The Rise and Fall of the Third Reich* ten months ago and it impressed me a great deal. Incidentally, my father has written a new book, a most interesting one, about the Marranos of Spain, and it would be worth your while to read it—*it really is extremely interesting*—a totally new theory on the Marranos, what they were, etc.

I'm sorry to hear that my letters bore you sometimes (you hinted as much rather indirectly, and that was really very thoughtful of you because thanks to this I didn't break out in tears of grief). Therefore let me implore you (how's that for style, chum) to mark with a colored pencil (preferably red or green; not blue because it looks like ink) all the lines that aren't up to standard, and I'll try to improve.

As to the elections, I'll write you later; I haven't the time just now. Sorry! No, really; I don't have time, believe me!

February 3, 1964

Koshe,

Look, although your letter was liberally seasoned with fulsome phrases and complaints, your questions were not clear enough. I tried to extract the central core, but found to my regret that there was none. I forgot that this letter was supposed to constitute a significant milestone in the history of Israeli satire, so forgive me if it doesn't contain the usual biting wit in the Netanyahu-Karpeles style.

I won't write you now about my father's book, but I hope to be able to send you a copy with the appropriate comments and explanations, and I hope you'll get a lot out of it.

As for me: how am I? Not bad, after the exams. I miss Israel, of course. I read William Golding's *Lord of the Flies* which attempts to determine the causes for the emergence of different societies. It is really worth your while to get a copy and read it.

February 12, 1964

Dear Koshe,

Koshe, I want to live. I want to hold on to something, to find some meaning and reason in life, and I can't. I got over my adolescence long ago, so this isn't some passing whim. This is the first time that I look at Israel and don't see it as an "escape-hatch." I know that in Israel I'll find a different life, a life that I'll enjoy more. Yet at the same time, when I think of the "gang" back there, I blurt out almost unconsciously, "My God, the thought that soon I'll be back with all of you almost repels me. Why, you live like small children!" And not only you, everyone, everyone is like that. I live with you in the same world, but our views of the world differ completely. Look, I'm not making myself clear. I don't think I've ever turned to anyone with this request; but for various reasons, despite all the wisecracks we write each other, I've always considered you different from the others. So do me a favor: don't explain me to myself, because I haven't told you anything here, and you have nothing to seize on. Instead of that, explain yourself to me. Koshe, what are you, who are you? What do you want out of life? What are you looking for? What do you think about?

Do you know, a moment ago I grasped the pen so hard that I thought it was going to break. I loosened my grip a little and thought—what do I really want? I've developed an entire philosophy for myself about everything that's ever concerned me. I can fascinate people who listen to me. When I bother to explain myself and my ideas to someone, I see him gaping before me, entranced. But Koshe, this gives me no satisfaction. Please prove to me that I'm wrong. Show me that at least one of the people I know is really worth knowing.

Actually, I have no desire to send this letter to you. I want to tear it up, begin a new letter, a nice one, satirical and slightly biting but at the same time full of wisdom. But I'll mail it just the same. Don't go to the trouble of answering it. Go on writing the way you always write. Despite everything I say, I enjoy reading your letters. I know you well and have no cause to doubt your sincerity.

April 4, 1964

Dear Koshe,

Remember my last letter? I wrote it in a mood of despair. Well, the letter to the class that I'm enclosing here was written in an excellent mood; seriously. I'm sending it through you because you know them so well, and I leave it entirely to you to decide whether to deliver it or not. If the letter doesn't reach the class (and that won't upset me at all), tell them I'm fine, that I miss them and wish them success in the exams, etc. (and I mean that with all my heart).

Since I spent all my energy on the letter to the class, I don't feel like telling you stories or splitting hairs on philosophical themes. If it was someone else, I'd say the reason was indifference or the lack of common interest or an inadequate relationship, but since it's you who's involved, this isn't the case. I feel that writing to you can only ruin a certain relationship that existed between us. Why—I don't know. Maybe because a letter serves merely to compensate for the lack of something else, and I don't want any compensations. I write what I feel, think and understand, and it's beyond my power to change or to add anything to this fact.

I'll be seeing you,
Yoni

April 4, 1964

Dear Friends,*

We had a nine-day spring vacation and I went down to Miami, Florida. The vacation gave me time to think, to reach a number of conclusions, and to get to the root of certain things that were troubling me. It was an opportunity for me to come to terms with myself. I'm telling you this

*To his former classmates.

because it will help me to explain to Bari, and in fact to all of you, the reason I haven't written: It's because I don't really know you. As a group, you're the finest friends in the world and I could never wish for better company. So it's easier for me to write to you as a group than to write to each of you separately. Did I ever meet with you after school, just to talk, to exchange ideas, or simply to be together? With Koshe a little, with the others not. I see nothing wrong in that. I could write to you, Bari, or to you, Shooky, or address a letter to each of you, telling you how nice and pleasant the weather is here, how large my school is, what the American girls are like, what's happening with the presidential elections, and lots of other charming details; but in the final analysis what would that actually tell you? That I'm alive? That I'm homesick? That I haven't yet forgotten you? Nothing more than that. I want to come back and do what I didn't do a year and a half ago—get to know you. I don't think I can do that in letters; perhaps you can. I'm incapable of it.

ZAHAL

(1964–1967)

The young recruit in the paratroops, 1964

I N JULY 1964, YONI RETURNED TO Israel to enlist in the army while his parents and two younger brothers remained in the United States. The closeness between Yoni and his family now found expression in the letters they exchanged and in repeated visits to Israel by his parents and brothers.

Upon joining Zahal (the Hebrew acronym by which the Israeli army is commonly called), Yoni volunteered for the paratroops, which were considered its elite corps. The paratroops were stationed in the country's critical area—the narrow ten-mile "waist" that separated the Arab armies from the sea before the Six-Day War. Yoni's military service began at a relatively quiet period, but by 1966 the situation had gradually worsened as Arab terrorists launched raids into Israel from neighboring states with increasing frequency. Israel finally had to retaliate by striking at the terrorist bases. Yoni took part in the important raid against Es-Samua in Jordan.

His letters from this period give an inside look at the remarkable process by which a young man became a superb soldier and later an outstanding officer.

July 8, 1964

Dear Mother and Father,

I've already been in Israel two whole days (this is the morning of the third). I arrived Sunday night and went straight to Jerusalem. I didn't cable Aunt Miri because I wanted, first of all, to be in Jerusalem.

When I saw the country from the plane I felt a twinge in my heart. Despite everything that's wrong here, and God knows there are many faults and evils, it's our country, and I love her as I always have. The young people here are more serious, thoughtful and mature than those in America, and the social climate—for us at any rate—is far healthier than in the States.

My room won't be ready for another eight days. Aunt Phirah is virtually trying to force us to stay at their home, and I think Bibi* will be there for a few days. He's already managed to contact Avishai and Uzi and is probably now with his friends.

I continue to work non-stop at my physics, and am really enjoying it.

In the meantime emotions are running high in the country around the return of the remains of Jabotinsky† and his wife. Ben-Gurion has announced that he would not come to pay his last respects, and the whole country is divided. I, of course, will attend the funeral when the coffin is brought to Jerusalem.

I haven't yet been inside our house, but from the outside it looks fine. The garden, however, is destroyed. I'll visit the Embassy‡ soon and see how the inside is faring. The storeroom is bolted and seems to be okay, but it's really a pity about the garden. Oh well, when we all come back to live here together we'll make us a lovely garden again.

The neighborhood, especially right by the house, is all changed. A marvellous road has been laid through the field adjoining the house. Jerusalem is more beautiful than ever. Perhaps I am a bit sentimental because I haven't seen it for so long. Who knows?

August 1, 1964

Dear parents,

We received a letter from each of you and there's no need to tell you how glad we were to read them. I was very happy to learn that you are managing to rest a bit and also succeed in doing your work, and that everything has straightened out.

I have plenty of clothes and hardly needed to buy any. We're both well-dressed. Anyone who doesn't know us takes us for American tourists, but of course we don't care one bit. You were right, Mother, when you said that guys my age have stopped walking around wearing khaki, and we did well to take the trouble to buy all the things we brought over with us.

*Then on summer vacation in Israel.
†Vladimir Jabotinsky, the leader of the pre-statehood Zionist Revisionist Party, which was at loggerheads with the dominant Labor coalition. Jabotinsky died in 1940 in New York and requested in his will that his remains be brought to Israel only by decree of a sovereign Jewish government. This was refused by Ben-Gurion throughout his years as Prime Minister and granted by Levi Eshkol when he assumed the post.
‡The foreign embassy that was renting the Netanyahu house.

As regards the army, I'm going in on August 10th. Quite a number of my friends left on July 23–25 and they have now been joined by those who volunteered for Nahal service.

I've just returned from a three-day (two nights) trip in the magnificent, wondrous Negev. We passed through the craters and even got to Eilat. I think this jaunt to the Negev marks the end of the series of trips I've made since my return. I'll spend the ten remaining days before going into the army taking it easy here in town. Maybe I'll visit the uncles and aunts; in short, I'll save up strength.

True to the ways of young men embarking on a new path, and in fact like any thinking person, a few of my friends and I often sit together talking for hours on end. Sometimes our discussions continue into the middle of the night. At long last I've found people here who are my match. Guys like Avi, Eli, Shlomo and others form a group which I'm happy to be a part of.

A short time ago I sat down and wrote you, Father, a very long letter; I wanted to try to put my thoughts and ideas in order, to present myself to you and Mother as I am. I wanted to connect the various "chapters" of my thinking and behavior and produce a unified "book." I wanted you to know me better and advise me as you have been doing in your letters. I got as far as page 9 and stopped. It's too big a job, but that's not what deterred me—it was too difficult, and my words failed to convey properly what I think and feel. I'll try again, perhaps after I join up.

My *genuine* friends, both male and female, are, as always, few. But that doesn't bother me in the least. I don't need people just to share *my life;* if that's what I wanted, I could find them in abundance.

You can't imagine how much happiness your letters bring me. I'm repeating myself, but I want you to understand clearly the importance I attach to what you write. I'm so glad all is calm at home, and I hope that you, Mother, aren't working too hard. So while the quiet lasts, make the most of it to work and rest (the two need not be incompatible).

I am reading a great deal now, particularly Hebrew literature. I'm studying Bialik and Tchernikovsky* as well as Hemingway and Goethe *(The Sorrows of Young Werther).*

Bibi can't find the math and physics books that he was supposed to bring with him, and this upsets me a great deal. He thinks you may have forgotten to put them in the suitcases. Please check; the books are very expensive, and I had to run about a lot before I found them. I don't have

---

*The two most eminent poets of modern Hebrew literature.

much time to be sorry, and of course I'm not angry at Bibi, whom I see very often.

Don't worry about the army. I'm not stupid and I won't behave rashly —*rest assured.*

August 1, 1964

Beloved Iddo,

Congratulations, Iddo, on your twelfth birthday. Succeed and excel in all you do. Just as Father offers me advice, let me suggest something to you—learning is important above all else. The desire to study and acquire knowledge, to solve problems, to read and understand— these are the things that make a man great. At the same time you have to get along with the society in which you live—with your friends and most of all with Father and Mother. Be a good son and don't upset them. Actually, you have always been good, and it seems that I'm the one, more than any of us, who used to irritate them sometimes. Learn from my experience, Iddo.

Your
Yoni

August 15, 1964

Dear Mother, Dad, and Iddo,

I'll try to describe some of my experiences in the last few days.

Well, on Monday morning (the 10th) we were loaded into cars at the induction center in Jerusalem, and taken to the *Kelet* (induction and selection base) where we are to be assigned our different duties in the army.

Every morning there's a general assembly: there they call out the serial numbers of those soldiers who have already been assigned to specific units and who are to leave for their bases. I wasn't included in the selections announced in the first three days—and I despaired. Yesterday they placed me in a new platoon where I suddenly discovered a number of familiar faces. Apparently the aptitude tests administered in Jerusalem had shown everyone in this platoon to be gifted. Then we were given medical tests and additional aptitude tests and finally sent to a camp called "Tel Nof" for pilot-school tests. These tests will go on for another week or two, but I don't believe I'll go into the air force. It means five years—far too long! In any event I'll remain in Tel Nof a few days longer, and then I'll probably return to the Kelet to be integrated into some other combat unit. The treatment here is really wonderful. The conditions are excellent and the fellows—great guys.

I want to put you at ease and promise that I won't do anything final before I receive your letters and advice. Soon I'll tell you my army P.O. Box, when I reach a more permanent base; then you'll be able to address your letters to me directly. I feel fine. Strangely enough, I think the army has improved my health.

August 19, 1964

Dear Mother and Father,

This is the middle of my second week in the army. As Father requested, I'll try to describe in detail what has been happening to me here.

It's funny, and perhaps most characteristic of army life, but the minute I thought I had the time to write, I was called and assigned a task: to clean the tent, which means scrubbing it "until the floor shines like a mirror." But I'll go on with the letter in the hope that I'll manage to finish it. Let me start at the beginning and trace events in chronological order. I suppose I'll have to write with interruptions.

Well, the most maddening thing in this whole army business is not knowing where you'll end up. As I've already told you, they sent me to Tel Nof for flight tests. I got there on Thursday afternoon of last week, and the next day we went on leave which lasted until Sunday morning. When I returned to Tel Nof on Sunday, they were about to start the flight tests which are designed to show if you're made of the right stuff. Now, to be a pilot, you have to sign up for five years. I knew that I'd pass all the tests; and then, without even asking me, they'd put me into an air force uniform and do their utmost to persuade me to serve there. It's very hard to get around them, and in fact, many fellows once they've made it through the tests tend to stay in the pilot-training course.

So there we were, about sixty of us in the roll call, and the commanding officer ordered anyone who didn't wish to go to flight school to step forward. I was the only one who stepped out of line. Then eight more joined me.

After a very long procedure we were taken back to the Kelet. I've already spent several days here, and I'm almost going crazy. Still I haven't had a moment's regret about giving up the air force. Then why did I say I was almost going nuts? It seems that I can stand anything except this state of ignorance, this dependence on the decisions and utterances of someone else; and this is precisely the condition in which I now find myself. I don't know as yet where I'll be transferred, whereas most of our recruits already know where they're going, and many of them have already been sent to various bases. Anyway, I hope that this week (today is Wednesday) or at the latest at the beginning of next week, all this anxiety will come to an end and I'll be able to tell you clearly where matters stand.

What do we do at the Kelet? We've been divided up into platoons of thirty men. Each of these is headed by a corporal. Nine other guys and I share a tent (the tents are large and quite spacious), and I don't know a single one of them. We are a collection of soldiers from all parts of the country. There is a large number of corporals in the camp, and as a rule, each soldier's mood depends on the mood of his corporal. Some of these section commanders are poor, miserable guys who have found here for the first time in their lives an opportunity to "express" themselves; some were complete nothings in civilian life; others have suffered all their lives from an inferiority complex; and only a few are normal human beings (like the one I have today). Commanders of the first type are a real horror. To be subject to the authority of such individuals, whom in fact I could teach almost anything, can be quite odious. Still, it hardly bothers me; I realize that it's all done to teach us discipline. What does disturb me, as I've already said, is not knowing where I'll wind up.

We have a lot of free time, interrupted occasionally by the "PWD" ("Public Works Department"). The work they give us includes washing military vehicles, cleaning latrines, working in the commissary, and such like. Every evening they show us a film, and a lecture is delivered by a commanding officer of one of the branches of Zahal. Apart from the time we spend on guard duty at night, we sleep well. The food isn't bad, although in my opinion it's rather meager, but one can make do. We have a PX that's open nearly all day here, and you can buy anything from shoelaces, drinks, popsicles and sewing things to a complete and tasty meal —all, of course, at half the price you'd pay in town. After all, the army doesn't pay taxes! Interesting how the civilians in the cities are urged endlessly to save and save, while here in a state institution, the waste is enormous. Discarded food and unused manpower are only part of this.

Last Saturday when I returned from Jerusalem, I remembered to bring some books back with me. At least I don't fritter the time away. One can die of boredom here with hardly anything to do all the livelong day. I brought along a copy of Plato, a book by Ayn Rand and a volume of poems by Nathan Alterman (he really does write beautifully). The only books circulating here are mystery stories and cheap paperbacks, and reading them is just piling futility on futility.

August 28, 1964

Dear, beloved Mother and Father,

There is much in those first two words—dear and beloved. It's hard for me to describe to you how dearly I love you. I have no wish to cause you any distress, and I'm truly sorry when I read in your letters complaints that I don't write often enough. Let me first explain why this is so.

Army mail is only sent out to places inside the country and not abroad. The letters are mailed without stamps, as military post, and are sorted according to the different sections of the country. Even so it takes a long time for an army letter to reach its destination, all the more if it's going abroad. Until now I used to wait for a leave to mail my letters. Since the leaves are irregular, my letters too were irregular. And now it's going to get even worse, because I won't get any leaves until I start basic training.

You appear to be worrying far too much. I really feel *wonderful.* I didn't experience any trauma in going into the army, and I really didn't need anyone's company to ease the transition from civilian life to military discipline. I believe I considered the whole matter quite carefully while still in the States and didn't act on any foolish impulse; I'm really glad I acted as I did. *You have not the slightest reason for any worry.* Believe me! If your concern is based on logic and not just on emotions which you cannot control, then you ought to be completely at ease and not think of me as someone all alone in a strange country. I am not alone and if I did feel lonely, I could always go to the aunts; after all, the country is full of them. The army takes up all my time, and in my free moments I sometimes go to Aunt Miri, although I must admit it's rather seldom. Don't be annoyed if I don't visit our relatives more frequently. In my opinion it's not a matter of obligation. In any case, the time I have at my disposal is limited, and I don't really see a need. If you want it very much, then of course I'll do it.

Well, I'm in the paratroops. The paratroop corps is known as a dangerous place to serve in—but that's not true. It's as dangerous as any other combat unit. The drills are hard but not all that terrible, and the food here is much better than in the Kelet. The instructors without exception are all decent, the people around me are human beings and not mindless bums, and there's no cause to complain about the treatment. I doubt if you'll become less anxious if I continue to tell you about the corps; I suppose nothing will help. But everything is really perfectly all right. Don't be frightened and don't worry.

I see I can't escape the impression I think my letters are making on you. But you know that I don't say things offhand; if I tell you something, I mean it. *Everything is just fine.* Mother has been planning to come to Israel, maybe this coming year—well, when you come, Mom, you'll see that everything is okay.

Now that I've got this far (and I hope you're calmer and convinced that your anxiety is groundless, especially you, Mother, because Father—in his relatively few letters—doesn't say whether he's worried or not, from which I've happily concluded that he isn't)—here's the main point of this letter: A Good and Happy New Year.* I hope you'll be able to have a really good rest, especially you, Mom dearest—you both deserve a rest very much. I wish you a successful and creative year, dearest Father. And to Bibi and Iddo, the best of everything! I hope and in fact feel sure, Bibi, that you'll achieve the goals you've set for yourself. As for you Iddo, what shall I tell you, beloved Iddo? To study well? To behave well? But you do that anyway. Go on doing so, go on and on.

September 8, 1964

Dear Father, Mother, and brothers,

Basic training started a few days ago, but the tremendous hardships we heard about so often haven't yet materialized. We got New Year's leave (which is still on), from Sunday 2:30 P.M. till Tuesday night at 11 P.M. I went straight to Savyon and saw everyone—Boaz and Miri, Luzi, Shai, Ron and Ori, Grandma, Uncle Ezra, Ruthie and the kids.

Grandma reminded me a dozen times to tell you how lovely it was to see them all—Ezra and Ruthie, etc., "and may the whole family be together in Jerusalem next year," and how nicely Miri received us. So I'm writing: it was really very nice. Since they all left on Monday, I did too —for Jerusalem.

*The Jewish New Year (Tishri), which, in 1964, began on September 7.

I have a girl friend here; her name is Tutti (Tirza), and she is very lovely. Bibi will bear witness to that. Too bad you don't know her.

Tonight I'm returning to the base. They say that from Wednesday to Saturday we'll have a march to "get to know your personal equipment," which means marching twenty-five miles a day. But that doesn't worry me. I've reached the conclusion that anything the army requires of a soldier, I can do.

We've already received our initial instruction in weapons and therefore have to memorize all kinds of details: type of weapon, make, caliber, mechanism, characteristics, description and name of each part, and so on and on. Our personal equipment—canteens, ammunition, full packs, etc., not forgetting the steel helmet—is very heavy. Iddo would be very pleased to see us—just like in the movies, except that in the films they probably wear "steel" helmets made of cardboard.

It's been a long time since I heard from you. I imagine I'll find letters at the base from both Bibi and Iddo, and then I'll answer each one separately, providing I have time. The day is so full and crowded that we barely manage to eat anything, never mind rest. At night we are so exhausted that we have to use every second of the two or three hours free time for sleep. The only time we can write is Friday evening (if we're not engaged in exercises). In any event, I'll do the best I can.

I'm enjoying military service more and more. Every now and then a new hurdle arises to be overcome, and every time you overcome it you feel you've covered a pretty long stretch of road, leaving a lot behind you.

Everyone says I've lost a lot of weight and look well. I weigh 150 lbs., and in my opinion I'd look considerably better if I had another twenty-four hours unbroken sleep. Out of habit I wake up while it's still dark outside, and it's very hard for me to fall asleep again. Lack of sleep no longer affects me so much and I manage fine, as I've already told you. In the two days I spent at Miri's I gained 3 lbs., which I'll undoubtedly lose as soon as I get back into the army routine. Miri did quite a bit of laundry for me, and I'm returning to camp all clean and shiny to the extent that it's possible. I'm writing all this because you asked for details.

If I'm not mistaken, today is the First of Tishri. Well then, I wish you once again a very happy New Year.

Thousands of kisses,
Your
Yoni

September 11, 1964

Dear Father, Mother, Bibi and Iddo,

Yesterday marked the end of my first month in Zahal. Now I know at last what "hard life" is, although everyone says that this is nothing compared to what is yet to come. The Sabbath days at the camp are relatively quiet, so I have the time to sit and write. But it seems we'll have a roll call in ten minutes, and I'll have to interrupt my writing.

Well, when we returned from our New Year's leave they decided the time had come for our "drubbing," and since then we've been on our feet day and night. Yesterday was the worst day. We exercised nonstop all day, and by evening everyone was thoroughly exhausted and praying for a good long sleep (i.e., four or five hours). We thought we'd earned it after being pushed so hard physically. But the officers had other ideas, for immediately after supper they started night training, which went on for a few hours. After the exercise, our hopes for a good sleep were dashed again when a five-mile high-speed march was announced. Let me explain: This is the worst thing in the army, worse than any running, because no rhythm is kept. You start running wildly to catch up with the others and close gaps. Anyone who can attaches himself to the few in the lead, and if he can stay there he's better off, because then he doesn't have to run to fill the gaps created by the stragglers. So far I haven't had any problems, and I'm sure it'll be the same in the future too. The truth is I'm capable of meeting all the requirements better than most people here.

Well, after the march, which was extended by an extra mile, we came back to camp, and then again, instead of sleeping, we were put through a "Tirtur," the like of which we'd never had. ("Tirtur" means we have to run and fetch the cot, then the mattress, then the kitbag, then the mess tin, then put on our winter clothes, etc.—all in a matter of seconds.) That was really too much. We barely dragged ourselves along. We thought, now they'll let us sleep; it was the middle of the night by then. But no, we were told we were having a "Commander's Review," which is a major inspection normally lasting three hours and requiring a full day's preparation. Everything has to be shiny bright, and when I say everything I mean *every thing*. As a result, they kept us up till about 3:30 in the morning to straighten up our tents, tighten the ropes, clean up the grounds and so on. After that, when we had only a little over an hour left for sleep, it turned out that it was our squad's turn for guard duty. So we stayed awake all through that marvellous night. And if you think that was easy, you're wrong. When a man's exhausted and worn down yet has to stay awake, he breaks down altogether, and by the morning nothing's left of him. Today (Friday afternoon) training started as usual and yesterday is already past and forgotten. Today is the only thing that matters. In the final analysis, it's not so very terrible.

I've described briefly what we did throughout the day to give you an idea of what goes on here in Zahal. I didn't dwell on the nature of the maneuvers, the running, the marching, the arms drills, the physical fitness exercises, the shooting practice, the obstacle course, and all the rest. If one begins with the assumption that one must pass it all and that everything comes to an end, you do pass and the end does come. I know I'll get through alright.

If I have previously complained about the army's treatment of soldiers, I have in the meantime become accustomed to it, and I'm gradually becoming more and more content with Zahal.

I'm sitting in the PX, which is totally empty. This is the only place where one can write at a table. The sales counter is closed and everyone has gone to sleep (you don't get such an opportunity every day!), and very soon I'll do so too even though I don't feel the slightest bit tired. I'll have all day tomorrow to rest. What's certain is that tonight I'll sleep well.

When I was at Miri's I discovered some thin little books, about fifty to seventy pages each, no larger than the palm of my hand, which fit inside a shirt pocket. This find has enabled me to take some reading material with me wherever I go; it's of great value because when we're given a few minutes' rest it's too little time to fall asleep, but it's also impossible to sit around doing nothing. Among these books I found Hemingway, Saroyan, Edgar Allan Poe and many others and have taken them with me.

As to the textbooks that got lost, I still hope they will be found. At present I'm doing the impossible: the other soldiers have stopped reading even the cheap Westerns and sex stories, while I'm still reading good literature. That's the way I am, and I really enjoy going off to the side for a moment's read. It's a kind of departure from the world of the army into another world. I manage to combine the two and thus enjoy every minute spent here.

Our next leave seems to be slated for the Sukkot holiday. Until it comes, they say, we'll pray so hard for rest that we'll fall asleep walking to the bus on our way home, only to wake up when we return to camp. Meanwhile everyone already looks half-dead. It's a comical sight.

September 18, 1964

Tutti my love,

The days pass so swiftly here that one loses all sense of time. Suddenly I realized that it was September 14th and that the day before you had been inducted into Zahal. Who knows when I'll see you again. Before, I was at least sure that on returning to town we could always be together, but now even this is no longer certain.

Tutti mine, I miss you more than I had ever thought possible. It seems to me for some reason that it isn't enough to see you once a month or even every two weeks, and I fear that the intervals between our meetings may put a greater and greater distance between us. The possibility that we may "grow tired" of each other doesn't exist for me, and at this moment, I think, for you as well; but the passing time weakens the bond between us and gives too profound a meaning to our meetings and too great an emptiness to the intervals.

You wouldn't believe—or to be more accurate, I didn't believe—that every time mail is distributed here I would stand there wishing so hard that there was a letter from you. Why? Because you are my only link with the world outside the army. Were it not for you, my military service would constitute the whole framework of my life for the next two years, plus, of course, my "personal life"—whatever of myself I'll give to the army. Were it not for you, I wouldn't have an interest in leaving camp. By "interest" I mean interest in other individuals, not in civilian life as such; *that* I'll never lose, and this applies not just to me; no one loses interest in the life he has once lived. For it is on the foundations of the past that we have built ourselves and will continue to build and be built. Lose you, Tutti? If I must, then it would be better all at once and not little by little over a long period of time, trying to cling to something that is flickering and dying. But I won't lose you that way. Never.

You sound in your letter pretty much the way I did when I was at the Kelet, except that in your case the cause is primarily the people around you, whereas with me it was the anxiety of not knowing where they would send me. Man's strength lies in his ability to adapt himself to new conditions and to reconcile himself to them. Needless to say, everything depends on you—on your state of mind, on your successes and failures both in Zahal and in life in general. Isn't that so? You have to try to find the positive core in the service, in the army as a whole, and use it to its fullest. If you extract from the army the good that is there, then you won't despair, and what is more, you might even be happy. I wish I could say that I'll be beside you along the path you must take. But it can't be; each of us must walk this path all alone.

We are told that the maneuvers become progressively harder. Every week the company commander and squad leaders promise us an increasingly difficult life. The truth is that the maneuvers as such do perhaps make greater demands on the soldier, but by now we've gotten into shape and the running and marching do not present a problem. The only serious obstacle is the chronic lack of sleep. During the classes we can scarcely keep our eyes open, and we all seem to be ready to drop. Our company has been getting a really awful drubbing, literally. The definition best fitting the life of our company is that we are enduring the drubbing of Base #4* together with the training of the paratroops. It's rather difficult to combine the two and stay on your feet.

There's no point in belaboring the subject. Actually, things are not so bad. I'm more satisfied in the paratroops than I ever expected to be. If the goal is to make soldiers of us, then it's quite clear to me that this goal will be achieved. Whoever remains here will be able to say that he is capable of accomplishing a great deal (physically, that is). It's interesting how great physical stress can rob you of the ability to think; yet you have to concentrate all the time on what's happening, to absorb and absorb and absorb, and then process it all.

I see that if I go on I'll start just babbling. I'm dead-tired and scarcely able to sit up (in the PX). Hope you'll forgive me for feeling weary while writing to you, but the situation is really pretty dismal. You see, I don't even have the energy to be cynical. I feel that my hand is beginning to move across the paper quite mechanically. I'm writing this just so you'll know that I'm thinking of you and I love you. As I write this, it sounds so very far away.

September 27, 1964

Dear Father and Mother,

The longed-for Sukkot leave has arrived. How we soldiers waited for it! After three weeks of exercises we could scarcely stand on our feet; another week under similar tension and the exertion would have broken the last remnants among us who were still able to move.

About a week ago I was called and asked whether I was a "lone soldier"† and in need of help. I'd heard that for anyone in such circumstances the

*Training base for recruits, often of noncombat units, in which the use of excessive disciplinary measures was common.
†A soldier who is alone in Israel without his family.

army arranges an "adoption" by a kibbutz or a private family. I didn't want this, since I wanted to remain as independent as possible and to be free to choose where I'll stay. So I told them that for the time being I can look after myself, and should I need assistance in the future, I'd turn to them.

I came to Jerusalem on Friday and investigated a number of possible places to rent, but none worked out. I spent that night with Aunt Phirah who received me very nicely. I needed a complete rest to recover from military fatigue. The last time I woke up was at 3:30 A.M. on Wednesday, so there was real cause for my being worn out. I slept from 4 to 8 P.M. and then again from 9 P.M. to the following morning.

In the course of my search for living quarters I stopped in at the home of Eli Barmeir, about whom I wrote you. I slept there the first week after returning to Israel and enjoyed his home and his parents very much. The next day I accompanied them on a picnic in the Presidential Forest, and while we were there his parents invited me to stay with them. I have never received such a marvellous offer. They really are excellent people, and in addition they have enough room. As for rent, they refuse to let me pay, but I hope I'll be able to persuade them to accept at least the sum the army allocates for my living quarters, even though the matter has no significance. Everything has worked out well, and we've already transferred my things here. In fact, I slept here last night (Saturday).

Aunt Miri still sends me packages to the camp which of course I'm happy to receive, although it isn't essential. We get food but at present it doesn't, in my opinion, provide sufficient energy for the work we have to do. I feel great.

September 28, 1964

Beloved Iddo,

Everyone tells me how tall you've grown. Suzy wrote me that she came to our house to ask for my address and scarcely recognized you, you've changed so much. I want to see you, Iddo mine, more than anything. If you can, send me some photos. For that matter, it would be a good idea if all of you would have your pictures taken and send them to me. Talk it over with Mom and Dad, will you?

Life is very hard in the army. You've probably read about it in my letters to all of you. But it isn't so awful. I'm managing to stand up to everything and to overcome all obstacles. The main thing is not to try to evade anything and to want to overcome. It's by will power alone that we can take the training. But don't get a wrong impression. There are also very pleasant moments in the service, and if you "accept everything with good grace," as we are told, you can even enjoy it. We're now able to do things I wouldn't have dreamed possible before, and we're told this is minuscule compared to what we'll be doing in the future. In any event, I'm not complaining and I'm glad that I'm able to meet this difficult challenge. After all, that's the very reason I volunteered for the paratroops.

October 2, 1964

Dear Mother, Father, Bibi and Iddo,

Friday's come at last and we're enjoying a thorough rest. We returned to camp Tuesday morning and right away started some strenuous exercises. These are actually our regular exercises, which have become so routine that they don't merit special mention.

Everything went on as usual until the evening of that same Tuesday. That night we set out on a twenty-two-mile march with full battle gear and weapons which ended at 3 A.M. The final six miles were turned into a stretcher-march—you lay the heaviest guys on stretchers and carry them. That's the hardest work you can imagine, especially when the march goes on for miles on end.

The next day, Wednesday, we got up and continued with regular training. But we got another hard "Tirtur" that night. We were ordered outside at 11 P.M. They claimed we were "tardy"—in other words, we may have been ten seconds late for roll call once. As a result, they kept us awake till 1:30 A.M. and we had to repeat our whole day's schedule at night: getting up, having morning inspection, shaving, shining our shoes, leaving for exercises, going to bed (by the way, we brought the cots and all our equipment out on the parade field, a distance of several hundred yards from the tents, all of course in pitch-black darkness)—in brief, it was quite dreadful. Everyone came out of this workout half dead.

On the following day, Thursday, we got up as usual. Again the exercises. And at three o'clock we went on another march, the second in three days. That was unheard of (at least among us). We had all come back from the first march, which was conducted at high speed, with sores, strained muscles, injuries and great fatigue. But it became clear that this was only intended as preparation for the second march. Well, on Thursday we set out on a march aimed at getting us "acquainted with the borders," with full packs (very heavy!). That day we marched until nightfall. We slept outdoors and continued in the morning until two in the afternoon. Morale was high. We entered all the Arab villages in the region and crossed the borders near our base.

The march was nearly forty miles long, and we covered the distance at great speed. Now all the soldiers are limping, barely able to walk. As for me—I have very few problems. Compared with the rest of our men, I'm in excellent physical shape. The marches aren't difficult for me. The running and all the other exercises leave me in good shape and unperturbed relative to the others.

Today the officers decided that this eventful week had been filled to capacity and they would now let us sleep. They say that tomorrow—Saturday—they won't assign us any tasks but will allow us to have a complete rest for recovery. In all the other branches of Zahal that's the normal situation (Sabbath is Sabbath), but not for us paratroops. These last four days were really crushing, and it's good that they're over.

Now that I've completed over a third of basic training, I can look back and see the long road I've traveled, see all that I've accomplished and what I'm capable of doing. I look back on it with genuine satisfaction. I think that so far I've gotten out of the army everything possible; and I'm sure this will continue in the future as well.

I want to encourage you all to write. The only moment of leisure in Zahal is the one devoted to reading letters. We read them while running to roll call, during our five-minute breaks, etc. But this gives us contact with the outside world and dispels the tension that prevails here. It's terribly important to receive letters, and the soldier who doesn't receive any is miserable. My need may be even greater than most because, after all, the others do get to see their families at every leave; though I'm not complaining at all and make do with what I have in the best way possible.

October 4, 1964

Tutti my love,

It looks as if you haven't managed to adapt yourself to the one critical thing in the army—to live as one of the crowd: to stand in line, and the like. On the one hand, I'm sorry because if you don't accept this reality, you won't have as easy and useful a time in the army as you could have. On the other, I'm rather glad; that's the truth. Actually you have no choice and must adjust to the situation. You said yourself, and you well knew, that this would be your main problem in Zahal. But you were certain you'd overcome it, despite everything. As a matter of fact, I think I was even more sure of that than you were.

Our problem here is a little different. I remain here all alone, live my life with and within myself and share my inner self with only one other person—you. At the same time I function well with the entire unit. I once told you that I help the guys with running, marches, and the like, but that I didn't like it. As I see it, this is not a fair basis for reciprocity, and I don't think I'll need help in return. But by now I've completely accepted the situation. I can't stand by and see someone fall without picking him up and helping him until I've exhausted my last ounce of strength. Not when he is trying as hard as he can. If he doesn't try, then he doesn't deserve help. With my tent-mates it's different of course. Here the rule is, "One for all and all for one." This also applies to me, and I've acted accordingly from the start.

Today I received a letter from Bibi. It was quite unexpected, and you don't know how happy I was to receive it! I think I love him more than anyone else in the world. I didn't take my correspondence with him as something particularly important. Bibi exists, and that was enough for me. When I was abroad I wrote few letters to Israel. Four months prior to my return I wrote a letter to C. He responded with a letter full of anger—how dare I write out of the blue without giving any explanation? Did I want to renew the ties between us which had in the interim weakened due to my neglect, etc., etc.? I had a good laugh when I read it and wrote him that he was talking nonsense, that despite all his anger and fury, I would still remain his friend because I knew him so well. He replied with a heart-warming letter, but again I didn't write. When I returned to Israel, I found I was right. It's the same with Bibi, except that you'd never get a reaction like that from him. He knows me better than anyone else does, at least I think he does. I'm always happy to receive letters from those I love, but if I don't, I don't, and that's that. Bibi wrote mostly about himself, his studies, his activities, a little about his everyday life. When Bibi writes about home, our parents and Iddo, I *believe* him. I feel as though I had actually been there and seen everything that was going on and had reported it to myself.

They say that next Thursday we'll go on field maneuvers. We'll have to march nearly forty-five miles to reach the place where the maneuvers will be held. If this rumor is correct (and it appears to be so), I'll be back three weeks from now. I hope very, very much that you will be in town at that time.

October 7, 1964

Tutti,

Fatigue and weariness are beginning to show. There isn't a class in which some canteens aren't emptied over the heads of those who've fallen asleep; everybody's walking around with eyes half-shut and knees sagging. The number of guys from Jerusalem in the company is diminishing daily. I hadn't noticed it till M. remarked today that only five of us were left. Pretty sad!

Not a day passes (today is the exception) that I don't receive a letter from you. Your letter is like a ray of light that scatters the dullness all around.

I want to write at length, but I can't. Sometimes I can write and write. Today I feel as if I'm writing a telegram.

By the way, take things as they come and don't let wild fancies get hold of you. The guys break down psychologically because they can't keep concentrating on what is happening *here*. In that state they are overwhelmed by thoughts of home, civilian life, etc., which just now are out of reach.

October 8, 1964

Dear Father, Mother, Bibi and Iddo,

This may be the shortest of my letters. In less than an hour we're setting out on exercises—at least ten days in the field—and then I probably won't have time even to write a letter as short as this. After the field exercises we'll get leave (two days apparently; that seems like a lot of time now). Everyone is madly getting ready, and there isn't a moment to spare. I'm writing this at top speed to make sure I send some word to you before we set out.

I received several letters from you and was simply elated. Bibi wrote a really *extraordinarily* good composition. In my opinion, it could be published anywhere. Bibi, I'd like you to continue to send me things you write at school.

When you tell me about the house, the garden and the work you do in it, about Father's work, Mother's activities, and Bibi's and Iddo's studies, I feel very very close to you—it's like actually living with you. I can see everything as though I was right there beside you. Write, write, write.

Our leaves are so rare that I think, Mom, you attach too much importance to them. All we want to do is to come home and sleep. It hardly makes any difference to me where I go (that is, as long as I can't go to our own home, of course). Look, I'm getting along very nicely and am happy that everything has worked out so well.

My weapons and equipment are ready. We're finishing the job of breaking camp, and then we're off.

October 17, 1964

Dear Mother, Father, Bibi and Iddo,

More than a week has passed since I wrote to you. I sent you a brief note telling you that we were going on field exercises to open country. Well, the location of these exercises was about forty miles from the base, and needless to say we covered this ground on foot with all our equipment on our backs. Everybody arrived in poor shape and everyone, bar none, was limping badly. I came through quite well (compared with the others). Since some of our group had trouble marching, the others had to drag them along—literally "drag" them. There were only six to eight among us who were able to do it. I "adopted" a very nice fellow who weighs about 200 lbs., and believe me, dragging a guy like that is no mean task. At least it helps make one fitter. Naturally it was tough, but it was hard for everyone and not just for me. Had I walked alone, I'd have felt free as a bird.

You wrote Miri that, judging by what I told you, you think that I'm having a hard time in the army. Please, don't misunderstand me. The army isn't easy for anyone. It's a great hardship, and it's meant to be. Even so, I'm among the few who don't find it too great an effort and manage splendidly.

This time it was firing exercises. All we did, day and night, was shoot, shoot, and shoot. We shot rifles, Uzzis,* machine guns, bazookas, anti-tank guns, mortars, etc., until our ears rang with all the noise. I've not enjoyed anything in the army as much as this exercise. Now we've been given leave until ten o'clock Sunday morning.

By the way, the Barmeir family sent me a large parcel. It was a total surprise as I didn't expect so much kindness from them. They are really very lovely people. I also received a parcel from Aunt Miri, and today when I visited Aunt Phirah, she loaded me with a harvest of wealth to

*Israeli-made submachine gun.

take back with me. So I have nothing to complain about.

I am receiving your letters regularly and am happy to hear that everything is okay at home. I'm terribly sorry that I'll miss Father's lecture. I would so much like to hear it.

Now I can enlarge a bit on Bibi's essay. Bibi, your composition is really extraordinary. You have an uncommon gift of expressing yourself in writing. I wish I knew half the English you do. You appear able to make use of all the English at your disposal. If you continue along these lines you'll be producing marvellous things. If you are capable of composing an essay like this in the tenth grade, who knows what you will write in the twelfth, and afterwards.

I'm overjoyed to hear that both of you, Iddo and Bibi, are doing so well in your studies. I'm sorry I'm not with you and can't see your progress with my own eyes. I'd also like to see the house, the garden, even the roads —but above all else, of course, I'd love to see you. Bibi writes that you, Father and Mother, look wonderful; I only wish I were in a position to make such a judgment myself at this moment.

October 24, 1964

Dear Mother, Father, Bibi and Iddo,

Last night we finished maneuvers and returned to base. On the way back we conducted an eight-mile stretcher-march across the dunes to Bat-Yam. Five of us carried a fellow weighing 200 lbs. It was gruelling physical torture. Just imagine, we had to walk not parallel to the dunes but across them—that is, we had to climb every single hill. With each step we took, our feet sank some ten inches in the sand. On the ascents we would drag one foot forward and then slide backward, so that each step only took us four inches forward. Tonight (Friday) we were allowed to sleep so that we might recover from the two weeks of training. Tomorrow we leave for the field again, but today we're enjoying a bit of rest and relaxation.

It's been some time since I wrote to you all, because it's impossible to write during exercises—I don't even have two minutes to spare. Even the differences between day and night disappear while the exercises are under way. Training doesn't stop for a second. The two hours' sleep they give us we use to the full, and even then with a sense of apprehension lest they wake us.

To tell the truth, I enjoy life in the field even more than in the base. From today on, the base will cease to be our regular living quarters and will assume its proper role—that of a rear base. Nearly all our time on exercises will be spent in the field.

At long last we feel like real soldiers, not green recruits. We've overcome genuine difficulties, we've mastered the use of firearms, etc. Soon we'll be taken to participate in the making of the film *Judith* (with Sophia Loren). Undoubtedly we'll be cast as both the British and the Arabs. We're waiting for that day as if it were a dream. At least, we hope, we'll be able to have some rest.

I'm writing this letter in installments and will soon end it. Just this minute we finished lunch; meat (a distressingly small amount) mixed with rice, beans, a pickle and an apple (not bad food, but not enough). Army food is so planned that all the calories you take in are immediately used up in work. If you don't eat your portion to the last crumb, you won't be able to move. Some guys faint from weakness.

Our numbers are gradually diminishing and only the strongest and most competent remain. Now it's a pleasure to be in such company. We have coalesced into a single body, and we function as a superb team, even though the road ahead is still long and we're only at the beginning.

October 30, 1964

Dearest Mother, Father, Bibi and Iddo,

Well, I got another leave and as usual came into town.

I hadn't had a wink of sleep for forty-five hours—and it showed. Five of us soldiers traveled by bus to Tel Aviv, and since the trip took about an hour, we fell asleep on the way. When we woke up we found ourselves in Tel Aviv. All the passengers, including the driver, had long since gotten off and only we five were left on the bus. In general, we've reached such a state that we use every free moment for sleeping. If I'm given a ten-minute rest, I'll be fast asleep within one minute, and at the end of ten I'll wake up fresh and alert. That's the only way to hold your own in this sleepless army.

I can imagine the excitement at home over the great success of Father's lecture. I'm so sorry I missed it! It so happens that I always miss his lectures. This is really frightfully bad luck. But if I couldn't hear it, I'll be able at least to read it. I suppose all of you will now rest a little. In any case, I hope so, because you have worked so hard.

The army continues to step up the demands it makes on us, and most of us succeed in meeting them. But many are still being tossed out. These are really people who don't belong here.

A few days ago we returned from the filming of *Judith*. We played both the Israelis and the attacking Arabs. But most of the day we slept. True, we were outside in the sun, but just the same we slept. There were infantrymen there too (from "Golani"*), and they claimed that being in the film was a pain for them, but for us it was tantamount to a holiday. On the last day of our stay there the film company loaded us all on buses and drove us to Nahariyah to see the movie *Tom Jones*. Such a thing is unheard of in the army.

In the next few days we'll go on a march of fifty to sixty miles, and immediately afterwards we'll leave for two field exercises aimed at individual and group training. Both are hard, and I'll write about them when the time comes.

When I consider why I was so drawn to the paratroops, or to put it more accurately, why I manage to bear up here, I reach the conclusion that the reason is the difficulty, the need to overcome obstacles and above all the chance to prove to myself that I'm capable of doing everything required here, and a lot more if necessary.

Dear Bibi, happy birthday! It's hard to believe that you're only fifteen; you've always seemed to me more mature than your years.

The army doesn't leave its soldiers much time to miss home. I think a person feels longing when he has the time to stop and meditate, to look into his inner self. In contrast, when he is up to his neck in the present, which weighs and presses down on him, he has to give all of himself to that present. When I have time, as I do today, and can stop for a moment and breathe in the quiet, I realize how much I'd like to see you.

I'll stop now. I'm going to wash my fatigues, and then I'll give the underwear to Phirah or to Mrs. Barmeir. I do the fatigues by hand because they have to be washed thoroughly, and I don't mind doing this work, even though Mrs. Barmeir insists that she wants to do it.

Your loving,
Yoni

October 31, 1964

Dear parents and brothers,

It's Saturday and tonight I return to base. This was the first leave I slept as much as I needed.

*"Golani"—an infantry brigade in the Israeli army.

A bit on "how I look." Everyone claims I look fine. My hands and face are very tanned because we're out in the sun all the time. The rest of my body is less so. What else? I don't think I've lost any weight. In any event, every time I come on leave, I put on a couple of pounds on purpose in order to counteract any loss.

You ought to see our fatigues, the uniforms we wear every day. They are tiger-spotted in three colors: brown, dark green and light green, perfect camouflage colors. They're made of such heavy fabric that the top can serve as a good, warm coat. In the daytime when the sun is hot, it's a virtual inferno to wear them (that is, until you get used to them; after a while you just don't feel them). But at night, when it's cold—especially as winter approaches—there'll be nothing we'll love more than these fatigues. Just imagine, in the night and in the morning, around 4:30 to 5:30, it's so cold that we sleep in these clothes, with a thick windbreaker on top. Until now we each had three "Grade 3" blankets, i.e., blankets 3 feet by 3 feet (no exaggeration) and with holes so big that if you'd wanted to use the wool left in them, it wouldn't amount to more than one square yard. Now these have been replaced by "French blankets," huge, thick, woolen blankets; if you sleep under these in your clothes, it's nice and warm. You should remember that in the field we generally sleep inside pup tents with a blanket spread on the bare ground. You can't imagine how soft the earth is when you're tired.

On the whole I enjoy the field exercises more than life in the base. They are much more varied and interesting. You know I've always liked living outdoors, in camps, etc. Now I have it in abundance, and it's a good thing I'm used to it and even capable of enjoying such a life.

The weather in Jerusalem is lovely. It does get a bit cool in the evening and you have to wear a sweater (and sweaters, thank God, I have plenty of). It's pleasant to feel the approach of winter, but in the daytime the sun still reigns supreme, and it's warm and pleasant. All in all, it's good to be in Jerusalem. A quiet, tranquil city.

November 7, 1964

Dear Father, Mother, Bibi and Iddo,

Again we're "somewhere" in the country, training in "individual combat." The purpose of this exercise is to prepare us for a situation where we'll be by ourselves—in daytime, nighttime, in enemy or friendly territory, in time of war, attack, assault, etc. We storm hills, infiltrate objectives, fire at hidden targets, hide out in the field, take cover, "fight" in built-up areas, etc. Quite interesting.

A week's gone by since I last wrote, and it passed *very* fast. It's the seventh of the month already, and I've been in the army three full months! Today's Saturday—and we're relaxing. I'm resting this letter on Steinbeck's *Travels with Charley*. I manage to read it exactly once a week —in moments like this.

It's good to hear from you about home. About the guests who visit you, about Bibi and Iddo's studies, and more. So much time seems to have passed since I left school, while actually it's all been very recent. Four or five months, right? And already I'm anxious to return to my studies! Well, I'll get back to them eventually.

Hey! Just now they called my name for my monthly pay. Got to go. That's it. I'm waiting in line now, about five soldiers in front of me. Naturally we're standing holding our weapons. They're "attached" to us, or as we say here, "we're attached to our weapons." Everywhere we go the rifle comes along. We've gotten used to eating while it lies beside us, to sleeping while we're "hugging" it—this for fear that it may suddenly disappear. Stealing in the army is on a scale that's hard to believe. Anyone caught cannot escape punishment—immediate incarceration. Trouble is, anyone missing any item of equipment has to fill out a "loss of equipment" form and stand trial. Just imagine, for the loss of an army cap, which costs less than one I£, you're made to pay 10 I£ (cost plus fine). It's quite obvious why stealing is so common in the army. I'm pleased to note that so far I haven't lost a thing and hope this will continue. Our company had relatively few thefts. Well, I got the money (17 I£).*

November 1964

(To Tutti)

It is inconceivable that the distance between us and the lack of letters may cause us to grow apart. What there was and still is between us will always exist, unless and until we both feel that we have nothing more to give each other, that being together adds nothing to our lives and is merely a burden or a forced routine.

Do we really feel that way? Of course not!

Two days have passed since I began this letter. In that interval we

*Equivalent then to about $8.00.

managed to conduct a forced march of thirty-five miles which took the whole night, and now we're starting group training. I set out on the march with a fever, a very sore throat and a bad cold, and now I'm a bit ill. It will pass in the course of the exercises. Next Thursday we'll begin squad training exercises, and in two weeks we'll finally go to jump school. That will mark the conclusion of our basic training, and we're counting the days to the beginning of that course.

Last night we slept like logs, and now we're full of energy. About a mile away from the camp ("Danger, No Admittance, Shooting with Live Ammunition!") there's a Bedouin well. This morning, Saturday, we went there, drew water up in pails, and "showered." We also managed, Yair and I, to get hold of three cubes of soup and built a small fire in the shade.

That briefly is what we did yesterday and today. I forgot to tell you that six of us representing our company had a talk yesterday with the battalion commander about the company's problems, its morale, etc. The things discussed were quite trivial, but since the commander is a very nice chap, this, too, was pleasant, although somewhat drawn-out.

What else? That's about it! There's no other news.

I miss you, Tutti, I don't have time to write.

Something happened recently that claimed my entire attention. I have a friend among the paratroopers, a wonderful fellow. There's no point in writing about him until you meet him because I won't be able to describe him. Well, about two weeks ago, during night training, he was hit. He's in the hospital now, being fed by means of plastic tubes, and no one knows whether or not he'll recover.

I'll try to write more, although the above was not the sole reason for my failure to write. I simply couldn't.

November 14, 1964

Dear beloved Mother, Father, Bibi and Iddo,

It's Saturday evening now and we're going to bed quietly (for the present; any minute may bring an alarm ordering us all to "battle stations" in full equipment; this is quite routine and can happen any time during the night). Some of the guys here sleep with their shoes on; they don't take them off for a full week at a stretch for fear of those alarms. As a result, there are many whose feet are rotting. Needless to say, I'm not one of them. On the other hand, all of us sleep with our clothes on, and the reason is obvious—to be warmer and avoid freezing during the night.

My companion in the pup tent, a fellow from Hadar Ramatayim, is now sitting outside the tent oiling his rifle (before he goes to bed) by the light of the candle beside which I'm lying and writing. I've already oiled mine. It seems to us that the type of rifle we're using rusts more easily than any other type of weapon. Neglect it just one night, and the next day it's all yellowish-red with rust.

We finished one field exercise and immediately set out for another one. Yesterday at 6:30 in the morning we completed a forced march of about thirty-five miles which took eleven and a half hours (with our regular equipment—light gear, battle gear and weapons). We've been doing a lot of these quick marches and will do many more. We maintain a pace of about 4–4 1/2 miles an hour (this includes a few minutes' stop approximately every two hours, and once during the entire march a break of fifteen minutes). After thirty to forty miles of marching like this, it becomes hard to go on because your feet are burning, actually flaming. I haven't developed any blisters, but, like everyone else, I felt that my feet were on fire. On the whole I'm in good shape.

At the conclusion of the basic training (very soon), we'll conduct a march of twelve miles at the same pace (the aim is to complete it in less than twenty-four hours). To tell the truth, when we started the last march I had a very bad sore throat and could scarcely say a word. Had I been at home, I'd have stayed in bed for a week like a good boy, but here it wasn't considered anything. When I finished the march—wonder of wonders!—not only had I not got worse but I'd actually improved somewhat, and today, after a rest and good night's sleep (Friday night), I'm fully recovered.

In a few weeks we'll go to jump school. We're all nearly mad with anticipation of this moment. Let it come! Let it only come! We've gone down such a long road that this course is like a treat that's awarded at the end (that's the general feeling), and now we're like little kids who've been promised candy but haven't been given any. The course itself, they say, is the easiest part of our army service. That is, the daytime training is not at all easy, but at least you sleep well at night and the food is excellent (the course is conducted in one of the central military bases, which has everything: food, showers, huts to sleep in, and more). There are altogether seven parachute jumps in the course; that's not too great a challenge (at least, not for us). What will follow later is another story. That's when the real "heat" will start. But time for that when we come to it.

You have only to remove yourself a bit from the burden of military life, and immediately you discover things that make you laugh. For instance, on our base we have latrines dating back to the days of the British, big holes in frames of concrete with a deep pit underneath. You can guess what happened. Naturally, one of the guys fell in and had to be pulled out on a rope. Or take another example—when someone wants to "fix" some soldier, he arranges to have the changing guards wake him up every three quarters of an hour. Just imagine the pleasure of being awakened every hour from one in the morning on! While it's happening it's most unpleasant, but later on it's possible to laugh at it. The trouble is we're under such continuous strain that we've almost forgotten to laugh.

At this moment I plan to shut my eyes. The height of bliss!

November 27, 1964

(To Tutti)

We finally got some leave, and I am now in Jerusalem—after a shower and a good dinner. On Sunday we're going to jump school, and all of us are looking forward to the moment when we'll be able to sleep in bunks and live like human beings. This past month has been a real "drubbing," but it finally came to an end and in fact marked the conclusion of our basic training.

It's sad to be here without you, although you already may have doubts in this regard. What can I tell you after receiving your letters? You're obviously right in feeling as you do—or, to be more accurate, I understand what you're feeling, but a letter won't help you (and me, as a result) to get rid of this bitter aftertaste. If I told you I didn't have a minute to write, would you believe me? Maybe not, because it's possible that I could have managed now and then to write a few words as you asked. Again: the root of the problem is imbedded in me alone because I fail to communicate my feeling to you. I can "live" with the present situation, so I think that you can too. At the same time, I am *really* happy when I get a letter from you, but when I don't get one, it doesn't cause me suffering and heartache. The letter is an add-on, not the foundation.

Tutti mine, I want to see you and long for the time when we'll have leave together. Then we'll be able to clarify things and to know, as you put it, "where we stand."

Yours with all my heart,
Yoni

November 28, 1964

Beloved Father, Mom, Bibi and Iddo,

It's been so long since I last wrote to you! I can well imagine the worry and anguish I must have caused you. My only excuse is that during the past month I haven't had even five minutes of free time. Can you believe it? It's hard to believe it's possible, isn't it?

So first of all, yesterday I finished basic training and tomorrow we're going to jump school—finally!

I think this past month has been the hardest we've had so far in the army. Incredible what we've gone through! I'll begin by describing the last week.

Let me just say in advance that we conducted many field exercises and did not leave open country for a month and a half. Upon concluding one exercise, we'd pack our gear and set out on a march to another location —to start a new exercise. In the meantime winter has begun, and it looks as though it's going to be a very hard one. For us it is virtually a catastrophe. Last week we had five consecutive days of torrential rain, which did not stop day or night; not for one moment did that cruel downpour cease. Nevertheless, training continued on schedule. We go on living in pup tents, which let in water very fast. But one thing at a time.

Well, last week we "moved" again and, after marching all night, arrived in an area on the border of the Valley of Ayalon. We got there in pouring rain and pitched the tents on the wet, muddy ground. That same day we began exercises at 12:30 P.M. and continued with them until 7:00 P.M. in rain the like of which I swear I never saw even in America. Raincapes are not standard issue in Zahal—they claim that soldiers wearing them are clumsy on the move. So we got soaked to the skin, the rain penetrating our clothes and running in streams down our bodies, where we felt it from our necks down to the soles of our feet, just as if we had no clothes on at all. We practiced taking a fortified position. Fortified positions are generally found on hilltops, with connecting trenches surrounding them, as well as look-out posts and foxholes. To capture such a position you have to go along the trenches clearing every post. The rain had filled the trenches with water two feet deep—the soil here does not let water sink in, so we stood in that terrible rain with our feet sunk in water above the tops of our boots, rifles at the ready in our hands. It was so cold that I had to use all my strength to reload the magazine. Imagine a cold so fierce that the hands don't obey their master!

Later, when I reached my tent, I couldn't even hold a match in my fingers to light a candle (our sole illumination). I had to grasp it in my fist and move the box of matches up and down with the other hand to kindle it. The candle slipped from my hand several times before I managed to light it. But I'm getting ahead of my story.

Well, there we were standing with our feet in the water and the rain beating down on us mercilessly. After a while our shoulders began to hurt and our backs to ache, and we felt stabbing pains in the neck and other parts of the body. Don't forget that all this time we're working with live ammunition and have to exercise great caution.

We finally returned to the camp and went to sleep. Because we went out to the field with minimum gear, some of the men had no spare clothing and went to sleep with their wet clothes on. Not me, thank God! I stripped to the skin, crawled into my sleeping bag and fell asleep. Next day, it turned out that one man was suffering from rheumatism and another had the symptoms. They simply woke up in the morning unable to move their shoulders. Two others were put on stretchers and carried into a command car, as they couldn't climb into it themselves, and were driven to the regimental hospital. Many others became ill or got colds or were drained of every ounce of strength and had to be transferred to the isolation ward at the base. Others who were sick were left to rest in their tents.

There were days when only sixteen men of the platoon's thirty-seven (that's our paper-strength) went out on exercises. That's how it was in the final days of this week as well. True, it wasn't as awful as the first day, but it was bad enough. The ground remained swampy and slippery and the risk of sliding and falling was very great. One of our men had managed to fall and break a leg, and another fell during a night stretcher-march, apparently spraining a pelvis bone. You have to take great care and exercise every caution. I don't treat anything lightly. I've learned that if I want to stay on my feet, I must devote complete attention day and night to what I'm doing.

Here, either you become fully hardened or you break down. There's no middle ground. I feel I'm now in top form. No march, no run and no other physical effort is really difficult for me. When I came to Jerusalem this time (I arrived last night at six), everyone who saw me said I looked wonderful. I was happy to hear it—it's a good sign. I know you'll be happy to hear it too, and that's why I mention it.

When I got to Jerusalem, I went directly to the Barmeirs. I ate Friday night dinner with them (having come just in time) and then went with Eli and another friend to stroll a bit (Tutti is not in town; she's at a squad commanders' course, and I haven't seen her for a month and a half). Then

I went to visit Ruthie H., whom I haven't seen for over three months. She's now studying Jewish and General Philosophy at the Hebrew University. She's very pleased with her studies and her teachers, especially the ones teaching Jewish Philosophy.

That night I went to bed around one o'clock and slept till eleven in the morning (today), without waking before 5:30 as I usually do. Normally I wake up at that hour as if I had an alarm clock by my side, but this time I slept uninterrupted till eleven. Evidently because I knew I didn't have to get up early. This probably affects that hidden alarm clock.

Mr. and Mrs. Barmeir received the gifts you sent them and were delighted with them and very grateful, though they stressed, of course, that there was really no need and that the gifts were far too extravagant and completely unexpected. Once I asked them to buy something for me and send it to camp. I left them the money because it was quite expensive. When I next came home, I found the money on the table. They have taken me into the family like another son, and I'm very happy with this. What better arrangement could one have?

This evening Bari and I went to a movie and then to a restaurant for supper. Thus I realized at least one of the dreams we all have during training. Some soldiers dream of coming home, putting on all the clothes they own, creeping into a warm bed with a quilt blanket, never to leave it, not even to eat (I'm sure some of them did just that). Now I'm devoting part of the night to writing this letter and when I've finished, I'll go to bed.

I've been receiving quite a few letters from you. There was even a letter from Bibi and Iddo. Of course, I'd like both of you to write more. I understand that Father is extremely busy with his work and that Mother writes for everyone. I seem to have acquired from you, Father, the habit of writing few letters and concentrating fully on the task at hand.

Sarah told me of your plans for the summer. I wouldn't like you to come back on my account but would prefer you to do what's best for Father; that's the most important thing, and I'm getting along fine anyway. In any case, I'm hardly ever in town. We get leaves about once a month, and it will stay that way in the future, or perhaps get even less frequent. Anyway, if you do come, even for just a summer visit, it will be real happiness, and naturally I'm impatient to see you here.

You wouldn't believe how much more I have to tell you, but I must finish. It's very very late and I want to try to sleep at least four hours tonight before I get moving. And I've still got to make my bed before going to sleep. Bari is making us some coffee.

December 5, 1964

Tutti,

Another week has passed and again it seems that we won't be able to meet. As you probably know, this Saturday we had to remain "on alert." Well, someone has to do it; and after all we were at home last week. Next week we'll go home again (I should add "probably"), but for us two that's not much help.

We haven't reached, and apparently won't reach, "nirvana"—at any rate not in our company. After completing jump school, we will have night exercises. Films are out-of-bounds for us, as is nearly everything else. And every now and then comes a hefty kick to cool us off a bit.

I want to see you very much,

Miss you,
Yoni

December 7, 1964

Dear Mother, Father, Bibi and Iddo,

I'm using a short break in the training to write this letter. Well, we've been at the course for a week now, and we are living magnificently. We have passed "from bondage to freedom." Conditions are superb, the exercises interesting, the food excellent and the sleep abundant. What more could we ask for?

Since we are now in what is called the "School for Parachuting and Light Warfare," it appears that the conditions are those of a real school (if comparisons can be made at all). Between exercises there are short breaks. We are not drilled too much during the day; and at night, at 10:30, lights-out. That doesn't mean we don't have night alerts, or that we don't have nighttime training after the day's exercises—to supplement some material we missed (usually theoretical stuff). It looks as if we are to remain alert during the day and not fall asleep. That's hard. Now that we are being given a chance to rest to a certain extent, our exhaustion bursts forth and shows itself throughout the day. Lassitude shrouds every part of the body and the eyes keep falling closed.

I must end. The break is over.

December 14, 1964

Dear, beloved Mother, Father, Bibi and Iddo,

We are approaching the end of the course. Life here is marvellous. Right now it is raining in torrents and we are sitting inside a warm cabin, protected from the wrath of the storm.

Yesterday we got leave until midnight, and I went to Jerusalem and slept properly. This has become a habit—to come home and sleep even when we're not tired. Sleep has turned into something you need to accumulate, not only to make up for what you've missed, but also to enable you to go without sleep in the future. I'm conscious that I refer to a visit to Jerusalem as "coming home." It's good that I've fallen into the habit of thinking in those terms. But that is also what I called my room on Shammai Street and every place I slept for a few successive nights. Of course, "there is no place like home"—i.e., your *real* home. This is such a true saying.

In the meantime I read a great deal. In the big leave (if we get it) I plan to resume my physics and then I'll get the feel of "studying" once again. I come to town and see before me the different notebooks (Bari's or his sister's), and I get the urge to pick them up and read them. By the way, I took some books in Arabic from Bari. I opened them to discover, believe it or not, that I remember a great deal. I can easily translate from Arabic into Hebrew, but the reverse is difficult, and that's quite understandable.

We have just been informed that the training has been postponed "until further notice." Here, when it rains, there are no exercises. Someone got hold of an accordion and a few soldiers are playing it and going wild. Fun.

December 24, 1964

Beloved Mother, Father, Bibi and Iddo,

At the moment I am on guard duty. It is past midnight and, luckily for me, all I have to do is sit at the base gate and note down which cars come and go. At this late hour traffic is light and I am free to do what I want.

In just a few days we will finish the course. I have three jumps behind me—two without battle gear and weapons, and one with. On Sunday we will have our first night jump.

A pity this is only an aerogramme with little space to describe the jump properly. Actually it's also hard to describe.

We finished our ground exercises very quickly (or so it seemed) and immediately afterwards we were arrayed in rows on the runway strip. We strap on our parachutes, receive final instructions from the instructors and walk toward the plane entrance. There are thirty-six of us in our plane. Eighteen men are to jump from the right-hand exit, eighteen from the left-hand. I am designated to jump first, left side, plane number one. The doors close behind us and slowly the plane begins to roll. Its thunder turns into a roar, the roar to a wail. As it picks up speed, we "help" it take off by shouting "On, On" and then burst into song. Suddenly the doors open, and immediately afterwards we hear the command "Attention!" which brings us to our feet, tense and ready. I am, as I've said, to jump first, but I have a fleeting moment until the next command. Once again the order is given: "Attention!" and I stand for a moment in the door, in the "ready" position, looking around. Far, far below is the ground. Here and there on the horizon scattered areas of settlement are visible, shading the earth with different hues. Ahead, just in front of me, I can hear the whistling of the wind and feel it chilling the palms of my hands, which are already outside. My head is raised, and I look straight ahead. My right foot is back, ready to give the kick that will catapult me into space. No time for fear. Fear will come later, in future jumps, or perhaps it has already come before this one! At this moment I dare not do anything that is not directly connected with the jump itself. No time for that. Must concentrate on the void straight ahead. Everything has to be done just right. "Jump!" I hurl myself out of the plane, the floor slips from under my feet, and I am out in space. I take the blast of the slipstream as it pushes me left toward the tail, and I feel myself falling down, down. I count aloud, "Twenty-one! Twenty-two! Twenty-three!" It's important to stay alert and keep a sense of time. During this first jump you don't feel yourself falling so much, you're conscious only of the eddies of wind all around you, chaining you and preventing you from moving your limbs. Your head is bent, your arms are crossed and your legs are curled up very, very tight. The chute opens.

I look up and see the canopy spread out. No cords are twisted, nothing needs fixing. I release the right side of the reserve chute and look around me. Behind me, all about me, parachutes are scattered. The second in which you find yourself free in the air is not a second but an eternity. You no longer feel yourself falling; you are floating slowly, slowly, between heaven and earth. Now the landscape is different: quiet, silent, filled with a kind of majesty. It's virtually impossible to describe those seventy seconds in the air. It's undoubtedly the most marvellous experience. You're master of the world and even more so—of your own self! The ground below grows increasingly larger; already you are only about fifty yards above it. The day is clear and there is scarcely a breath of wind. A slight drift to the right, which you must stop so the chute won't drag you once you've landed. Forty yards, thirty, now the ground is drawing closer with ever-increasing speed and you get into "Prepare to land!" position. You must observe all the rules. Your legs and feet are pressed together tightly, glued to one another. If both don't strike the ground with equal force, there's a good chance you'll break a leg. Your legs are slightly bent. Your head is lowered. Your arms tighten on the steel helmet. The ground approaches fast. Twenty yards, ten, and then it's over. Landing, rolling correctly, and you're on your feet, running around the chute to grab it.

Apparently, the landing was a bit too fast; I hurt my left foot slightly. Evidently my legs did open a bit. Next time we'll have to improve this —thus we decide and thus we do next time. You glance upward and there, across the face of the heavens, are scattered the parachutes from the planes that followed us: several hundred yards around you can see figures dropping, landing and immediately springing to their feet. Is everything all right? All landed safely. One sprained his foot; he didn't do everything as he should have. Trucks take us back to the base. Over and done. We've jumped!

Second jump. You know what's ahead of you, and for this reason you are more afraid. It isn't real fear but only an oppressive, unpleasant feeling. In all honesty, I expected a much greater apprehension, but there is no time for that. Again you jump. You unwind the twists made in the cords by the blast of the wind. This time your approach to the ground seems to be slower. You roll correctly and stand up. While in the air you do not feel that you're falling at all; you feel it only toward the end.

The third jump was the most successful even though it was done with full gear. There's time for everything. There's no need to hurry. By now you're able to direct your gliding in the air, exchanging cries with friends floating around you and getting up to watch the others land.

What shall I tell you? I haven't room to describe it all. This is such a unique experience that unless you've been in the air you really can't imagine it. The jab of the chute as it opens, the world drifting about you, the ground approaching from below, the soil beneath your feet, the parachute lying inert on the sand.

As a young paratrooper, after a jump, 1965

December 26, 1964

Beloved Father, Mother, Bibi and Iddo,

Lately I've received lots of letters from you, which made me very happy. Father's letter arrived a short while ago and afterwards two more—one from Mother and the other from Bibi. I had no one to whom I could brag about my two excellent brothers, but actually there's no need for that. It's enough that I know. It's so good to hear how well both of you are doing in school! I'd really like to be with you and see you sitting there studying and making such progress! But never mind; I get a complete picture of all that's happening at home through all your letters, as each of you describes what goes on from his own point of view.

As for me, a few days ago I completed jump school. I was surprised that Mother wrote that she could not understand how anyone could enjoy such horrors. What's the matter with you? That's precisely what I volunteered for! Didn't I think about the jumps before I joined the paratroops? No horrors are involved here. Quite the contrary. There is much in parachuting that is grand and splendid.

Bibi asked me to describe in detail how a person is trained to become a parachutist—to overcome fear and finally to jump. Well, since this is Saturday and I've got more than eight hours before I return to base, I have time to describe each step.

The course takes three weeks, of which the last is devoted to the jumps themselves and the rest to ground exercises. The training includes instruction on how to enter the plane, how to sit inside it, and what to do from the moment you get into it to the moment you reach the ground. Every step requires a different drill and is important in its own right.

"Via dolorosa"—that's the nickname for the jump-training installation. But it's not really painful at all. "Knowledge Prevents Fear" is painted on signs placed all around. There's much truth in this, although, in my opinion, it's entirely a personal matter: one man will be scared to death where another will pass with a smile on his lips.

The underlying principle in the training is practice, practice and more practice, until the fear that's present in the initial exercises disappears, and you discover there's not much to it. The execution has got to be perfect, and the instructors—superb. Anyone failing to pass the ground exercises is not allowed to jump.

The course included seven jumps, two of them at night. After the final one (a night jump) we conducted a march with full packs and reached the base at 2 A.M. The following day we received our paratroop wings.

Now I'm a full-fledged paratrooper, and as such I have to carry a greater burden; but I have to admit life is no longer so difficult. True, we have to bear up under the same hardships as before, and even greater ones, but these no longer seem to be genuine difficulties, and I am capable of doing everything. We've just finished a thirty-mile march which is only a "baby" march, carried out at a speedy five miles an hour. And bear in mind that each of us carries with him full gear, weighing some thirty-five to forty-five lbs. When the march ended I knew with utter certainty that I could turn right around and retrace the entire distance we had just covered.

January 6, 1965

Beloved Mother, Father, Bibi and Iddo,

I don't remember if I told you that we were given a nine-day leave. For that whole time, I must admit, I hardly stirred out of the house. Every morning I'd take the physics texts left in my possession, go to the National Library at the University and study for three to four hours. Then I'd go back home for lunch, after which I'd read and study some more. Most of the time I'd go to bed early and rise early.

For a week now we've been engaged in what is called a "finishing course," performing more complicated and much more taxing exercises. It is raining continuously, but I got used to it long ago and get along very nicely in conditions which to another person might appear quite terrible. I returned from the leave feeling invigorated and happy, unlike many others who were bored to death because, as they insist, there's nothing to do in town. I spent the entire time at the Barmeirs, and they were nice as usual.

By some miracle the rain has stopped but the air is still saturated with a chilly moisture. The sky is completely grey and the sun is all but invisible. It's now possible to sit outside the pup tent; so at the moment I am perched on a rock, beside one of the Bet Govrin caves, and writing this letter to you.

By the way, I managed to do something I didn't believe possible: to read a book during field exercises. I am incapable of drilling all day, then dropping onto the blanket in the tent to sleep for a few hours, only to begin drilling again without an interlude devoted to thinking or reading. Somehow or other I always manage to dig up some time to read. Right now the book is *Atlas Shrugged* and I'm making good progress.

I'm sorry you're finding it difficult to read my handwriting, but my letters are written under field conditions; that is, the paper is on my knee and the pen is of poor quality.

Again the Jordanians have begun to shoot and again we have problems. I have to stop and present myself for roll call. I'll continue later.

January 18, 1965

Beloved Mother, Father, Bibi and Iddo,

After weeks of tough maneuvers in the field we were taken to Jerusalem. We'll remain here for a while along the front lines,* then we'll go out on a number of short field exercises, and finally on a long one of five weeks in a row.

Since we are in Jerusalem, I'll tell you a bit of what we're doing here. We sit in positions that are very well fortified; it seems that even a direct hit from a shell couldn't destroy them. Actually, each post is a house occupied by three to five soldiers, each of whom is assigned to several hours of lookout duty, usually five to seven hours a day. The rest of the time I am free inside the post. There is a refrigerator here, a cooking range and food in abundance. But the main thing is the free time. The truth is we're having a most wonderful, relaxing break. We hardly do anything all day long, and we stay here simply because there must be soldiers in this city, just as their presence is essential in other parts of the country.

I haven't heard from Bibi for a long time, and certainly not from Father. It would be very nice to hear from all of you occasionally even though I know that these times will be few and far between and that you don't write only because you do not have time. I realize, of course, that one has first to do one's work conscientiously and only then allow time for things of secondary importance.

February 18, 1965

Dear Mother, Father, Bibi and Iddo,

In another week I'll leave for an entire month of field exercises, and my writing during that time will be very limited. These will be large-scale maneuvers for the paratroopers, in conjunction with tanks and other

*Before the Six-Day War, Jerusalem was a divided city and the Jewish part faced the Jordanian border.

vehicles. We're sure to have an extremely strenuous month, but at the same time a most interesting one.

Clearly, there are better ways of spending one's years between eighteen and twenty, but since I am in the army, I try to get out of it the maximum benefit, interest and knowledge. During the past two weeks we studied classroom topography (i.e., from maps, not on location). The standard maintained in this course was very high. To conclude our theoretical studies we went with our instructors on a small group march (four to five men in a group) which lasted two days. We traversed the Carmel region, and never in my life have I seen such beautiful country. Here you can come upon mountains that look as if they had never been trodden by a human foot, and jungles of trees and shrubs that are all but impenetrable, inside which you find numberless brooks that form pools of cold water within the woods.

During the past few weeks of training, we simulated many interesting raids. Of special interest was the raid on a military camp, which began with a parachute jump at twilight. Immediately after landing we assembled in previously designated places; we prepared landing zones for helicopters, and when these arrived, we boarded them and flew toward our objective. When you fly in a "Nord" plane (for parachuting), you feel the whole plane quivering throughout its huge body, whereas the helicopter seems like a magic carpet, devoid of vibrations; it simply lifts up and flies. We disembarked about three miles from our destination, carried out the raid very successfully and returned to the helicopters, which took us back to our base.

The number of men in our company grows ever smaller. Where others find great hardships or boredom, resulting from their refusal to rise to the challenge, I find much that interests me; this is my great advantage over them.

The Barmeir family is nicer than ever. If I don't praise them to the skies, it's because I assume you know all about them and not because I am taking the current situation for granted.

February 21, 1965

Dear Mother, Father, Bibi and Iddo,

Today we finished a spell of navigation, this time without instructors. We walked from Jerusalem toward Dimona. But we didn't merely cover the distance—we climbed each mountain and went down into each ravine we encountered on our way. Our method of advancing is based on walking from one designated point to the next, until the final destination. These designated points may be a ruin in the Jerusalem mountains or an immense abandoned pit somewhere in the vastness of the Negev.

At noon today we reached the camp and got organized. We'll remain here in the Negev for about five weeks more.

You can hardly imagine how well you get to know a country on your feet. Try traveling on a flat desert wilderness and come suddenly upon an enormous canyon, which has created a stream, or on huge ravines, which bisect the mountains, and you'll see what an extraordinary experience it is. Then try crossing on foot these same canyons and mountain ridges, and only then will you feel how deep the gorges are and how high the mountains.

In the Negev when you're passing some remote spot, you may encounter a number of Bedouin tents with camels and donkeys and some sheep. An interesting way of life. It's remarkable how they're able to exist in these desolate regions. I think their only fear is of armed soldiers. They are prepared to extend their best hospitality to the soldier so that he leaves well satisfied and, more important—so that he leaves as quickly as possible.

You may have noticed that my handwriting is not uniform: sometimes the letters are large and sometimes small, etc. The reason is that I have to shield the paper from the wind with my left hand while I hold the pen in my right, so the letter keeps jumping around to the left and right with nothing holding it down. What's more, the light is very poor. But this is the only time I'm able to write, and it would be a pity not to use it for letter-writing, especially since I don't think I'll have such opportunities in the near future.

March 7, 1965

Dear Mother, Father, Bibi and Iddo,

Three weeks have passed since I last wrote you, and if I don't use my free hour from six to seven this evening, several more weeks may elapse before I manage to write again.

At present we're in the thick of maneuvers conducted "somewhere" in the open ranges of the Negev. To give you an idea of what is happening here, I'll describe the last few days, which were especially absorbing.

We went out on a battalion exercise on Wednesday at 2:30 in the morning and returned on Friday at 3:00 in the afternoon. During all that time we did not once shut our eyes.

At 3:00 A.M. we got into trucks, which took us to the spot where the exercise began. At the appointed hour we mounted tanks and armored half-tracks and swallowed mouthfuls of dust. All through the day we carried out impressive attacks on a variety of targets; present at these operations were the Prime Minister and the Chief of Staff. The maneuvers were accompanied by blazing fire from jets diving on the targets, with artillery shells and very heavy fire zooming over our heads. On Thursday evening we marched to a specified objective, and all through the night we dug in on the hills. In the morning we set out on a long march.

We reached our camp half sick and weak from exhaustion and from taking in too much dust and too little food. Because of the strain, the lack of sleep and the dirt, most of the soldiers fell ill. Only seventeen of us were still on our feet. Luckily, I came through the whole thing safely and in good health (as usual). As soon as we reached camp, I popped into the field shower and had a good wash, despite the freezing night air and the ice-cold water. I think most of the others got sick because they fell on their cots with all the filth still clinging to their bodies; they simply couldn't overcome their fatigue. It all started with the wake-up roll call on Saturday when two fellows standing in the line-up swayed a little and fainted. The epidemic came after that, with temperatures of 38.3°C to over 40°C. Nearly all were evacuated from the field infirmary to the hospital in Beersheba. But don't let me worry you. After a whole Sabbath's rest, I feel fine. This morning (Sunday) we trained lightly because in about half an hour we are leaving for a night march, which will include both laying and setting off explosives. No doubt we'll dig in again for the whole night. We plan to return tomorrow at noon.

Although the exercises are hard, I find much interest in everything that's happening. We're now seeing a far larger force acting as one superior team. In about two weeks' time these exercises will end, and only then will we go home. After that they plan a Sappers course for us, following which we'll take part in the Four-Day March to Jerusalem. For us this will be a real rest. Imagine, only twenty miles a day and nothing else. On top of that, a leave of several days seems to be in the offing, but to be honest we have some doubts that it will materialize.

Soon we'll start squad-commanders course, and I should be finished with it by the time you reach Israel. In the paratroops, ranks are awarded very slowly.

In six more days I'll be nineteen. The year passed quickly, didn't it? And

68

SELF-PORTRAIT OF A HERO

with that what a vast change has taken place in our lives this year, and what a great distance separates us! Like you, I await your visit here most impatiently.

March 18, 1965
Dear Mother, Father, Bibi and Iddo,
The maneuvers are over and we've returned to our base. After five weeks in the desolate, arid Negev we came back to the greenery and the orange groves of the country's center. A brief moment of peace. I am finally resting on a *bed*, dressed in clean clothes and immaculately washed. Most of the guys have not yet returned from supper (at long last eaten at tables with clean mess tins), a transistor is playing in the tent and there's still enough light outside to write a letter. Hey! At this very moment we've been told that an alert is on and a roll call will be held in an hour. This may mean that we will not go home this weekend after such a long period without leave; but we shall see.

I have a lot to tell you in this letter. First let me describe the past week. On Thursday morning (4:00 A.M.) we packed our gear, broke the camp and left our location in the Negev. We traveled by truck to Rosh Zohar and from there navigated on foot to Ein Gedi. Again we set out in small groups, carrying only light packs and loaded weapons.

I got to know an area that was entirely new to me—the Judean Desert. The streams here are so deep that it's impossible to walk in the riverbeds, you have to climb up to the ridges instead. Every stream is flanked by immense cliffs which rise vertically upward. In every wadi there are breathtaking waterfalls, and the whole view is magnificent and awe-inspiring. Sometimes we had to leave the ridges and get down into the wadis, and in places it took us an hour and a half to cover five yards! That should give you an idea how difficult the crossing was.

In previous navigations as well as this one, I was group leader, that is to say, the one responsible for the welfare of the men under my supervision and the final arbiter in differences of opinion as to the path to take. I navigate well. On Thursday evening I was the first of the company to reach the night's camping place. Some men even got stuck on the cliffs and had to be pulled out the next day. To tell the truth, it's a pretty dangerous business if you don't know how to find your way about.

On the first day of navigation we were supposed to reach Massada. We reached it not from the seaward side but from the mountains to the west.

We were climbing a huge mountain when suddenly the cliff of Massada was revealed to us in all its splendor and glory with the Dead Sea behind. When you see Massada you understand at once why it was so hard to defeat its defenders.*

We spent Saturday at Ein Gedi and the next day set out on an exercise that lasted two days and concluded the entire maneuver. As night fell, the exercise began with parachute jumps and helicopter flights. After that we marched on foot to the target, and at 12:30 A.M. there began an orchestra of fire, followed by the storming parties. On the heels of the attack we dug in until daybreak and the next day marched from Maaleh Akrabbim to Oron (the phosphate works)—a truly difficult march since we were carrying a great deal of equipment on our backs.

They are just coming now to let us know whether we'll be going home today.

March 19, 1965

Well, we got the okay.

Toward evening we reached the helicopters and began to board them, when suddenly we were informed that a technical mishap had occurred causing a "slight" change in plan—in other words, instead of flying by helicopter to the nearest airstrip and continuing north from there in other aircraft, we now had again to march the entire distance. So we had another sleepless night. In the morning we arrived at our destination, having marched in fact very well and in high spirits. Food and water were parachuted down to us all along the route, and if there was a shortage of food before, we now had far too much. You should have seen the amount of food each soldier was carrying—real plenty for the first time!

March 26, 1965

Beloved Mother, Father and brothers,

Mr. and Mrs. Barmeir are preparing to go to the States for about three months and will leave next week. I'm sure you'll want to meet them. I'll

---

*Massada was the last fortress held by the Jews in their rebellion against Rome. It fell to the Romans in A.D. 73, after all its defenders had committed suicide.

give them your address and will try to write again to let you know when they will arrive, as soon as I know.

On April 4 the Four-Day March to Jerusalem starts and we'll take part as the representatives of the paratroops. We've been preparing for this. During the past four days we marched some one hundred miles. It's now so easy for me to devour great distances that I didn't even feel I was walking. And these were substantial stretches that we covered at a murderous pace.

I received Father's excellent letter; how much I'd like to see your book finished and printed!

I'm glad to hear that you will probably be able to remain in the U.S.A. this year and apparently for a few years after that. For I believe your work there is easier (if that is possible, the truth is I've yet to see you take a real rest). Maybe now, when you leave the Encyclopedia for good and devote yourself solely to teaching and writing, you may find greater satisfaction and serenity.

I gather that you, Bibi, intend to finish high school in the U.S. This seems to be the right step, but we'll have plenty of time to discuss it when you get here. In the final analysis you make the right decisions, Bibi. Since you use your common sense, and since ultimately you will do what you really want to, it stands to reason you won't ever regret it—just as I don't regret being in the army. True, now that I look back I realize that perhaps it would have been better after all to have studied first; but had I not enlisted, I might have been tormented by regret for not doing what I considered right. The point is that I'm not *losing* these two years. I am after all acquiring something in the army and getting to know another side of life, which I'd never have known had I not been in it. Since I am in the army and obliged to serve, I'm especially glad I chose the paratroopers. For if you want to extract all that is useful from the service in the way that seems right to me, you have to follow the most difficult road. And this is without a doubt the most difficult.

April 14, 1965

Beloved Mother, Father and brothers,

I am at the moment serving as deputy commander of the guard—a job that is the easiest and most comfortable of the various guard duties. All I do is sit at a table and answer a telephone, which never rings. It's a wonderful opportunity for writing letters; who would be fool enough not to use it?

In the meantime I am beginning to wrestle with the problem that confronts every soldier when he finishes the squad-commanders course. After the soldier makes corporal, he faces the choice of either going on to Officers' School or serving as squad commander and ending his service as sergeant. To clarify the problem somewhat, you must understand that every officer in Zahal must sign on for an additional three to four months before he can be awarded officer's rank. Although money matters don't trouble me, they should still be considered. An officer receives 400–500 I£ a month and his living expenses are practically nil. There are other aspects that deserve some thought. It's important for me to know when the school year begins, both in Israel and abroad, to find out whether I'll have to prepare for any exams, since as corporal or sergeant I won't have any time free for studying. And although as an officer I might have some time to study, it would mean postponing school for a year in any case.

Of course, the work of an officer in Zahal is more interesting than any other work, and there's much that's captivating about it. In the paratroops there's an additional problem for officers. Not all who go to the Officers' School return, on completion, to the battalion. Some of them are sent to serve in other branches: Golani,* the armored corps, etc. To be assured of returning to his unit, the paratrooper must sign on for another year of service. If he doesn't sign on, preference is given to those who did, thus lessening his chances. If the soldier excels in the course, he might end up instructing Officers' School classes. If I become an officer, my chances of ending up in the paratroops or in the Officers' Course are quite good, even if I sign on only for the three additional months. The last point, which no one considers but which I do take into account, is that of reserve duty. The period of annual reserve duty is considerably longer for an officer than for a sergeant. Even though many argue that reserve duty breaks the tension of everyday life and gives it interest and color, this fails to excite me since I don't picture my life as a civilian as being boring and bereft of meaning. If that's what it's like for others, woe to them!

The more I think about the problem, the more I approach the conclusion that I won't commit myself to even one additional day in Zahal. I'll complete the two years and two months, and that will be it. Although, to be honest, there is still room for further consideration. Very few succeed in getting sent to Officers' School from the paratroops and it's

*An infantry brigade in the Israeli army.

hard to pass up the "honor" and the great attraction involved. In any event, by the time the course starts, I'll manage to reach a final decision. Our squad-commanders course will end a few days after you are due to arrive, and then a few days' leave will be due us, so I'll be able to discuss it with you.

April 30, 1965

Dearest Mother, Father, Bibi and Iddo,

I received a letter from Mother and another from Father, one on the heels of the other. They contain a great deal of news. The first, which saddens me, is that Father will not come to Israel on June 24th, but at a later date. I do, of course, understand that important reasons were involved and realize that you, Father, would also like to spend the summer with all of us. But there's nothing to be done except hope that you will somehow manage to join us during the summer. I was glad to learn that you decided to part from the Encyclopedia—and I hope this time it will be final—and that you are devoting all your time to writing your book. How I'd like to have it in my hand already!

I don't believe I wrote you about the Seder. Well, it was a wonderful Seder in the bosom of the whole family. Aunt Phirah labored hard and prepared a model meal, Uncle Saadiah chanted with great enthusiasm, and I've got to say that he really does have a very pleasant voice. Recently I have managed to visit Aunt Miri several times at her home, and there was no end to Grandma's joy.

You asked me, Mother, whether I'll get a few days' leave when you come. I assume I will. Besides, several days after your arrival we're due to finish the squad-commanders course when most of us will be given a relatively long leave, so we should have plenty of time to spend together, and it makes no difference to me whether it will be in a hotel or in an apartment, or any other place.

May 29, 1965

Beloved Mother, Father, Bibi and Iddo,

This past week, except for half of one night, I got no sleep at night. From time to time we slept, a few hours at the most, in broad daylight. Many things keep us busy—navigation by night all over the country, lookout duty on the borders, ambushes at the borders and along the roads that can serve as infiltration routes to the country's interior, drills and exercises of all kinds that continue day and night without pause, without sleep and almost without food. The situation in Israel, as you doubtless know, is not too good just now, particularly after the latest incidents. But we feel fine and are in the best of spirits.

You will arrive in exactly one month from now, or rather, three weeks from the day you receive this letter. I'm looking forward to that moment most impatiently. A whole year has passed since we parted! Now we'll see each other again. What a pity that Father won't be with us. I'm confident, however, that if not next month, then we'll meet shortly afterwards.

It seems that tomorrow we will parachute again; and if all is quiet, we'll go on sea maneuvers, which include shore training, landings, and the like.

June 27, 1965

Dear Father,

Only rarely do I count the passing days in anticipation of some future event. When you do that, you lose the meaning of the moment—today, right now—and skip over weeks of your life longing for a day to come. There are men in the army who from the beginning of their service count the days to their discharge, thus seeing their period of service as a waste of time—which is a mistake, for there is always value to the present. Yet now, as the time approaches for the arrival of Mother, Bibi and Iddo, I too am starting to "count the days."

I'm sorry you remained alone in America and will not be with us. How marvellous it will be if you really can manage to get to Israel after all. To my regret, I don't know how many days' leave I'll be able to get while the family is visiting here. I'm sure I'll obtain a few days at least.

As to Officers' School, I delayed telling you my decision until the qualification tests were completed. Actually, I finally decided some weeks ago that I would go to the course, but I didn't let you know this as long as I wasn't sure I was accepted. Before a soldier is sent to this course (and needless to say only a few soldiers are sent, especially from the paratroops), he has to pass three days of qualifying exams. You find yourself in a group of seven candidates accompanied by two experienced psychologists who administer the tests. By the time the tests are over, it appears they know all there is to know about each individual. They get to know your capacity to make judgments, to control yourself and the men under you, to solve problems, to be a leader and to make decisions, as well as your optimism and pessimism, your strengths and weaknesses, and no doubt dozens of other characteristics of which I know nothing. When we get a chance, I'll tell you about the examinations; they are really remarkably interesting.

The test results are graded 1 to 9. 9 is the highest grade one can attain, 1 the lowest. 3 means that it is doubtful if the man is suitable as officer material, while 4 indicates he is.

Our battalion sent about sixty men to be tested, and the results arrived only a short while ago. A considerable number failed altogether. There were some who received a 7. One fellow succeeded in obtaining an 8. I received a 9. Whether I am suitable to be an officer will, I think, be determined only in the future, when I'm actually serving as one, and not by preliminary tests prior to that. But I thought you would be pleased to know, and that is why I'm telling you this. It was, after all, a test involving me and one which I passed.

Three days ago I met Mr. and Mrs. Barmeir, who returned to Israel last week. I should tell you that most of their stories were endless paeans of praise about you, and that is not surprising. I hope you liked them too.

In another week I'll finish the course for squad commanders and receive the rank of corporal, after which I'll go right away to the Officers' School course, which will last six months.

July 22, 1965

Dear Father,

In the two weeks since I last wrote you much has happened. First of all, Mother, Bibi and Iddo arrived—and there's no limit to our joy. All three look wonderful; Mother looks younger and healthier than ever. Bibi and Iddo have grown and developed, both physically and mentally, to such an extent that it's hard to believe that one year could have produced such a transformation. Every chance we have we all get together and spend some pleasant hours. They really came just at the right time. Had they come only a few months earlier, it's possible that we might have seen one another only once or twice during their entire stay in Israel, whereas now we meet every weekend and sometimes in the middle of the week as well.

Next Monday I'll be going to the Officers' Training Course, having finished the squad-commanders course yesterday and received the rank of corporal. This followed a week of nighttime navigation in Galilee. "Navigation" means finding your way with the aid of topographical maps. At night navigation is very much harder than in daytime—for obvious reasons. Each night we walked some twenty to twenty-five miles, thoroughly covering the entire northern section of the country. The last two nights we made our way without the aid of any map, following our route from memory. This requires serious study, since you have to know not only the route, i.e., all the wadis, hills and mountains you must cross, but also the entire area several miles on both sides of your line of march so that you'll be able to find your way in case of error. In our little country there is always the possibility, a very real one, that you might cross the border. The navigations were unusually successful, and now I feel completely confident about walking in any area with a map to guide me.

I'm so sorry you're not here in Israel. I hope you're at least resting a bit after the effort you put into your last work. You wrote me that you went to the country to visit the Morris family. Tell me about this visit and your mode of life in general, now that you are alone. I miss you, Father, very, very much.

Your loving
Yoni

August 1, 1965

Dear Father,

In the past two weeks Mother and Iddo came to visit me at the camp gate, but we managed to see one another for only a few minutes. The military framework is restrictive, and it's impossible to free oneself from its yoke. I was with them also last Saturday in Jerusalem and enjoyed their company very much.

I feel very sorry for Mother. In the course of her entire stay here she will be able to see me so rarely that my heart aches terribly each time I leave her. If I only had more free time! Mother doesn't make any demands on me—it seems she thinks that if she did, my joy in seeing her would be spoiled. She wants so badly to do things for me and to look after me when in fact I don't really need anything. We have so little time to spend together! I'm glad she doesn't sit at home all day but goes on marvellous trips around the country. As far as I can see she enjoys them very much. Mother is a practical woman and knows how to use her time to the best advantage.

What about you, Father? I hear so little from you.

Officers' School is in full swing. The physical effort is almost nil compared to the effort in the unit I came from, although there are some who claim that the exertion here is an exertion nonetheless.

August 4, 1965

Dear Father,

We returned to the base at 3:00 in the morning after two days of squad-deployment in the field. This morning we got up late, at six o'clock, and from then until now—suppertime—continued with our studies as usual. Now we have a free evening which will be devoted to a little studying, some reading, and going to bed earlier than usual.

The Officers' Training Course is primarily a study course into which exercises and physical effort are occasionally interwoven. The theoretical studies are numerous, and some are quite interesting. Time passes rapidly. The instructors in this course are, in my opinion, generally of a lower caliber than the officers we've had in the past. You could sense the feelings of respect for an officer in the paratroops; the commander is a man to be emulated. Here in Officers' School this isn't the case. Except for a few, who are really excellent, most of the officers serving as instructors are pretty mediocre. Everyone here is very pedantic about small matters of order and discipline. At the same time, they rely a good deal on cultivating mutual trust rather than on administering punishments. The heaviest punishment here is, of course, dismissal from the course. That, in fact, is the only punishment that has any effect. This method appeals to me. Evidently here they seek to complement a person's other facet, the side left insufficiently developed by the combat units.

By the way, conditions here are excellent. "For a change," I sleep at long last in a room with a bed, a mattress, tables, electric lights, wall cupboards, sheets, pajamas—and not in a pup tent shared with another soldier, on the ground, and in the same fatigues that you wear day and night, sometimes for weeks on end.

August 21, 1965

Dear Father,

I received the letter in which you enclosed the university catalogue, as well as the letter you wrote after your visit to the Morris family. I see from the contents that the subject that interests you most as far as I am involved and the one you wish us to discuss concerns my studies. I'll try to sum up my feelings in this letter as well as I can at this stage.

Well, it is still early for me to consider the matter with any kind of finality. Not because I don't regard it as exceedingly important, but because right now I haven't the time to deal with it and give it the appropriate thought and action. I'm in the army and under a regime that demands every minute of my time. I am not master of my time and the moments of leisure granted me are very few. In the normal course of events, I get leave once every two weeks; that's when I'll try to do as you suggest and contact Mr. Segal,* even though in my opinion the matter is not urgent. Right now the problem is to finish the Officers' Training Course. After the course I'll have more time to myself, at least I hope so, and I'll be able to devote much of it to this subject.

I will say goodbye to Mother, Bibi and Iddo in about ten days' time. I have just returned from a special leave that I was given last Saturday to enable me to see them (that, by the way, is one of the advantages of being an officer cadet: one is treated more liberally and privileges are greater, so if a request is reasonable and there's time available, one is given leave).

Next Saturday I'll get another leave, which we'll spend, at Mother's request, in Jerusalem. On Tuesday they'll be leaving, and again I'll be left alone. I do hope, Father, that you will manage to come at a later date so that the two of us will see each other. On Monday I'll request leave until their return back to you in America. I assume that loneliness troubles you a little, or perhaps more than a little, and can imagine the joy at being reunited.

I have more opportunity to read during this course because I have much more free time on the base (though not in the field) than I had before. As a matter of fact, there is no comparison between the previous year and the months I'm passing now. Nevertheless, I prefer the way I lived last year. Although I am learning a great deal in this course, and although I've got more liberty with my time and activities, I don't particularly enjoy the course and am looking forward to the end. After all, the aim of this course is to develop our ability to command and to bring us up to officer standards, and that is the only reason I am here and am working at it for these six months. Despite the freedom we enjoy here, one cannot overcome the feeling that one is a sort of object on display, around which they stand all the time with pad and pencil in hand, noting every move and every

*Admissions officer of the Hebrew University.

deed. Believe me, this is not very pleasant. Of course, there are many positive aspects too, and I don't feel that I'm wasting my time.

September 3, 1965

Beloved Mother, Father, Bibi and Iddo,

Again I am writing to all of you together.

Before you left here, certain people were asking me in Mother's presence whether I'd be happy to be "free" once more, and they even insisted that it's good to be alone. What fools these people are! I don't think they know what it means to be alone in Israel, without one's family, for another year or two. To be fair, I didn't know myself.

It was so good to come home and find all of you there, and besides, with Mother here life was so much easier. You took care of so many things for me, Mother, that I could allow myself a complete rest. Although I can turn to Mrs. Barmeir or to any friends of yours, Mother, and ask them to buy for me things I need, I don't; I just can't. Whereas you, Mother dear, attended to my slightest need, bar none. Yes, in these months I came to know the full meaning of the word "home." If only Father had been here, too, everything would have been almost perfect. Why "almost"? Perfection would come if we were all together in our house without having to be separated again.

There was no end to my enthusiasm over Bibi and Iddo. Now I have *two* grown-up brothers. Bibi I've always treated as a mature person, but Iddo has changed to an unbelievable degree. I'm so happy with these two brothers of mine. No one could wish himself a better, more complete triumvirate.

Mother has also changed so much for the better, looking younger than ever and full of life. I almost didn't recognize you, Mother, when you got off the plane.

I want to ask you something. As you know, there is a great hubbub in Israel now with the elections approaching. The newspapers deal with hardly anything else, and in the army, despite the fact that it's forbidden, hotheads are prepared to devour one another during free moments in their rooms. None of the parties satisfies me, and none of them represents what I think is right. It is said that a citizen's duty is to vote, but I have no desire to vote in support of views that are not mine. Must you vote for something that is merely preferable to something else, to prevent a certain party's coming to power, even if the party you vote for doesn't represent your own ideas?

At the end of each week you hear the cry here, "One more week!" Not only the weeks are counted, but the days and the hours as well. Each passing day brings us closer to the end of the course. With each week that ends, a considerable amount of new knowledge is implanted into the future officers of Zahal. The material is quite interesting, some of it very. Today is Friday, and the weekend has just begun. I have a great many things to read and plan to return now to my physics.

September 29, 1965

Beloved Mother, Father, Bibi and Iddo,

A good and happy New Year to all of you, a year of success in everything and satisfaction from everything! I remember beginning last year's letter in the same way. I only hope that next year we'll be able to express our good wishes to one another verbally and not by mail.

This year, too, I won't spend the holidays at home. Again we are lying in ambush on the borders at a time when the entire House of Israel is happily celebrating at home.

It's extraordinary, the distance between soldier and civilian. In town people are having parties. In brightly lit rooms there is music, and people stay up until morning. I, too, was up until morning, the only difference being that I was lying on the ground on a dark cold night without a single ray of light to brighten my surroundings, alert to every suspicious sound and movement around me. When you lie like this without moving hour after hour in a cloud of mosquitoes, gazing at the lights of a city in which you can't set foot even on leave, the enemy's city, with only a field of clover drenched in dew separating you from it, your eyes begin to close and you have to struggle with the desire to lay your head on the ground, to which your body has been joined for hours, and drift into deep sleep.

Behind you, a few yards away, you can hear the monotonous sound of the "booster"—the water pump for whose safety you are responsible. From far, far away every now and then sounds of song and laughter of "our own" burst out—some kibbutz is holding a New Year's party. You lie there and count the hours. You know that in another eight, another seven, another six hours you'll be able to get up and go to the nearest assembly point where a military vehicle will pick you up. At 4 or 4:30 A.M. you will be sleeping your "nightly" sleep, which begins the second your head hits the mattress.

You spend the days of the holiday in total rest: sleeping, reading, writing letters. After all, it is a holiday, and with a holiday comes relaxation. Tonight we'll be lying in ambush again, and again and again on the nights that follow.

Despite all this, there is a magic in everything we are doing now. I have lain like this in ambush more than once and shall do so many more times. I just wanted to share with you some of my impressions on the eve of the New Year.

October 5, 1965

Iddo my beloved,

It seems to me that you turned thirteen years ago. When I saw you coming down the steps of the plane about two months ago I couldn't believe my eyes. Some people look on a younger brother as a nuisance, but for me, my chief pride is in being blessed with two such brothers.

I don't know whether you noticed it, but I was sorry I saw so little of you during the summer. I think that you often refused to come along with me because you supposed that you would be a burden to me—a supposition altogether without foundation. For you know very well that if I had thought any such thing, I would not have suggested that you come along. I'm so sorry we spent so little time together. I'm privileged to have such a wonderful brother, and yet I am unable to be in his company for longer periods.

In another year—who knows, perhaps more than that—we'll see each other again. By then, you'll be a high school student (the truth is that even now it's hard for me to think of you as someone in the eighth grade) and I will still be putting out my "sweat and blood," as the saying goes, somewhere in this army. What will our next meeting be like?

It was always hard for me to express my feelings. When I write "Iddo my beloved" at the beginning of this letter, I want you to know that I say it from the depths of my heart. Nothing is dearer to me than my two brothers. It is because of them that I see myself so blessed and so lucky.

What shall I wish you on your bar mitzvah? You are marching on the right path and anyone who does that and who looks ahead cannot help but reach his goal. You see, I'm so sure of your good judgment that the only thing I ought to wish you is to continue doing in the future as well as you have been doing until now.

Your loving brother,
Yoni

October 18, 1965

Greetings, my beloved ones,

Last Sunday we were given a leave of nine whole days. Today is Monday, and tonight I must return to the base. I decided to use my leave to travel around the country and acted accordingly.

On Sunday I left with Tutti (by the way, we're not going steady any more), bound for Upper Galilee. Among the things we did, we climbed the lofty mountain ridge known as Mount Galilee. At its summit we were able to see clearly almost half of our country, from huge Mount Hermon in the north to some points south of the Sea of Galilee.

One of the most beautiful sites we visited on this trip was the "Cave of Alma," named after the settlement nearby. This is an enormous cave full of stalactites in dozens of colors and shades. At one end of the cave there is an opening, the beginning of a huge underground labyrinth stretching hundreds of yards to an end no one has yet reached. I got inside along the rope tied to its entrance, and it looked as if there really were no end to this magnificent cave. We passed the Dishon ravine, which is full of rabbits, climbed Mount Meron (the Jarmak), and slept on the shore of the Sea of Galilee. We returned home on Wednesday afternoon.

I rested at home for two days and on Friday went on another outing, this time alone. Since on most such trips in Israel a weapon is mandatory, I took an Uzzi with me. I wandered about the Judean Desert. I visited some of the places that Mother and Iddo went to see during their trip here, such as Arad (and you were right, Mother, it is an enchanting place) and Ein Gedi. There is not a mountain around Ein Gedi that I haven't climbed, and anyone who hasn't seen the landscape from the peaks of the mountains overlooking the Dead Sea has missed the most spectacular sight of his life.

I think I made the fullest use of my leave and am going back to the army pleased and satisfied.

October 23, 1965

Dear Mother, Father, Bibi and Iddo,

Last week I told you that I visited many places in Israel. I managed to tell you about a number of these places without going into great detail as to what I saw because I was limited in space. I won't go into detail now either, for even if I wrote expansively about the beauty of a place, the written word would never approach the sight itself—and when you return

I'll make sure that you see the whole country thoroughly.

All of these hikes and trips made a profound impression on me, and that's what I want to touch on now. Until now, I must admit, I never *felt* the country, if you can put it like that. I think Bibi felt it much more than I, and also Father spoke more than once of "our land." Never before had I felt this so powerfully. I knew the country existed, that I was living in it, and that, if the need arose, I would fight for it. But really to feel the place, the soil, the mountains and valleys of Israel—this sensation I have now experienced for the first time.

When you are in the army and cross the length and breadth of the country in marches, your enthusiasm for the beauty of a place is somehow pushed aside by the monotonous, ceaseless rhythm of the march, by the burning sun and the sweat streaming down your face and body, by the dryness of your parched tongue and your almost empty canteen, by the weight of the pack on your back and the weapon in your hand. You cannot marvel at the beauty of a hill when you are storming it and the whole place is deluged in gunfire. At most, the picture flits through your brain, kindles a tiny spark and vanishes.

In the army I have learned to appreciate the beauty of life, the immense pleasure of sleep, the taste of water, which is irreplaceable, the matchless value of will power, and all the marvels a man can do if only he will. But it's rather hard to love a place in the midst of all that. Then I decided I had to know the country, and by "know" I mean be familiar with every tree and rock in it. This is the unique opportunity I now have, and I intend to use it to the full.

I have seen and felt the beauty of the Judean Desert, the might of straight, steep cliffs rising vertically for hundreds of feet with only one thin white trail winding through them like a tiny trickle of water, the beauty of dry, parched earth and the whiteness of the salt caked on the stones, the strength and power of the fortress of Massada, and the life of our ancient ancestors in the oases of the desert. All these have now taken on a profound meaning for me. I saw places of beauty, which were created before and after the establishment of the State. I saw Nature the destroyer and the builder.

All of this, together with the special sense of life I have acquired in the army, has now become enmeshed in my being, creating the full circle of a life that is whole.

I have always said that my time in Zahal is something I have to live through and make the best of. Now, although this period is not going to set the course of my future life, it has become deeply meaningful for me. I know now that without this period I should have missed something. I would probably not be aware of this lack but for being in the army, and in all probability my life would have gone on quite normally and have been as complete as before. But since I am here, I find, to my great joy and surprise, a life that *has no equal.*

October 23, 1965

Bibi,

Mother told me that you wrote an excellent essay on Jefferson. Why don't you send it to me, or a similar one? Encourage Iddo to do the same.

By the way, you mentioned that the physics text you use is not the best, and you are right. Before I left, I spent a lot of time searching for a really good physics textbook—and found one. A good book, also used in universities, is *College Physics* by Sears and Zemansky. Another like it is *University Physics* by the same authors. But this one is for a later stage, when you're up to calculus. Both are excellent books, suitable for independent study, because they are written in very clear language. They're available in nearly every bookstore. I recommend them highly. Try to get them and see if they suit you.

I see, Bibi, that you had to release the surplus energy you stored up during the summer. There's nothing wrong in that. But it's too bad you sprained a finger in the process.* In my opinion, there's nothing wrong with a good fist fight; on the contrary, if you're young and you're not seriously hurt, it won't do you real harm. Remember what I told you? He who delivers the first blow, wins.

November 10, 1965

Beloved Mother, Father, Bibi and Iddo,

We had more field maneuvers, which were extremely significant. Every day brings more substantial knowledge, which will ultimately result in an excellent "product"—an Israeli officer.

I heard from all of you about the lessons Father is giving Bibi and Iddo. How sorry I am not to be with you. To sit and hear Father teaching— I could ask for nothing more. Mother herself was so impressed by the lessons that in her last letter she wrote a summary of the one she had just heard. I only hope you won't stop doing this after a while. I'm afraid this

*Benjamin was involved in a fight following an anti-Semitic remark directed at him.

may happen because of Father's heavy work load and Bibi's and Iddo's studies. Just remember the value and usefulness—and I may add, the pleasure—of these lessons, and you're bound to reach the necessary conclusion.

You told me that Father may be able to come to Israel for a few days and asked when the Officers' Course is due to end. Well, the date is January 5th. On that day the graduation exercises will be held with parents and other invited guests present. It promises to be a very impressive ceremony. On January 6th, all the cadets will disperse, each assigned to his unit. If you really do come, Father, on that date or at any other time in the near future, I'll be overjoyed.

Tomorrow, Thursday, we are scheduled to carry out a raid (as part of the course) and the day after—a parachute jump. After five months without a single jump, I'm not too eager to parachute. There's something weighing me down that I can't get rid of; a taste in the mouth that is not so sweet. But it goes without saying that I will jump, and it is clear that I'll come through safely. It's just not so simple to stand once again in the open doorway of the plane at the top of the world. The required motions are no longer automatic after such a long interval. As our sabra slang puts it, you need a little more "blood" than usual to jump. But it's obvious that, despite all, it would be a pity to miss the jump. And it's clearer still that if I don't jump now, the next time will be even more difficult. Once the course is over, the paratroopers will have a "finishing course" of their own, and then I'll be jumping a great deal.

One of the interesting programs in the course is the one called "educational sessions." It takes an entire week and consists of a series of lectures on problems of education, leadership, the War of Independence, the Sinai Campaign, the lessons and achievements of previous battles, and more. I once participated in a similar program in the squad-commanders course, and I'm now full of curiosity about these lectures in Officers' School. They will start on Sunday, right after our return from leave.

A little more about myself—and this may be of special interest to Bibi and Iddo. I run a lot. Whether I am on the base or in the field, I go out every day for a run of several miles. As a result, I feel just—how do they put it—"super." On Saturday two weeks ago, when I was home, I ran in the university stadium and made six miles in forty-five minutes, and it was as easy as pie. To run a distance like that on a track wearing sneakers rather than on sand wearing heavy boots is a pleasure, not an effort.

Your loving
Yoni

November 17, 1965

Beloved Mother, Father, Bibi and Iddo,

The "educational sessions" are now in full swing. In a few minutes a lecture will be delivered on "The Characteristics of Adolescence." The lecture that will follow is on "Reward and Punishment in Education." In the afternoon we'll hear lectures on the "Heritage of Heroism as a Value in Education," and later on "Factors Affecting the Will to Fight." As you can see, the course is rather interesting, and I am quite satisfied with it.

I told you that on Thursday we would conduct a raid and on Friday we would execute a parachute jump. The raid was very successful. Since we returned to the base at about 2:30 in the morning and had to get up at 4:45 for the jump, many of us did not get up. Some, of course, were afraid to jump and therefore gave up this privilege. If three days earlier I had felt apprehensive about the forthcoming jump, on the day of the exercise my apprehensions vanished. I have never had such a successful jump. Perhaps it was even better than the first one. It seems to me that if you pay scrupulous attention to all the instructions and act correctly without losing your head, nothing can possibly go wrong. Actually, there are not many mishaps. In my opinion, the greatest concern is the fear of committing some non-routine action that may result in an accident. When someone is injured in a jump, in about 90 percent of the cases it's his own fault.

Bibi, in your last letter you referred to the border clashes between Israel and her neighbors. Well, I don't know how familiar you are with what is going on here. I assume that the American press mentions only the most serious of the incidents, or those with the most far-reaching repercussions. And indeed these offer sufficient cause for worry and distress. I won't list each and every incident. Let me just say that instead of becoming fewer, the border incidents are lately increasing, not only in number but also in the depth of the penetrations, in the intensity of sabotage, in the number of neighboring countries involved and in the reactions resulting from the acts of terror. But apart from those incidents that the press reports, there are *dozens* that create no stir in the world. Some are not known even to the Israeli public. The responses of Zahal are also becoming more numerous and more vigorous. Our own penetrations across the border are essential, genuinely necessary—this after years of quiet and no need to react.

There is some tension in the air, especially within the civilian population, but it's actually not felt too strongly. In the army, to be sure, there's recently been a bit more activity and alertness, but that is all. The country as a whole is now resting after the mud-slinging campaigns, which have just ended. Political parties have come into power, coalitions have been formed and dissolved, pacts have been made and broken. The debates have ended, tempers have died down, and by and large the atmosphere is peaceful.

December 4, 1965

Beloved ones,

I think some two weeks have passed since I last wrote. These were most interesting weeks for me. I learned a number of things that I consider very important from both the military and civilian points of view. I learned to understand the significance of the administrative staff, which, behind the scenes, organizes and takes care of all the little details of the soldier's everyday life, from supplying food and water to the field and fuel for the cars to dispatching needed vehicles, distributing ammunition, caring for the cleanliness of the camps, conducting inspections, and a great deal more. This responsibility was assigned to me throughout this past week; I was the commander of the entire course, and I must admit that administrative work is extremely hard.

This week we were in the base all the time. We spent two days on the range practicing shooting with a variety of weapons, ours and the enemy's (a military secret no doubt). We spent many hours studying a number of essential subjects; yesterday (Friday) we took the "fitness test," and then went home. This test is meant to measure your physical capability, and marks and medals are awarded; the top is the silver medal. Of course, I won it without any difficulty. Not many did. The course is quite lax from a physical point of view, and practically no one was up to the test. As for me, because I do so much running, I was equal to the effort.

When I wrote the date on this letter I suddenly realized that exactly thirty days remain to the end of the course. I cling to the hope that Father will come to Israel at the end of this month, if he possibly can. How I want to see you here! Of course, I'll understand if you are unable to make this wish come true, for no one knows better than I, Father, how badly you want to come here, if only for a few days.

Recently you sent me such a beautiful letter, Mother, that it made me think that our whole family consists of writers. You also mentioned that Bibi wrote a lovely story, well worth reading. Once you sent me a composition of his about a ride on a bus climbing to Jerusalem. It gave me so much pleasure! Why don't you do that again, Mother? It won't be hard for you to copy Bibi's latest composition and mail it to me; you need only decide and do it.

By now the snow must be coming down in Elkins Park, and the cold should be at its height. Here we have a downpour of rain every now and then; the sky changes from red to black to white and occasionally blue, and the sun no longer warms as it did. Winter is felt not only in the air but also in man—his behavior changes; he withdraws more deeply into himself, becomes more silent, bursts out less frequently, meditates more. He and the coat that wraps him are one; he is completely enveloped in its warmth. The weather is somber, and under its influence man, too, becomes somber, so that one tends to look back, to react more slowly, to give more thought to one's actions. I am simply voicing my impressions of those I observe around me. I don't usually form too many impressions, and the impressions made on me by other people generally flit through my mind. Maybe winter has also changed me somewhat; the fact is that I pay more attention to what I see.

Your very loving
Yoni

December 22, 1965

My dearly beloved ones,

At long last I've been granted a bit of rest and peace during which I can write to you as I wish. It is midnight now and I'm sitting in my room at the Barmeirs', next to a table lamp, listening to Brahms. Outdoors a great frost runs rampant, borne by the winter winds of Jerusalem, clinging to the panes of the closed window; on one side is the winter, and on the other the warmth of the heated room. Can you imagine a more fitting background for writing you a letter?

I don't know where exactly I ought to start the story of my adventures in the last few weeks. I think I'll begin in chronological order.

Well, three weeks ago we went down to the Negev for what's known as Half-Track Company exercises. The purpose was to drill us as officers in a more advanced phase of the work of the infantry, when it functions jointly with the armored divisions, tanks, half-tracks, heavy artillery, and the like. The exercises were most interesting, but I won't go into detail because if I get started I'll never stop, and I'm not at all sure that all the technical points will be of interest to you. But I will tell you about one exercise in which I was directly involved.

As you know, the Officers' Course is conducted, at least in the final months, mostly by the cadets themselves, with the commanding staff limiting itself to supervising and directing us. The highest level that a cadet can achieve is to direct the entire course for a brief period. I've already told you about that, but that was only in administrative work.

We are also put in charge of exercises. For each exercise the staff of commanding officers selects one of the cadets to command the entire force. They test the cadet (when they *want* to test him) in his ability to command, in the soundness of his judgment, in his capacity to implement plans, and the like. It goes without saying, that the better cadets are given command over the more difficult exercises. At the conclusion of each part of the training a summary exercise is conducted, which is the hardest and most complex of them all, and for these they naturally choose the top cadets. This is particularly true when the commander of the school is present at the summary exercises; the staff, it appears, is then anxious to make a very good impression. It's like the host who sweeps his house when he is expecting guests even though, as is known, it's not always clean and often even dirty. In any case, I was chosen to command such a drill (by the way, this was the second time I've commanded a concluding exercise in the presence of the school commander; this has never happened in our course before). I think this was the toughest assignment I've had so far.

The general idea of this exercise was to carry out a raid on simulated targets deep behind enemy lines with jeeps, half-tracks and tanks, combined with an attack on the enemy from the rear. My assignment in the initial stage was to go with a squad of soldiers in two jeeps and a command car and navigate on the far side of a mountain ridge, for a distance of about ten miles, in the dead of night. Navigation in these mountains is difficult and complex—the ranges and ridges are very numerous and at some points become as sharp as blades, with chasms and cliffs on both sides of the spine of the ridge, spelling certain death in case of a fall. It was my job to mark, with the aid of signs previously agreed on, the path that the entire force was to follow as it came behind me. This task was no less difficult—and perhaps more complicated—than the navigation, since up to this point the mountain ridge had taken at least four to five hours to cross, with the force losing its way more than once, vehicles getting stuck, etc. Then, after all this, I had to command the attack. Well, I won't go on since I have a great deal more to tell you. The entire force crossed the ridge safely in less than two hours, and everything was carried out perfectly. The school commander summoned me to appear before him and, in the presence of the whole staff, heaped such praise on me that, despite my successful "career" in the army, I had not heard such compliments before. Later on, when he summarized the drill, he mentioned the model performance and added, "I only wish that all the exercises conducted in the school might attain such a high standard of achievement," etc. My feeling when it was over—general fatigue.

Three days before the end of the maneuver, we had a remarkable experience. I've been caught in many a sandstorm during my army service and have got out of them by the skin of my teeth; but the like of the sandstorm I want to tell you about now has not been known in the Negev for many years.

This sandstorm raged on for three full days without a moment's respite. It was so powerful that it was impossible to discern a company of tanks a yard away, and I'm not exaggerating. Our pup tents withstood the onslaught by a miracle, and even though they were tightly sealed, we still found a layer of sand a foot deep on the blanket spread on the ground in the tent when we came back from exercises every day (again, I'm not exaggerating). To open one's eyes against the wind was impossible, and since we couldn't see anything anyway, we felt our way like blind men in the dark. Needless to say, we ate hardly anything, and when we did eat, the sand grated in our teeth. We went about with our faces wrapped in handkerchiefs and only the slits of our eyes open to the wind, and we didn't take off our handkerchiefs even when we slept. The blast of cold that swept in with the terrible wind made us shiver—in our hot Negev! —at 11:30 in the morning, even though we were wearing sweaters and windbreakers. I suppose we had to undergo this experience in order to grasp the full meaning of a sandstorm.

Finally, however, this maneuver also came to an end, and we set out at once on another, which was quite short—"sea maneuvers" this time.

This included landing drills conducted in boarding craft, torpedo boats and rubber dinghies, used for landing on shore, rescuing survivors from a sinking vessel, for attacks launched from the sea and the like. The final drill included landing on shore from our craft and conducting an attack a considerable distance away. Let me make it clear: From the landing craft you rush into the water up to your neck (the short fellows are sometimes submerged completely), make for shore with your gun held over your head, get organized and immediately, weighed down as you are—socks and fatigues sodden and full of water—set out on your way. If you add to this the torrential rains, which fell that night in the bay region, you'll understand that it wasn't too pleasant. As a result of the wetness most of the soldiers got hard calluses, and the coarseness of our trousers as they rubbed against our bodies caused serious scuff-burns. Some just barely managed to walk, and it was evident that each step was torture. As for me, I enjoyed the whole thing. I suffered no pain or injury, and altogether it reminded me of a tiny fraction of the hardships I had endured in the paratroops.

Bibi, I want to say something to you on a subject that is troubling me. You think, it seems to me, that I belittle your studies, or at least the difficulties you have to overcome at school, as if you had heard me say: "What does this little guy know of difficulties?" You couldn't be more wrong. Look, I can't go back to high school again, whereas you will be able to jump from a plane, if that's what you make up your mind to do. Perhaps you don't really understand the importance of doing what you are engaged in at the *present* in the best possible manner. And if you do understand this, as your actions and your successes indicate, then how on earth can you belittle your activities in this way? Just the opposite: do you think that I don't realize what difficulties a student has to face? After all, it was only a short time ago that I attended the very same school you are in now, and I don't think I learned half of what you are learning, or in any case I didn't invest as much effort in my studies as you are investing. I don't regret those years because I think I fulfilled my part as a student in the best way possible. But if we were both students in the same class right now, I believe you would outshine me in a substantial number of subjects. Don't you ever again denigrate the value of the things you are doing now when you compare them with what I'm doing. I'm not at all sure that such a comparison is appropriate, nor am I sure how the scales would tip if the comparison were made just the same.

January 9, 1966

Dear ones,

To hear your voices is almost like seeing you. I tried to imagine you in my mind's eye and could not avoid biting my lips. Nearly seeing you, and yet not seeing!

I see that it's important for you that I describe in detail the ceremony at which I was commissioned an officer—so now I'll do what you ask.

Well, after six long and very interesting months we finished the course.

If I had to evaluate the course in one sentence, I would say that it achieved its goal successfully. This really is an excellent Officers' Training Course. By the way, it is also considered one of the best Officers' Training Courses in the world (only a few can compare in standard, and it is easy to check this out).

At the conclusion of the course the top cadets are chosen. Each platoon selects its best cadet, and the choice is usually very difficult to make, since as a rule the cadets include a number of genuinely superior men. Then from the four platoons one is chosen as the top cadet of the company. This is, of course, the highest honor one can win. By the way, it is interesting to note that of the five outstanding men—the company winner and the four platoon winners—four were paratroopers and only one came from another corps, a great guy from the armored reconnaissance unit. This may serve you as a criterion by which to gauge the standards of the paratroops among the units of Zahal.

I was chosen the outstanding company cadet.

The graduation parade, conducted in the presence of the Chief of Staff, was planned for January 5th at three o'clock in the afternoon. Luckily for us, it was an enchanting day. I don't think there were many such days during the last few months. A light breeze drifted through a world drenched in green, and the sun warmed away the chill in the air. The ceremony began with the four platoons marching as four solid blocks onto the parade grounds. A few drills were performed and then the flag of Israel was unfurled.

After the company was brought to attention, the Chief of Staff* showed up. He passed between the ranks reviewing all the graduating cadets (I even have a picture taken just at the moment when the Chief of Staff passed opposite me). Then he returned to his platform and was asked by the officer conducting the ceremony to award officers' pins to the top cadets.

Up to this point we had been standing in the ranks. Now the five of us, who had been holding our guns "at the shoulder," lowered them to the ground on hearing the words: "Outstanding cadets!" Then we heard the call: "Outstanding Company Cadet—Netanyahu, Jonathan!" I had to come to attention, call out, "Sir," and then run lightly to present myself in front of the Chief of Staff's platform. After me were called, one after another, the four outstanding platoon cadets. The Chief of Staff came down from the platform, approached me, pinned the insignia on the lapel

*Yitzhak Rabin, later Israel's ambassador to the U.S. and still later Israel's Prime Minister.

of my jacket, exchanged a few words with me, congratulated me on my achievements, shook hands and wished me success. Then he passed on to the four top platoon cadets and pinned insignias on them as well. When the five of us returned to the ranks, the platoon commanders passed among their men (each platoon was arrayed in rows of three so that every row made a squad, and each squad commander pinned the officer's insignia on the men of his group).

Later the Chief of Staff delivered a speech, which was quite to the point, and following his speech, a symbolic ceremony was held in which roles were exchanged between our former commanders and us, the fledgling officers. I went over to the lieutenant colonel, the company commander, saluted him and took his place at the head of the company. Next the other outstanding cadets changed places with the platoon commanders—captains and majors. The staff of instructors left the parade grounds. Then we, too, left it, marching in front of the Chief of Staff. I marched behind the flag-bearers, and behind me—the four platoons. I have a photo of this too. Needless to say, everything I've described was accompanied by music of army bands and all kinds of military pomp, which took considerable time.

Later on, in a large hall filled with guests, the ceremony of "revealing the ranks" took place. If you studied the snapshots I sent you, you must have noticed a white ribbon on our shoulders. Each course in Zahal has its particular identifying sign; that of the Officers' Training Course is a white ribbon. Underneath these ribbons were our officer bars, and the point of this ceremony was the cutting of the ribbons to reveal our rank. We were called to the platform in alphabetical order, went up, shook hands, received officer certificates, and then the white ribbons were ceremonially cut off, and we left the platform as full-fledged officers. I was called to the platform "last but not least." Don't ask how many documents I've got: officer's certificates, class photos, certificates of excellence, outstanding cadet certificates, etc. I also have a picture in which I'm shaking the hand of the major, my company commander, after he uncovered my rank. The mayor of Petah Tikva, which is close to our base, delivered a speech and then called the "most outstanding cadet" to the platform to be awarded Petah Tikva's special gift: an album of that city with a dedication; so my literary treasures are that much richer now. Following that, I was called upon to speak on behalf of all the cadets. I said what I said, and, of course, it was O.K., there was thunderous applause and all the rest. Then the colonel who is the commander of the Officers' School—a genuinely charming man, a very special person—had

(top) *Outstanding cadet at Officer's Training School, 1966*
(bottom) *At the graduation ceremony of the Officer's Training Course*

his say. At night we held our graduation party with our girl friends present, and on the next day we scattered, each man to his assigned unit. But before that, each *officer* was called to the commander of his platoon to receive the grades he had earned at the end of the course. I received the highest marks in the company, and the major, who is the commander of my platoon, began to tell me how marvellous I am and how in the six years he has been instructing in the school he has never met and has never had . . . etc., etc. I packed my things and left the base for the last time.

Very few of the paratroopers who are sent to the Officers' Training Course return to serve in the ranks of the paratroops. Each branch of the army sends a certain number of men to the course, according to the number of officers it needs, but since many fail to graduate from the course, the branches request that their original quotas be met, if necessary, by other men. All of these gaps are filled by the paratroops. Since our human material is better, and since our men rarely drop out of the course, the paratroops send a larger number of good men to the course in order to fill those gaps for Zahal. Our battalion, for example, sent some twenty men to the course—all of them good paratroops, knowing full well that only four or five officers would come back to the battalion. Since most of those who are sent want to return to the paratroops, the army has ruled that anyone returning to the paratroops as an officer must sign up for at least another full year, on top of the four months already committed.

Without signing up you cannot return to the paratroops. Usually this condition is met, for most of the good men among us are kibbutz members, and they don't hesitate as much about signing up (although a good number of city men do that too). Some of the graduates of the Officers' Training Course are appointed as instructors in the Officers' School—a job I'm not interested in. Since I finished the course as the outstanding company cadet, a keen struggle ensued about my assignment between the Officers' School and the paratroops, for both wanted me to serve with them. (The minute we came to the course we passed from the authority of the paratroops to the supervision of personnel, whose job is to place new officers in the various army units.)

In short, I'm returning to the paratroops as a platoon commander without signing up for a single additional minute.

We were given leave from the day we were dispersed (last Thursday) to next Wednesday; then we'll have to present ourselves in one of the paratroop bases for advanced training for paratroop officers. I've heard that this is one of the most interesting courses in Zahal (if not the most interesting of them all).

How am I spending these six days of my leave? Well, this is my third big leave, and I decided to take it easy. I want a breather after the long course. I've become so accustomed to sleeping so little every night that now one of the most difficult things for me is to sleep well. This is definitely a desirable goal. This morning (Sunday) I rose at eight o'clock, ate a good breakfast and then sat down in good spirits to write you this letter. I even managed to finish the first seven pages. Now, before supper, I'm continuing it.

Dani Litani (whom you know) is also on leave, and when I told him that I was staying in Jerusalem and was planning to run every day in the stadium,* he decided to join me. He showed up at about 10 A.M. and we walked to the campus together. The weather in Jerusalem is marvellous now, neither hot nor cold; it's hard to believe that this is the winter season. And if the farmers aren't too pleased with the brilliance of the sun, those responsible for its sparkling light should know that not all are ungrateful.

Well, this morning I ran ten miles very fast, showered in the locker-room adjoining the track and went back to town. In the afternoon I read a great deal and listened to music; I'm doing that a lot lately (Bari has acquired a large number of classical records). I enjoy lying on the sofa with my eyes closed, half asleep and half awake, listening while my body rests. After supper I'll go, again with Dani, to a play at Habimah.†

Since most of the young people of Jerusalem are in the army now, there's no one around to disturb my rest. Occasionally I go out with a girl, but most of the time, as I've said, I spend running in the stadium or reading, listening to music and sleeping. By the way, I'm now reading *The Young Lions* by Irwin Shaw and am enjoying the book very much. The more familiar you are with military themes, the more critical you become of war literature. At the same time, your interest in this literature increases because you no longer read it as an outsider, observing an alien world from the sidelines.

The play that Dani and I went to see was Harold Pinter's *The Birthday Party*. Let me make a general comment.

When a person goes into a café and instead of sugar pours salt in his coffee, he won't drink it, of course. The same applies to a book—you don't

*Of the Hebrew University.
†A well-known Israeli theater.

finish it if it doesn't interest you. I sat in the theater and observed the audience. At least half of them were not enjoying the play, I thought. I couldn't understand why they didn't leave.

I'm incapable of enjoying a presentation of distorted lives and abnormal, psychopathic characters, or plays whose content can hardly be understood, or if understood have dubious significance. In any event, I left this play in the middle, and I think I was better off. Zvi Barmeir told me that you all attended a Pinter play together in the U.S.A.; I'd like to know your opinion. Of course, now I can sit for hours and discuss the nuances of the play, etc., but in the final analysis I find it tasteless and pointless.

February 5, 1966

Beloved Mother, Father, Bibi and Iddo,

Again we've had a lengthy silence on both sides of the ocean. I waited in vain for letters from you after that "masterpiece" I wrote you when the muse descended upon me, after I finished the course. You did receive the letter and the snapshots I sent, didn't you? I now realize that you must have sent me letters addressed to the military post number; if so they've all been lost, because I've already changed addresses twice and will change at least two more times before I'm given a permanent address; and, as is well known, in this army, 80 percent of the letters that don't reach their destination right away never reach it at all. In any case, since our wonderful telephone conversation I've received only one letter from you—from Father, who wisely sent it to the Barmeirs' home.

After finishing Officers' School, I began advanced training for paratroop officers, which takes over a month and a half. Now another week and a half remain to the conclusion of this course. The number of participants is very small; it comprises the cream of the cream of the paratroops —in fact, the finest of Zahal's young officers. The demands here are very great, and I must admit that it's pretty difficult. I think I must have lost four to six lbs. in the past two weeks from insufficient nourishment and lack of sleep. Soon we'll conclude this training, which is extraordinarily interesting. I have yet to experience such an interesting period in the course of my military service.

Only four officers who finished Officers' School are returning to the battalion from which we came. As for me, I won't have even one day's respite, for immediately following the paratroop officers' training, and possibly even two or three days before, I shall be going, alone of all the graduates, to an additional course, which will last a month and a half—an officers' course of heavy mortars' deployment. The company in which I'll serve as platoon commander consists of men drafted in February. It's slated to be the support company of the battalion: that means that, in addition to being a regular company, it will be supporting the entire battalion with heavy weapons. After finishing the course, I alone will be responsible for the execution of that task. This involves skills worth acquiring, on top of the job itself. Aside from this, I'll be a platoon commander in the paratroops, which I've always wanted to be.

February 10, 1966

Beloved Mother, Father, Bibi and Iddo,

The paratroop officers' advanced training is finished, but I came out of it bruised and gashed.

As I wrote to you, the course ends with a most difficult exercise. Well, in one of the stages of this exercise we had to parachute in an area that is not a proper drop zone—"somewhere" in the Negev—under cover of smoke and planes, to take over an emergency airfield, capture a number of targets in the area and after that mark the airstrip and land several planes carrying equipment for the continuation of the mission—all of this at night, of course (and this was only a small part of the exercise).

Well, the jump zone was more or less level ground, but the earth there was harder than the floor you walk on; what's more, it was strewn with stones. The heavy equipment we jumped with exceeded the maximum loads allowed under the security regulations, and the French parachute we used brakes the speed of the fall much less than the larger American parachute. Although when measured in the airfield, the speed of the wind did not reach the maximum permissible for jumping, it did reach it in the jump zone (and the maximum applies to a regular jump zone, i.e., one that is sandy and has no obstructions). All this, and the pitch darkness of the night, caused me to land with such force that I finally got hurt in the course of a jump, thus ending my good luck. For until then I hadn't taken the slightest knock on any of the jumps, coming out of all of them unscathed.

To put your minds at rest: after taking X-rays the doctor said that I had suffered merely a heavy blow on the knee and that the pain would pass after a while. At first they thought I might have gotten a sprain or "miniscus" of the knee, but the doctor reassured me it wasn't so. That would have put me out of action—and brought an end to my service in the paratroops. You can't go on if you have miniscus; it completely incapacitates a paratrooper and compels one to return constantly for treatments. It's happened here more than once. Luckily for me, I received the blow in the final exercise of this training, so that I could finish the course. Even though I can barely walk now, I already feel an improvement, and soon I'll be fully recovered.

On Sunday I leave for a course in heavy mortars and machine guns. This course doesn't demand much exertion (if it should, I'll opt out in the beginning), and it would be a pity to miss it! The course offers so much knowledge, which so few of us possess, that I'd be a fool to pass it up.

March 5, 1966

Beloved Mother, Father, Bibi and Iddo,

When I got home yesterday on a Saturday leave I found two letters waiting for me, from Father and Mother. I gathered from them that I had caused you a great deal of worry by telling you about my little injury. It's a pity, because it's not worth worrying about.

I'm eagerly awaiting your book, Father. How I'd like to see you right now! All of you! I think some two years have already passed since I left home, and I haven't seen you, Father, even once in all that time.

In my previous letters I asked Mother to try to take care of my American driver's license, and now, even before my letter reached you, I got your letter with the license form for me to sign. You're a real "woman of valor," dearest Mother.

Reading your letters, Bibi and Iddo, I try to picture you as you must look now. The result—help! (as Bibi often says). I think that if I were to walk down the street with the two of you, people would take you for my bodyguards—two giants keeping watch over their poor brother.

You cannot imagine how I long to see you. True, you say it's only four short months. You're even counting the weeks, but I've never been able to view time as "short." Quite the contrary, my time is crammed with things to do. The plans for those months and for the months following them and those coming later are all made, and everything tugs me onward. I can look back on four months that have passed and say they went by very fast, but not on four months yet to come.

Lately we've begun to work and to study (in the mortars course) at a feverish pace. The more the course progresses, the better I understand how great a responsibility it entails. At times it's downright frightening to think about it. You have to learn to do a great many calculations with slide rules and log tables, as well as proper radio procedure, technical mastery of the instruments, control over the men operating them, fire direction and a great deal more. In brief, total concentration is a must. To sum up, I am very well satisfied.

Kisses,
Yoni

March 25, 1966

Father,*

Do you know what is in my heart right now?

Words cannot express all I feel upon the completion of your great work, which is in fact only the beginning.

I have never told you how proud I am of your being the man you are, of my being your son.

Your loving
Yoni

March 30, 1966

Beloved Mother, Father, Bibi and Iddo,

I am now in the region of Arad, close to Tel Arad, in the heart of the wilderness. The only dots of light you see here at night, and then only from a high mountain overlooking the area, are those of Arad (about which you waxed so enthusiastic last summer), not counting the few rare lights coming from the Bedouin tents that surround us. We are well into our second week here.

After weeks of summery weather, the elements have turned topsy-turvy, and the rains have come pouring down. It's been raining with such force and at such a rate that for three days now the newscasts talk of little else: electricity poles were toppled; Wadi Beersheba has overflowed its banks, blocking the road to the Negev; trees have been uprooted; and much more. Although the rain came late and did not prevent a drought, it still managed to turn our lives into the "usual nightmare." Again I am in a

*After receiving a copy of his father's new book, *The Marranos of Spain*.

pup tent with a fellow lieutenant, continuing the exercises and drills despite everything. And believe me, with a forty-five mph wind in the area, with hail battering us, with a tent that is leaking and dripping all over and without proper clothing, this is not the most agreeable of times.

Next week I'll finish the mortars course and return at long last to the paratroops.

The last few Saturdays I went out on a number of trips. The preceding ones did not entail much effort as I did not want to tire my leg, but last Saturday I was finally able to walk well and indeed did so. A week ago, on the 12th of the month, one day before my birthday, I went with a girl friend to Tabha on the banks of the Sea of Galilee. I had forgotten that it was my birthday, but when I got home I found a lovely cake that Uncle Saadiah had brought the day before and left there for me. Since I came home very late at night and by five in the morning had left for camp, I have not thanked him yet, but I'll do so next Saturday.

On the day before last, Friday, the sun suddenly came out, and the entire universe was beckoning me to set out on a walking trip. Even before that, I had arranged to meet Bari and a couple of friends at Ein Gedi and spend two days there. Well, instead of hitchhiking to Ein Gedi, I took along only the minimum essentials—windbreaker, water flask and machine gun—and set out alone on foot on the road leading from Arad to Massada. Actually this was not a real road and my walking was really a navigation trek with the aid of a topographic map of the region. But that is what is so interesting in these trips. Again I got to know another route in our country.

I reached the hostel at Massada toward evening and from there traveled to Ein Gedi by the Sodom Road. I arrived there exactly as Bari and his retinue came with all their baggage. Bari has an excellent tent, purchased abroad years ago. The girls had prepared plenty of food, and everything was arranged for two days of comfortable living (I can always count on Bari for that). I arrived tired and thirsty and ready for complete rest. Well, we pitched the tent on the shore of the Dead Sea, lit a bonfire and cooked supper. Then we sat beside the fire and sang and talked until late into the night. From this point on a number of things happened that we had not planned for, but that made the outing all the more exciting.

During the night the wind started up again. "And it came to pass at midnight" that we three young couples felt the tent giving way and collapsing. Luckily, it dropped on us like an enormous blanket, thus shielding us from the wind and the rain. When we had put it up, we had expected summer weather, never anticipating such a development. The only thing I feared just then were floods, which could have swept us into the sea, since rain that falls in the Hebron Mountains ends up as great torrents of water flowing in the wadis to the Dead Sea and sweeping everything before them. But my fears didn't materialize. That night we didn't pitch the tent again but merely wrapped it tightly around us. In my opinion, it was delightful; I slept very well.

In the morning, as soon as the sun shone through the clouds and the fog, painting the Dead Sea and the Edom Mountains with those marvellous shades of color that are so uniquely theirs, we packed our belongings and prepared to move on and pitch our tent in a different place. At about ten o'clock, the world became bright, and we went for a walk in the Brook of David along the enchanting waterfalls and the extraordinary vegetation that fills this oasis. We had a picnic in a hidden corner beside a little pool of water, and in the afternoon we pitched the tent, but this time I made sure it was pitched properly. And in fact, despite the wind and the rain that came later, we didn't feel them in the tent, where we cooked on gas stoves and sat by candlelight. Late at night we dismantled everything, loaded it into the car and drove back toward Arad. I got off on the main road and continued to our camp by foot.

March 31, 1966

Dear Tutti,

I'm surprised I can write; my fingers are virtually frozen. Today is Tuesday and the rain, which started on Saturday, doesn't even "think" of stopping. What a disgusting situation! To sit in a dripping pup tent three whole days with the rain striking five to six inches from your face, depending on how the tent moves in the wind!

The defense drill, which was scheduled for today, was cancelled; the rain is so strong that all the wadis in which the mortars are normally set up have turned into veritable rivers. The command cars broke down already yesterday, so that in effect we are completely cut off, and anyway it wouldn't enter anyone's mind to carry out mortar drills here now. The only food we have is what was brought here on Sunday. All the Indian tents were ripped in the wind and are utterly useless, i.e., they no longer exist. Half the ammunition is ruined, and the weapons are sunk in mud. Only the pup tents are still standing—worthless, but standing nevertheless. The last rainfall, which started at 2:30, did not stop until just now, 4:30. Many a time I've been on exercises during long rains, but I've never had to sprawl in them for hours without a break. Only now do I grasp the meaning of ceaseless rain. How much can one sleep or read, for heaven's sake! Someone found a box rolling around containing some 5,000 envelopes. That gave rise to ideas of how to get rid of the stupor.

When you dropped me off beside the sign pointing to Mount Tzia, it soon became clear to me that our camp was about six miles from the road, not four. To cut it short, I was lucky that you dropped me off right there, for things happened in a way to make the Saturday perfect. It's just as well you didn't continue on in the car because the road ended after about two hundred yards; it was breached across its width by the streams. Even command cars can't cross it—as I said, we are cut off.

Well, I began to walk when I was suddenly caught by that extraordinary rain, which must have hit you as well. The road vanished and the only thing that remained was a rather doubtful azimuth. After several falls into an equal number of wadis, I reached the conclusion that at the very worst I'd spend the night exploring the area—a sort of night navigation exercise. As soon as I arrived at this conclusion, my spirits soared—and why not?

But fate willed otherwise. When I thought that I was approaching the camp, I saw a light blinking in the darkness, or rather it blinked once and disappeared. It was so dark that I couldn't see anything, so I decided it must be a Bedouin camp or, if I was lucky, our own. Not until the dogs started barking did I know for sure what I had stumbled into. The tent at the far end, which I entered, was one of a group of ten. It was an awkward situation considering that no one knew I was strolling in the area. But one thing is certain—the poor Arab who got up in the night probably cursed my arrival. He was just afraid. I must thank you again for suggesting that I load my Uzzi. True, I'd have done so anyway before going into the area where the lights were blinking, but it was nice of you to think of it just the same. At first he was rather surly, especially when he saw that I was alone. But when I said Shalom, and quite "by chance" tapped my Uzzi as a reminder, he quieted down and took me inside. When I got used to the dark, I discovered all around me a great many camels, donkeys, goats and dogs. I explained gently that I didn't intend to leave until the rain stopped. It was fun talking to him, since we scarcely knew a word in common.

To cut a long story short, we sat for about two hours by the fire he lit, the host totally unprepared for guests. After about half an hour, when he became convinced that I wouldn't eat him up and was just enjoying the fire, and as a sign of trust I took off my weapon and laid it beside me, we became real buddies, and he even suggested that I sleep there, which I had absolutely no intention of doing. We sat and talked, but mostly we were silent.

At about 12:30 the rain stopped, and we parted, to his sigh of relief. The truth of the matter is that I had grown so accustomed to the fire and the shelter from the rain, to the weeping of the infant that awoke on the other side of the partition and to the snoring of the camels only a few inches away that I regretted having to leave. But in good time I at last reached our camp and found it in an even worse state than I had described to you. Now it has undergone improvements.

April 5, 1966

Beloved Mother, Father, Bibi and Iddo,

"Concluded is the Passover Seder in accordance with tradition."

We held a Seder with the Barmeir family, Martha's sister and her family and myself. What shall I tell you? I had not taken part in such a Seder for years and years. It was so lovely, so heartfelt, so earnest, so full and overflowing, that all one can do is sing its praises. Zvi conducted the whole Seder, beginning with an introduction and explanation of his own —and I was truly impressed. We read the Haggadah from beginning to end, and there wasn't a detail that we failed to consider. Zvi drew our attention not only to the meaning of the words and benedictions but also to the beauty of the poetry, the rhythm, the problems of vocalization and much more. Martha prepared a lavish meal, after which we continued to read the Haggadah and to sing until after midnight. I didn't even notice that the time was already 1 A.M.

I've been a platoon commander in the paratroops for some time now, and all I want to say is: Never before in my military service have I drawn such deep satisfaction from my work or gotten so much out of it as I have in the last few weeks.

April 9, 1966

Dear Father,

I began to read your book, Father, and find it fascinating. I don't want to take it with me to the army because it may get torn in the field, and it is too precious to me.

Zvi has also read the book and cannot stop praising it—and you. He simply can't calm down. He has probably written, or will write to you soon.

May 15, 1966

Beloved Father, Mother, Bibi and Iddo,

It seems that weeks and weeks have passed since I last heard from you. Or perhaps I'm mistaken; lately, time has lost its usual meaning for me.

The day is devoid of a beginning, continuing from sunrise into the scorching noon sun, on to the cool of the evening and from there to the darkness of night and further to the shade of the pale moon, the stars after midnight, and on to shutting your eyes after two o'clock in the morning and forcing them open at four-thirty to begin a new day.

One day of drilling like this makes a man wake up the next morning with a sense of exhaustion that is all but intolerable, with a feeling as if his strength had been sucked out of his body—the hands are weak and the brain is not yet cleared, remaining foggy for a few more hours. Two such days make you forget that you have ever been at home and that anything exists besides work and ceaseless tension. Two such days are the beginning of eternity.

And week follows week like so many passing seconds. Time does not crawl; on the contrary, it sprints. You don't have a chance even to reflect on the meaning of those seconds. Time is just one great chunk.

In the past, when I was just an ordinary soldier, I thought I was going through the greatest difficulty. Now as an officer, I see how wrong I was. First, the drills that my men are carrying out are far more intensive, I believe, than those of other recruits. Really hard! They drill for eighteen to nineteen hours a day and the exercises are simply gruelling. The word "gruelling" will not properly describe them, since your concept of the word will not be the same as mine. It's incredibly hard. And after midnight, instead of sleeping, they have to go on enduring the constant tension of night alarms, sudden alerts, roll calls and drubbing of various sorts. The soldier who sleeps two hours a night is lucky. Just try for weeks on end to be awake twenty-two hours a day, and take into account that the effort the soldier makes here requires at least nine hours' sleep—this applies to someone accustomed to great exertion—and you will perhaps understand what I mean.

I once thought an officer could get more rest than an ordinary soldier, but I couldn't have been more wrong. During drills I am with them through each of all those long hours, and all that time the work keeps me continually on edge. The burden of worry and responsibility leaves its mark, and I feel the full weight of command resting on my shoulders.

We have been in the field for two solid months. We have not seen any kind of military base or camp. With all the gear on our backs and with our feet pushing hard at the ground, we pass each week from one training area to another in quick marches dozens and dozens of miles long. We pitch our pup tents and continue the drills. Yesterday we interrupted this way of life for a while. The recruits had finished their basic training, and now we've reached jump school (three and a half weeks). The soldiers will then wear the red berets and will continue farther. I used to think that "farther" meant to the completion of squad-commanders course, but now I see that for some people there is no end to the "farther."

After the relatively relaxing months of the courses I took, which were a means to an end, the time has come to accomplish that end, and the fact is that to attain it in the best possible way, the investment in the courses was necessary and worthwhile.

The situation in the country is becoming more and more serious. In the past few weeks a considerable number of border incidents have occurred and the number of casualties on both sides was great. Several weeks ago, two members of Kibbutz Mei-Ami were killed and two were badly injured. One of the men killed was a fellow from Tel Aviv who finished the Officers' Training Course with me. We were in the same squad, in adjoining rooms for six months and then together again for a month and a half in the mortars officers' course. Two weeks after our graduation he went to join the Mei-Ami settlement as part of his service in Nahal and was killed while attempting to rescue a wounded man. Immediately afterwards, there was a succession of incidents, including the border incident in Devira, which took place only a few days ago. Here, too, two men were killed, one of them an officer in the paratroops, a fine, well-known fellow. Just a minute ago there was an announcement on the radio of a mine explosion in Almagor, which resulted in the death of two farmers.

Two weeks ago we initiated reprisal raids, one in the Beisan region and the other in the Hebron Mountains. Two large, separate forces crossed the border. We blew up a number of houses belonging to people who are known to be collaborating with the Fatah, after first evacuating the inhabitants. We then returned to our lines in small forces, grouped according to their missions.

There is a restlessness throughout the country, and in the army it is felt

Lieutenant in the paratroops, 1966

more deeply than elsewhere. After weeks during which I did not get home, I have to remain here until tomorrow as the duty officer of the parachute course. Tomorrow another officer is due to relieve me until Friday, but I don't think this leave will materialize. For there has seldom been such a miracle—that a whole week should pass without the paratroops being put on alert. In spite of this, I hope we will yet reach a time when we will not have to live with the enemy's sword swinging over our heads.

I think I even forgot to tell you about the surgery I underwent to remove my wisdom teeth, or perhaps I haven't written at all since then (it really happened quite some time ago, relatively speaking). I had something similar to what Father had a few years ago, and surgery was necessary. After the operation I stayed in bed at Ollie and Anna's (they live near the hospital), and for two days I was spitting blood and eating nothing. I even went back to the hospital twice for additional tests, since the doctors thought it should all have been over soon after the operation. Ollie and Anna were very kind, and I am very grateful to them. An infection developed, and I had to swallow pills all the time as well as medication to lessen the pain, which was so bad that I couldn't sleep a wink at night and wanted to scream out in agony; I couldn't sit still for a second, and when I lay down the whole sheet became stained with blood running from my mouth, which was slightly open. Now, of course, everything is all right, except that one of these days I must have the lower left wisdom tooth extracted and thereby get rid of this trouble once and for all. This tooth is not infected and does not hurt, so that it is only a question of having it pulled out.

The date of your arrival is approaching—only another month and a half. Since we haven't written to each other lately, it seems like a much longer period of time. Every one of your letters brings me closer to you, but when I don't receive any, I don't even have time to think much about home. It has happened more than once that in the course of a day's drilling I didn't even manage to roll up my sleeves. That's how pressed I am for time. To write even a couple of words is too much. There just isn't time! On the few Saturdays I got home, I was so exhausted that I fell straight into bed and slept till the next day, when I had to go back. But I'm sorry you, too, don't find time to write a few words. It's hard to believe that you can't even find ten free minutes in which to tell me what's happening at home. Or perhaps you are waiting for a letter from me before you reply? What nonsense! That way we'll hardly ever exchange letters.

It is typical that whenever I try to tell you something of what is happening at home or in the streets of Jerusalem, I am struck dumb. I have no idea of anything going on outside the army. I hope that now we'll have a break in the training, at least during the course, so I'll once more be able to take an interest in what is happening around me. As a soldier, even when I returned after midnight from drills, I found time to read a few lines in a good book, but now even that is impossible. There is so much to do, prepare, plan and care for that every free moment is used up. The fact that I've already written five pages testifies to the change in the situation. Blessed rest.

What else shall I tell you? About my little experiences in the army beyond the training? About the moments of relaxation after the tension? I think I'll tell you a little episode of drunkenness related to this subject.

Among the paratroops we have the best fellows you could find anywhere—men who work from morning to morning indefatigably and usually without a moment of relief. We returned, one platoon commander and I, after midnight from navigation in the area and found an officer, who was about to be discharged, packing his things. Beside him were several bottles of cognac, which he had brought along to celebrate the completion of his service. The party had not taken place for a simple reason: the entire staff had fallen asleep. Needless to say, we woke them all up and at one o'clock in the morning began to eat and drink. We were all so tired that it was not surprising to see them getting drunk from just a few sips. Little by little they shed their fatigue and finally turned into a raging crowd: tossing steel helmets, weapons and shoes at one another; they wrecked a partition that served as a wall, broke light bulbs and only by a miracle did not kill one another. It was impossible to stop them. I took two blankets and went to sleep outside.

This was no ordinary drunken spree. What happened here was something quite different. There was so much tension stored up inside these fellows, such a heavy burden, that when relaxation came suddenly, something exploded in them that had been pent up for too long. Every one of them, commissioned and non-commissioned officer alike, lost control of himself. Maybe this is the way men turn into animals, kill and maim one another, destroy while their minds are dulled and reason abandoned, lose the essence of the consciously thinking man—who controls himself and is the sole master of himself—and turn into a wild mob. I think it is only because I'm incapable of allowing myself to give up full control over my actions at any time that I didn't lose consciousness and act like them. And I was more tired than all the others—that's for sure.

As I write this, various pieces of news reach me about what we are doing with regard to the border incident. Every time something happens on the border, the whole army stretches taut as a spring, then returns to its previous state of tense relaxedness.

May 18, 1966

Beloved Mother, Father, Bibi and Iddo,
In another twelve days you'll be here! Really on the 29th? If you could only advance your arrival by a week, we'd have so much more time to spend together! On the 24th we're going on a whole week's leave (until June 1st).

It's been a long time since I wrote to you, but it's hard for me to write when I know that soon I'll see all of you here.

I miss you all.

Love you with all my heart,
Yoni

August 3, 1966

Tutti my love,
In my imagination I now see the two of us borne upwards into the blue skies above my head. Not ascending in a storm but cutting through the azure like an arrow. Floating motionless. For some reason this picture has planted itself in my mind and refuses to leave.

It is now noon and a light breeze is tempering the heat. We are in the heart of an olive grove, and except for us there isn't a living soul. The tree trunks are ancient and dry and the dusty leaves are barely moving. Even the soldiers around me appear to be moving as if in a dream. I want to be here with you, alone, with time and the world before us.

These are hours of rest prior to the start of a big exercise. All the preparations have been made, and we can enjoy the calm. This is my kind of relaxation. Not idle rest, but rest that comes after days of hard labor —hours between the "before" and the "after."

I love you.

August 5, 1966

Beloved Father and Mother,

I am exactly a mile away from you.* If you go up to the pool above Arad and look down the road leading to Massada, you'll be able to see our camp. Never before have I been, while in the field, in such a comfortable and "central" location. As a rule we are in the middle of nowhere, without a road, and many miles from human habitation. What luck!

I'm sending you this letter because I won't be able to visit you next Friday and Saturday. Today we're leaving for a spot some distance from here, to conduct an exercise that will last until Sunday night. But don't despair! Maybe I'll be able to hop over to Arad in the evenings during the week, or for a while at night, and then we'll see each other.

Enjoy yourselves.

Kisses,
Yoni

September 5, 1966

Beloved Father, Mother, Bibi and Iddo,

On the eve of your departure I was still hoping I'd be able to come and see you, but in vain. Five days earlier I had again assumed the full burden of my military duties, and I haven't been home for three weeks now. This week we were in the Syrian border sector where all the recent incidents occurred—incidents that have become only more frequent and more serious since you left.

It would seem that during your visit in Israel I found it somewhat difficult to live the military life. Leaves were too important to me, I couldn't devote myself totally to my work, and as a result I may have been a little edgy. Now that there's nothing to deflect my thoughts, it's easier for me, and I can enjoy the army more. Or maybe I feel that way because during your stay here our military activity was relatively limited, whereas now it is once more on the increase.

How shall I describe those marvellous summer months? It was so good to be together with all of you or separately, either with Bibi and Iddo, or with you, Mother and Father. While you were here you showed me so much love and consideration and made such efforts on my behalf that I'm afraid I didn't show you all the love and gratitude I felt toward you. You

*At the time Yoni's parents were having a few days' vacation in Arad.

worked so hard for me and my comfort that at times it seemed exaggerated. For you didn't come here just to make things easier for me (that's what I want to believe), but for your own sakes; or perhaps the two blend together.

I received a letter from Harvard informing me that I must take a number of exams. Precisely what these exams will require I don't know as yet; I'm waiting for the instructions and booklets that Bibi will send me. The university also indicated where I can write if I have any questions about the exams. Once again I am placing this burden on you. It is now really hard for me to deal with the whole subject of my studies. You have given this matter so much thought, and undertaken so much, that at times it seems rather funny; after all, I am the student and the problem is mine. I think that, in the past two years, I've solved all my problems by myself, and then you come along and take everything upon yourselves—and what's strange about it is that I let you do it. But it really was difficult for me to think about it and to delve deeply into each point at this time when it is necessarily peripheral for me, if only temporarily.

It seems I'll have to take some exams in March (that is also according to Harvard's requirements as set out in the letter you left in my suitcase). Since it's obligatory, I'm not too apprehensive; either I'll pass or I'll have to wait another year. In any event there's no point in worrying.

I came home for a short while, and I'm leaving at once for the northern part of the country again, which on the one hand is so beautiful and peaceful and on the other—so turbulent and embroiled. I noted the exemplary condition in which you left my belongings, Mother—and I'm full of admiration. Simply marvellous! I also found all the letters and instructions that you, Father, left me, and everything is perfectly clear.

September 9, 1966
Tutti,

After two weeks of a "thrashing" I find myself lying in the shade of a pine wood in the distant north. In another hour we'll have breakfast and from then until nightfall—almost uninterrupted rest. During the night there will be a bit of action, but tomorrow—more rest. We have it coming to us. This "vacation" will end in a few days. I managed to turn up a two-legged bed in the junk of the kibbutz storage room, so now I sleep on a bed, at least during the day.

We had a big exercise, which took several days, "somewhere" down south, and in the past week we did navigations up here. Each platoon functioned independently. It pitched camp on one of the mountains and set out from there to navigate, while the platoon commander remained in camp. Since I can't see my men setting out and me staying behind, I went every day along the routes my soldiers followed and checked the target points of all the groups; this allowed me to meet my soldiers on the way, evaluate their standard of navigation and correct their mistakes. But the best part of it all was that during the week I "plowed" alone through the northern part of our country (twenty-eight miles by day and eighteen by night). I was given battle rations for the platoon for this period and was told, "Goodbye; see you in a week's time."

Yesterday my family went abroad, but I couldn't see them off. To prevent unnecessary waiting and disappointment in case I couldn't get to the airport, I told them on Saturday definitely that I wouldn't come, and we had a nice farewell.

September 9, 1966

Beloved Father, Mother, Bibi and Iddo,

I am working hard day and night. No leaves, no rest periods, and not even time to write long letters or to take care of those things that require attention and are postponed for the chronic lack of time. All our days and nights are devoted to a single purpose—to turn our troops into real troops; to make the good soldiers superior soldiers, and the superior soldiers good officers. The only subject being dealt with at present is soldiering, and more soldiering, and yet more.

It is not so jolly in Israel at present, as you no doubt gather from the papers. Explosions, mines, and acts of sabotage of all kinds, deaths and many wounded—these are events that are repeated almost weekly, and at times daily. It was good that things were relatively quiet during your visit here, although, as I remember it, the ruckus had begun already before you left.

I received some letters from various universities in the States, including Yale and the University of Pennsylvania. I've hardly had time to look at them. Yale writes that they will agree to delay the decision on my acceptance until they get the results of my exams in March. I'll mail you all that they sent me.

September 20, 1966

Tutti mine,

You write that your heart is wrung with love. My first reaction was that you must be very lonely. In fact you wrote this, but I failed to grasp the full meaning of your loneliness until that last sentence! Or perhaps I am mistaken and am only imagining?

I was in Jerusalem on Rosh Hashanah and decided to visit everyone who had ever been close to me. Koshe and Dani are in Eilat. The truth is that I don't have many friends, and never did. But I saw all the girls I used to go out with every now and then. It was interesting to see how much they had changed since we were in school together. On the last day I went to visit Shaham in Kefar Hadar.

The more I think about the subject of you-and-me, the more I fear that one day we shall part, each of us to live his life separately. Actually, it's not this that I fear, but the fact that I'll never meet someone like Tutti again—and then, by the time this is clear to me, it will be too late. On the one hand, I'd like you to be here now very, very much. On the other, it suits me that you're still abroad and that I have time to be alone and "organize" myself; to see myself among people without Tutti.

Two weeks ago, shortly after you left, I strolled by the sea all by myself, and I was sorry you weren't with me. Believe me. Yet it was good to be alone. I see that I've learned to toss on paper everything that comes to my mind at the moment. It is easier to write letters this way—and perhaps this is the only way.

October 25, 1966

(To his parents and brothers)
Kisses to all of you,

I received your letter telling me, among other things, of your visit to Haverford. Honestly, it's hard for me to get as excited as you do over the prospect of entering a university, while I'm still engrossed in the military effort. For some reason it seems to me that you attach enormous importance, more than it merits, to the continuation of my education, whereas I'm not that concerned about it. It's clear to me that I'll resume my studies right after my discharge, but at the same time I think that the two and a half years I've spent in the paratroops have given me a somewhat different perception of life—a perception that you, despite your rich experience, will never be able to have.

As you no doubt know from reading the papers, the situation in Israel is, in a word—catastrophic! War is hanging over our heads like a swollen balloon that the merest pinprick can burst. Not a day passes, literally, without a border incident, sabotage, mine explosion, murder, ambushes, shootings and setting fire to fields. During all the years of my service and of my living here the situation has never been so tense. In the army, everyone is impatient—when are we finally going to strike back?!! We have complete confidence in our strength. We are capable of anything.

My company is now the senior one in the battalion. Morale runs high among the men, and the level of their soldiering is superb. Did I tell you that I parachuted down to the Sea of Galilee? It was marvellous! Somehow it seems to have happened a very long time ago.

October 27, 1966

Beloved Father, Mother, Bibi and Iddo,

In your letters you asked for a first-hand report on what is happening in Israel from a military point of view. In about ten minutes it will be eleven o'clock, time for the evening news broadcast. I am waiting to hear about the latest incident, which occurred only minutes ago and about which I'll tell you now.

The recent incidents are in effect of two kinds: those committed by bands of terrorists who infiltrate from the Syrian border and those committed by terrorists from Jordan. The prevalent view is that those responsible for the actions are Al Fatah bands, aided and financed by the Syrian authorities. At any rate, this is the view that the government circles are spreading. They place all the blame for the incidents on Syria and try to minimize Jordan's responsibility. I can understand the logic behind this; placing all the blame directly on Syria is an attempt to isolate her internationally.

Before I express my opinion of the reprisal actions, I want briefly to mention what has occurred here most recently.

Last Tuesday a command car of the Border Guard was on a routine tour along the patrol road that runs close to the demilitarized zone, in the vicinity of the Syrian post Tel-Azaziat. Near Hirbet Nebi Hoda the car struck a mine and was completely demolished. One soldier was wounded. Last month a jeep struck a mine on the same spot and three soldiers were wounded.

Two days later a fierce battle took place between our forces and an enemy reconnaissance group, in which one of our men was killed while the enemy's losses were three killed and one wounded (all signs point to encouragement or support from the Syrian army).

On Saturday afternoon the Syrians *again* opened heavy machine-gun fire on a tractor that was plowing east of Kibbutz Ha'on.

Between these two incidents, chronologically speaking, a kiosk near Kibbutz Ein Gedi was blown up. Luckily, a mine was discovered about 150 yards from the site of the explosion, planted there deliberately to injure those who would drive over to investigate the cause of the explosion (something that has already been done successfully elsewhere and caused us casualties).

All of these are incidents of the very last few days. There is no need to remind you of the blowing up of the new buildings in the Romema neighborhood of Jerusalem (near the gasoline station at the entrance to the city).

The battalion was informed just this minute that, at 8:30 this evening, a freight train bound for Jerusalem struck a charge of explosives, which had been laid on the tracks near Beitar. A number of cars were derailed. Not content with this, the terrorists then opened fire on the passengers who were pulling themselves out of the overturned cars.

In the meantime I think they're waiting too long here. They should have responded to these terrorist acts long ago. The fact that they've waited this long necessitates a reprisal action of major dimensions now. Any minor act after such an extended silence would not be appropriate and would miss the mark.

Israel is, as I've noted, attempting to isolate Syria politically and to obtain support for its future actions. This may be the reason also for our long silence, and possibly at least part of this goal will be achieved. But all the indications point to actual war on an all-Zahal scale. Let's hope it will not come to that. In any event, we have faith in ourselves and our ability to carry out whatever task we are given.

Don't worry, because we're not worried.

November 16, 1966

Beloved Father, Mother, Bibi and Iddo,

I was in the Arab village of Samua, about six miles inside Jordan. My company was one of four that made the crossing. It was very instructive. Evidently there are people who lose all sense of reality under fire and don't know what they are doing, while others feel no change at all. In any case, that's how I felt—the same degree of concentration, the same sense of judgment, the same grasp of reality, and almost the same level of tension as I usually have on any other day. We suffered virtually no casualties except for one man killed, although a few officers were wounded—among them (you will be sorry to hear) M. (the son of your friend with whom you toured the north), who was hit by a bullet in the chest, apparently through carelessness on his part: he exposed himself too much instead of taking cover, as one should when cleaning out a village.

The three soldiers killed on the eve of the operation, when their command car struck a mine in the Hebron Mountains near Arad, were also our men, and one of them was a good friend of mine; the others were soldiers from the ranks, a year behind me.

At the moment I'm busy in the front lines in the south (we were moved up north from here for the reprisal action). I am doing the work of an officer with the rank of captain and am quite successful at it. A week before the operation, I caught five infiltrators, and, as a result, another spy network was uncovered in the north, in Um-el-Faham.

In the meantime my army service is drawing to a close.

Your loving
Yoni

November 30, 1966

Dearest Father, Mother, Bibi and Iddo,

Much has happened, much is happening and much will happen before my discharge. But the date is approaching (around the end of January).

A rather tense quiet now reigns in Israel. A full month has passed since I had my last leave, and chances are that until my discharge I'll get home only once or at most twice.

Yesterday our pilots shot down two Egyptian MiGs on the Sinai border. Incidents seem to be happening and developing on all fronts. The shooting in the north never stops and we've had casualties. Tomorrow the convoy is going up to Mount Scopus.* We are prepared for anything. Waiting.

*The Mount Scopus enclave in East Jerusalem consisting of a hospital and university facilities, remained in Israeli hands after the 1948 War of Independence. It was supplied by weekly Israeli convoys, which were occasionally interfered with by the Jordanians.

I received your letters and regret I have caused you so much worry. Even Bibi gives the impression of being a bit "edgy." Yesterday I went over the book on the SAT;* it turns out the math is very easy, but I'm sure to have trouble with English, especially with the vocabulary, in which I'm particularly weak. I'd like you to send me samples of past SATs so that I may see also the time constraints involved.

I play a lot of chess, almost the only thing that can be done with interruptions and taken up again at any free moment.

December 25, 1966

Beloved Father, Mother, Bibi and Iddo,

The battalion is very anxious for me to stay on in the regular army. I refused, of course, even though there are positive sides to this. I find the army to be of great interest, but I fail to see my future in it. There are so many things I want to do, and it is difficult for me to see myself as an army man all my life. In any case, if it comes up at all, the question is whether I should remain in the army or leave it. The answer is—leave it. The thing, therefore, should be settled at once. Be discharged and that's it. Without signing on for either long or short additional periods.

On January 4th my soldiers will finish the squad-commanders course and make the rank of corporal. I've come a long way with them. It seems to have taken ages. And maybe all that we've experienced during this time really did stretch the year and make it seem almost infinite.

I'm still receiving letters from universities, but I don't even have time to fill out the many forms; each university sends about fifty papers to fill out (I'm exaggerating a little just to make the point), and to do it would require hours of free time that I simply do not have. When I get home, I'll pack all these papers together and mail them to you. Just recently a letter came from Princeton; I'll send you that too.

In the army the work is feverish and demanding, both physically and mentally, to the very last minute. In nine days' time I'll finish training my men, but I'm scarcely aware of that. The only thing that is alive and clear beyond a doubt is the present day and the present moment.

I still run a lot even when I come home. In the army this is work, while at home it's pleasure. Best of all, after two and a half years in the army

*College entrance exams in the United States.

(a long time when you consider the kind of corps I'm serving in), I haven't tired of the effort and can do it all. In three and a half years' time, Bibi, you may understand the meaning of the term "weary soldier"—an all-too-common phenomenon.

January 17, 1967

Beloved Father, Mother, Bibi and Iddo,

My plans have not yet fully crystallized, but I have managed to draw up something of a plan for my immediate future.

First of all, I haven't yet been discharged. The date for that is January 31st. I am now on discharge leave and living at the army's expense.

Yesterday I took the TOEFL* at the ZOA House, and despite the heavy cold that made my eyes water and gave me a headache, I passed the exam very successfully. A very simple exam.

Last night I decided that the only way to get rid of this illness that has afflicted me is not to shut myself in the house with a hot stove and allow two or three days of rest to do their work, but on the contrary, to go out into the cold air with a firm determination to be well—and get well. I ran seven miles in the night and got well, of course. Now I am fully recovered.

Now to the main point. I've decided not to return to America right after my discharge, but to stay on here for a while. I'm not reconciled to the idea of "forsaking" Israel so soon after my discharge. To come to Israel, to serve in the army, and to leave immediately? That's not the way. Or to put it differently: I haven't yet satisfied my hunger for Israel.

Another thing I want to do concerns my living quarters. As long as I was in the army and came home, on leave only every two or three weeks, I didn't feel I was imposing too much on the Barmeir family, but as a civilian living at home day in day out, I see no justification for remaining here and burdening them. I want to rent a room and live the way I did before I enlisted.

By the way, have I told you that I'm already a first lieutenant? I received the promotion over two weeks ago, and that cost me a few bottles of cognac, as is customary. I received a gift with a really fine dedication from my men, all of whom are now corporals. We also had a wonderful farewell

*English test for foreign students wishing to study in the United States.

party about which I won't tell you now. It is difficult to describe casually an experience that represents the conclusion of a whole year's work—twelve full months, which are made up of weeks and days and hours and minutes and even seconds. It's hard.

RELEASE AND CALL-UP:
THE SIX-DAY WAR
(1967)

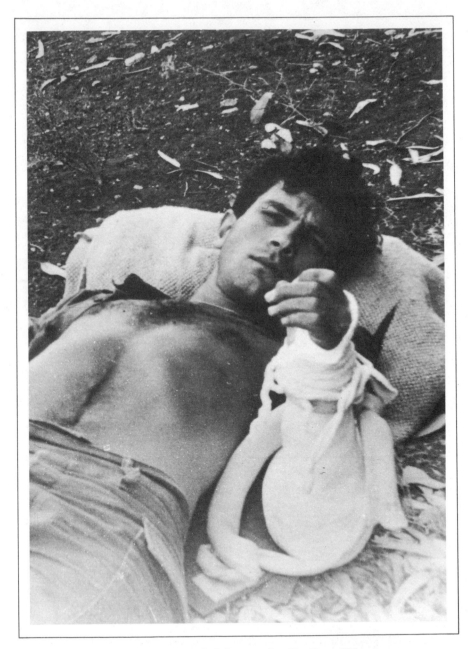

Yoni wounded during the Six-Day War

AFTER HIS RELEASE FROM THE ARMY Yoni decided to put off for a few months his planned departure for the United States to study at Harvard. Times were bad. Israel's economy was at its lowest ebb, suffering from a severe recession and unemployment. Yoni eagerly "cast himself into this stream," as he put it. Working at odd jobs, he soon found that he could make a handsome living.

In the meantime, the political and military situation was rapidly deteriorating and hovering dangerously on the brink of war. Without any provocation, and in violation of international law, Nasser's Egypt blockaded the Straits of Tiran, thereby effectively checking Israel's vital southern sea lane. This was tantamount to a declaration of war. There was faint protest from the United States and some of the European countries, but no action to open the international waterway. Soon thereafter the Egyptian Army, 100,000 strong, poured into the Sinai peninsula. Radio Cairo promised that the annihilation of the Jews was imminent, and to ensure this outcome Egypt arranged for a unified military command with Jordan, Syria and Iraq, Israel's neighbors to the east. An iron ring now surrounded Israel, and the world did nothing.

At the first signs of tension, Yoni decided to postpone his departure for the States again. Shortly afterward he was called up as Israel mobilized her army, made up largely of reserves, to meet the threat from without. For an agonizing three weeks, the entire world waited to see what would happen.

Finally, on the morning of June 5, 1967, war broke out. After a surprise dawn air strike, which wiped out the Arab air forces, the Israeli army burst through Egyptian defenses in Sinai and swept all the way to the Suez Canal. Jordan, not heeding Israeli warnings to stay out of the fighting, shelled Jerusalem. In response, Israel defeated the Jordanian Legion and captured the territory all the way to the Jordan River.

During the last two days of the war, the Israeli army finished the toughest task of all—conquering the formidable Golan Heights, which for nineteen years had been used by the Syrians to shell and harass Israel's villages in the north. By June 11, the war had ended with a total Israeli victory.

As a reserve paratroop officer, Yoni took part in several of these decisive battles, including the breakthrough battle at Um-Katef, which opened the way to Sinai. Landing with helicopters behind Egyptian lines, the paratroop force to which Yoni belonged attacked the Egyptian fortifications from the rear. Later Yoni was transferred north with other paratroopers for the assault on the Golan Heights.

Four hours before the end of the war, as he was reaching to help a wounded fellow soldier, Yoni was severely wounded in the elbow by Syrian fire from the Jelebina outpost. Bleeding heavily, he summoned all his strength and crawled for a long time under crossfire toward the Israeli lines. Reaching safety, he collapsed and fainted.

Yoni was operated on twice in hospitals at Safad and Haifa and was released as a disabled veteran.

February 1, 1967

My beloved ones,

Since yesterday, January 31, 1967, I've been a civilian. I returned all of my military equipment (except for one uniform with all the ranks and decorations on it), received a reservist's booklet—and the whole thing was over.

As I've already written, I've decided not to return to the U.S. right away, but to remain here a while longer. I think that in March I'll still be in Israel, so I'll be taking the College Boards here. Are there any special arrangements I have to make? Do I need an admission card for the examination like the one I had for the TOEFL?

In the meantime I've left the Barmeir home, accompanied by their best wishes. The time has come to live alone. To stay in their home once in two weeks is not the same as being there every day, since the work and effort this would entail for them are in my opinion too much to ask. In addition, I want—and I think it's high time—to live alone for a bit.

How do I spend my days? Well, I study mathematics a lot. Sometimes I can sit at the desk without stirring from eleven in the morning to seven at night. I don't even feel the time flitting by. Apart from that, I read a great deal. I've never had enough leisure to read as much I really wanted to. The days are too short and sometimes it seems I'm barely accomplishing anything.

February 21, 1967
Beloved Mother, Father, Bibi and Iddo,
Again I'm sending an urgent letter and hope that this one will be the last.

I forgot to write an essay for Harvard. Since the only subject I remembered of their suggested subjects was "Autobiography," I wrote an autobiography; therefore, the enclosed has to be sent to them. I'm not too good at writing about myself, but I did the best I could at the moment.

You asked for a list of books I've read, which is to be submitted to Harvard. I recall the following few titles, which can be added to those I gave you:

Crime and Punishment, by Dostoievsky
The Loneliness of the Long Distance Runner, by Sillitoe
Humanists, by Paul Landau
Night, by Elie Wiesel
Amok, by Stefan Zweig
The City of Fortune, by Elie Wiesel (a remarkable book).

March 8, 1967
(To his parents and brothers)
Beloved ones,
I have not yet decided when I'll come to the States. I think I must first hear from the different universities about the results of the exams.

Since the exams are now behind me, I've renewed my interest in chess. In my spare time I read a great deal; right now it's Machiavelli's *The Prince.* I'm also continuing with my math studies and doing very well. At the same time I continue working—now also in gardening. I really feel fine, although I miss you very much.

My dear Iddo, your letter was charming. In all seriousness. Please write lots more. Mother and Bibi, I'm so happy to hear from you about all that's happening at home. What an enthusiastic review you sent me of Father's book! If you can find the time, Father, write. You know how eagerly I await your letters, even if they're only a few words. When I visited the storeroom on Haportzim Street,* I looked for photos from our childhood

*The Netanyahu residence in Jerusalem.

days. Are there any? I found none. Do you remember where they are, Mother?

March 23, 1967

Beloved ones,

In the past few days you've flooded me with letters wishing me a happy birthday. Needless to say, I was very glad.

Since today I've finished another chapter of my life, it would be appropriate, I think, to say something about it.

As the time of discharge approaches, everyone is confronted with the problem of what to do as a civilian. For those who intend to study, the future is mapped out, but those who have a trade, or need to earn money to finance their studies (and these are too many to be counted) are faced with a serious problem. Israel is in the grip of a grave economic crisis. The recession causes unemployment on a scale the country hasn't seen for many years. It's all but impossible to find any kind of work. Even men who had regular employment or acquired some trade before enlisting in the army haven't found a place in the civilian market.

One of the things I wanted to do upon being discharged was to dive into this stream and make the attempt to hold my own in this difficult race. Everybody in the army and in Jerusalem predicted a very black future for me—that is, when I became a civilian. "Impossible!" This is the slogan of despair to which everyone clings. And since it's "impossible," they let themselves do nothing. To hold one's own in such an atmosphere is therefore a serious challenge. For some reason I was sure I'd manage to get along, but I put off dealing with this problem until after the exams, the filling out of forms for the universities, and such. Then, too, I wanted to study. As you know, when I decide to do something, I devote myself completely to the matter at hand and cannot do anything else, since I have to do things perfectly. It's not a matter of principle or calculated decision, it's simply the way I am. That was my attitude toward my studies, which I now plan to resume with renewed vigor. That's the way I behaved as a soldier, that's the way I run, read, hike and march; and that's the way it was also with my work.

Well, I started, as you know, as a porter. All your worries are unnecessary, for although this is hard work, it is, believe me, far easier than what I've been doing in the last three years. In the hardest kinds of work one either holds his own or breaks down, and I have always held my own, and believe I always will. Portering started out as hard labor, but became easier and easier. I am built in such a way that I can take it, and I haven't felt any special strain. Quite by chance, I also went into gardening. This work began with a payment of I£2 an hour and after a short while brought me an offer of I£700 a month, with conditions and hours left up to me. The truth is that I recognize my value as a worker and know my own ability. Whoever I work for is bound to benefit, whatever the fee he may pay me (I'm not saying this boastfully, but simply as a statement of fact).

Lately I've begun to work privately in gardening, or, to put it more accurately, in supplying soil to various people—for lawns and similar purposes. As I am a self-employed worker, the job is done by contracts, and the work is much more rewarding for me as a contractor. I rent a tractor, a cart and assorted tools from the gardener with whom I worked before, and in one day I earn from I£60 to I£75, and in a month about I£1500. All this as an unskilled laborer with no knowledge of my calling. Had I continued in this, I believe that in less than a year I'd have been able to earn more than I£2000 a month, would have become a partner in many small businesses and be making a very good living. Even though I have had to pay rent, buy food and other necessities, I've managed to save hundreds of pounds a week.

One of the most interesting phenomena that I observed in the course of my work is what I call "the gold rush." When a man begins to earn money, he wants more and more and finds it terribly hard to disengage himself from what looks like a gold mine. But reason and the knowledge that this isn't my future won out, of course. I had to force myself to refuse all sorts of employment offers, both as an employee and as a self-employed contractor. I gained the confidence—which previously I felt, but with no real justification—that I could manage to get along anywhere in the world and earn a living. In the course of the various kinds of work that I did, I became acquainted with a whole new world of people I'd never come across before: street cleaners, rubbish collectors, porters, relief workers and many many others. Some of them I got to know in the army, and with all of them I managed to find a common language—that of fellow sufferers, a breed praying for a fixed monthly salary, with a philosophy of its own and worries of its own. "Each man carries his own package," as they say.

Well, enough of that. This coming month I'm planning to travel all over our big-little country and then come back to my math and finish the high school material.

Right now I am engrossed in *The Third Reich* and the Bible at the same time and find it hard to stop even for a moment. As Bibi once suggested, I've bought myself a little pad and note down every English word I don't know, so that my vocabulary gets bigger. Before I forget, could you renew my driver's license?

Bibi, I owe you an explanation. Do you really think that I sit here worrying about being accepted by universities? Since I did everything I was supposed to, and can do no more, I don't even think about it now. That's that; for the time being I've finished with it. My pessimism? Believe me, I'm pessimistic for your sake; I don't want you to pin too much hope on the exams, the results of which I don't know. The last few years taught me not to "fight windmills," unless I really felt I could match myself against them. I do all that is required of me completely and to the best of my ability, but when I've finished doing it, it's over and done with.

April 22, 1967

(To his parents and brothers)
My loved ones,

It's too bad that there were so many long disturbances in our telephone conversation. I could hardly hear a word. I understand that you phoned out of concern for my welfare, as well as to know my plans.

Well, it's clear that I plan to come to the U.S. to study. Did you think otherwise? On the phone you sounded as if you doubted it all.

You asked why I hadn't written for so long. It's happened more than once that you, too, didn't write to me for weeks on end, and Mother, who is the "writer" in the family, assured me that this didn't mean you weren't thinking of me. It's the same with me. My failure to write doesn't mean that I wasn't thinking of you or that I didn't miss you; the opposite is true —I miss you very much. It may be that this trait of mine—becoming so deeply immersed in what I'm doing, no matter what it is—I inherited from Father. For you, Father, haven't written me for ages. I realize that that does not mean that you give me no thought, but simply that you are busy. True, one can say that no matter how busy a person is, one can always write a few words, but since I am your son and am like you in many ways, I understand it very well.

Bibi, since you are to enlist in August, it would be a good idea to come here a little earlier. I gather Mother also plans to come for a while. But as I know nothing of your actual plans, it's hard for me to make any firm plans for myself. I am certain of only one thing—that Father is going to Spain to work, so that apparently we shall meet only in the U.S., or perhaps I'll stop in Spain on my way to the U.S.A. and spend a few days there. I don't know as yet; as I've said, I'm waiting for more detailed information from you. I'll probably get a letter shortly.

By the way, have you received the results from the College Boards and TOEFL?

I've just returned from a bicycle trip to Eilat. Once I went by bicycle north, to Rosh Hanikra, and then the idea occurred to me of taking such a trip to Eilat. The roads in the southern part of the country are different from those in the north; they are neither well paved nor very wide. Also, there are many ascents and descents, such as the dizzying one, eleven miles long, down to the Dead Sea, as well as the one called "Maaleh Groffit." Yosi Karpeles (Koshe) and I cycled three days, alone in the desert, with sleeping bags strapped to the carriers and food in our knapsacks. Despite the strong southern wind that was blowing, the sun that blazed on our faces, and the sandstorms we passed through—it was a marvellous trip. I want to take one more before immersing myself again in books and in the atmosphere of Jerusalem—a hike into the Judean Desert. Around Passover all the wadis fill up with water, and in the empty vastness of our wilderness, far from any human settlement, little pools of cold water form in the cliffs. Our country is remarkable, and it's worthwhile to know it.

April 24, 1967

(To his parents and brothers)
Beloved ones,

I received your letter, Mother, in which you described in detail the scholarship awarded me by Harvard. I must say, it's very impressive.

I'd like you to inform the university that I *am* interested in the work they're offering me. If in the course of my schoolwork I find that I cannot both work and study, then of course I'll give up working. I know you are prepared to give me the necessary funds, and I'll have to take them, because by myself I'll never manage to earn enough to pay American tuition fees while I study. But I am interested in their offer of work.

Bibi, Mother wrote me that you were even happier about my being admitted to Harvard than by your own acceptance to Yale. I think you could say the same for me; the part of the cable that announced that you had been accepted by Yale made me happiest. Iddo, you're a delight; I already want to see you and not just to hear about you from Mother. When are you all coming to Israel? I miss both of you terribly.

This is the eve of Passover and the whole House of Israel is celebrating. Where are you having the Seder? When shall we finally be together on Passover Eve with Father at the head of the table? Happy Holiday!

May 20, 1967

Beloved Father, Mother, Bibi and Iddo,

There is probably no need to tell you about the situation here and the balance of power in the Middle East. Here the papers are full of it, and yet, although the subject is on everybody's lips, there isn't an atmosphere of fright or panic. I hope it will not come to war. How absurd! Not a soul in Israel wants it! But if war breaks out, I'm positive we'll come through it victorious, not only because we are strong enough—such is my opinion and apparently that of all Israelis—but also because we *have* to win. It's essential for the very existence of our people. The spirit in the country rouses my admiration. True, when you're traveling in an interurban bus and the newscast comes on the air, everyone listens with a worried look on his face, but except for this, behavior is as usual. All are calm and ready.

My finger is better now;* I'm not wearing a bandage any more and the nail is growing in nicely.

Tomorrow, Sunday, if I'm not called up by the reserves, I'll begin to learn to type.

By the way, don't let the mobilization worry you. It's routine and occurs in every period of tension, and such periods are not infrequent in this region. In any event, if anything should happen, I'm glad I'll be here and be able to take part. This is my country and my homeland. It is here that I belong.

From your last letter, Mother, I understand that you are leaving for Europe early in June. Will Bibi and Iddo join Father and you, or will they leave later? When do the two of you plan to reach Israel? Probably in July, right?

I brought a table and a chair up to the roof of my house and I sit here,

*Yoni's finger was caught in a car door and was badly hurt.

unseen but seeing everything around me. The weather is excellent, although a little warm. Right now, it's 29°C and I'm wearing a bathing suit. It is Saturday today, and I spent the entire day up here. Now the sun is already in the West, it is 4 P.M. and a cool breeze is beginning to blow. I managed to study a lot today.

I'm eager to see you all, and to be with you.

May 21, 1967

(To his parents and brothers)

My loved ones,

Part of the initial excitement is over. As you can see, I haven't been called up for reserve duty yet. True, they did call me in for a few interviews, one with the commander of the paratroops and others; and I have already been designated platoon commander within a parachute battalion. But first, as yet there hasn't been any general mobilization for the entire country, only a partial one, which has already been completed; and second, by law no citizen can be called up for reserve duty for six months after his discharge. To be sure, in an emergency a special military order is put into effect, order #8, signed by the Chief of Staff, but we haven't yet reached such a crisis. I've got to sit and wait for some communication. The truth is that if something does happen while I'm in the country, I would rather be a soldier in the army than a civilian in Jerusalem.

May, 1967

Toots,*

I've met the world and his wife here. All the men who were ever with me, almost without exception, are here now, and it's quite jolly. Actually, it's not so much fun—you're not here; or rather—I'm not with you. Tutti-frutti, I'm waiting for you to smile.

I love, love, love you.

Have to go.

Yoni

*After being called up to the reserves.

(top) *Just before his discharge from the paratroops, 1967*
(bottom) *At a family celebration, 1968*

May 27, 1967

My Tutti,

We sit and wait. What are we waiting for? Well, it's like this: an Englishman, an American and an Israeli were caught by a tribe of cannibals in Africa. When they were already in the pot, each of them was allowed a last wish. The Englishman asked for a whiskey and a pipe, and got them. The American asked for a steak, and got it. The Israeli asked the chief of the tribe to give him a good kick in the back side. At first the chief refused, but after a lot of argument he finally did it. At once the Israeli pulled out a gun and shot all the cannibals. The American and the Englishman asked him: "If you had a gun all the time, why didn't you kill them sooner?" "Are you crazy," answered the Israeli, "and have the U.N. call me an aggressor?"

It's a long time since we stopped listening to the hourly newscasts on the radio; the morning and evening broadcasts are enough. Today is Saturday, and we're even organizing a soccer tournament now. There are a few clowns among the guys here who can tell jokes twenty-four hours a day, stopping only for food.

Tutti mine, if anything does happen, we can't lose. Our men are just too good.

Your
Yoni

May 28, 1967

Beloved Mother, Father, Bibi and Iddo,

A few hours ago I received your letter, Father. How much love and understanding are expressed in those lines!

How can I put your minds at ease? Everything I tell you will leave you doubting and worried. But don't worry too much! There is really no cause for it. I've promised Tutti and I promise you too—I'll take care of myself. Why, it's obvious. Haven't I always been careful and thoughtful?

Like all the other paratroops, we were mobilized several days ago. I found here the best guys in the world. Fighters, each one of them! Friends and companions, each one! What joy meeting comrades-in-arms!

The morale in the army is high, you might even say sky high. There are many married men here, some of them fathers, and not one among them wants war, but we all know for certain—we shall be victorious! If war breaks out, we will come out on top, both because we are better and because we must win.

Every evening, when the day's work is finished, we light a bonfire, heat up tea or coffee (in empty cans) and sing together, pause to tell stories and sing again till one or two in the morning—merry songs and songs of longing, songs of love, of war and of peace.

Only in times of crisis can we see that our young people are cast of pure gold. But not only the young, the entire civilian population deserves to be admired.

True, this spirit always finds expression in the army—our young soldiers have no equal. But now—long live Israel! They are all as one. Every bitterness is forgotten. They've all forgotten how in the good days—when it really was good—they all remembered how bad it was, whereas today with the threat of war hovering over our heads, we're all united, concerned for one another's welfare, helping and loving each other.

Here, where I am with my buddies, there is no fuss and no panic. It's the same in the cities and in the kibbutzim, except that here we've turned it into a sort of joke. We listen to the radio twice a day at most—just to find out if there's been any change—but no one is particularly worried.

And let's not forget that this is the mood in the reserves! Imagine what the morale is like among the regulars.

Tutti discovered my whereabouts and came to visit me. She brought me post-cards so I could write you. She will also mail this letter by civilian post, special delivery, and maybe it will reach you before you leave for Europe. She sends all of you her warm regards. This morning I wrote you another letter, but it got lost. Perhaps it will still get to you in the mail.

Mother dear, I can imagine that you're a bit worried. It goes without saying that Iddo should not come to Israel now—there's no sense in that. But maybe, Iddo, when you do come, all the smoke will have blown away and the whole affair will be forgotten. Maybe! Despite everything, I'm glad I hadn't left for the U.S. and that I am here. If something happens, I want to be here in Israel, and not abroad. I think that if I were in America now, I'd go crazy!

Don't worry, and start smiling. For heaven's sake—why all this sadness?

I love you with all my heart,

Yoni

May 29, 1967

(To Tutti)

My beloved,

After you left we set out on a little "stroll," and it was nice to march again (at last!) with a load on my back.

When we got back, a few of the guys made coffee, and when we were getting ready to go to sleep we heard music from the nearby lot—the entertainment troupe of Central Command. What's there to say? Since there were two girls in the band, whistling and shouting broke out as if a group of striptease artists was giving a performance. When men put on uniforms, they become soldiers. Nearly all are married and some are fathers, but despite everything—soldiers.

Everything was done good-naturedly, and when the performance was over (at about 8:30), no one felt like sleeping. So we lit a bonfire, drank strong tea and spent nearly the whole night in its light.

The combination of soldier and civilian creates a much more complete human being.

How good it was that you came.

I love you.

Yoni

June 2, 1967

Beloved Mother, Father and Iddo,

What a surprise! Bibi appeared, healthy and fit, strong and handsome.* I was so happy to see him. He had so much to tell.

You are brave parents! It's not easy to send another son into the turmoil in a country so distant from you. But as yet nothing has happened and all is quiet. As soon as I get leave I'll go to Jerusalem and make sure Bibi is set up properly.

These days in the army are difficult for me in only one respect—being apart from Tutti. (The fact that Bibi is now so close to me and I can't see him makes it even more difficult.) I don't believe I could leave her, even if it's only for a year or nine months.

You've no doubt heard that the former Chief of Staff, Moshe Dayan, has been appointed Minister of Defense. I think this pleases everyone (in

*Benjamin returned to Israel to enlist in the army.

the army). I don't know the mood of the civilian population, but I think they feel the same way.

Don't worry; we'll be together soon.

June 2, 1967

(To Tutti)

Beloved,

Guess what? What a surprise! Bibi arrived. We walked and talked for hours. Now I won't see him either.

By Monday I was supposed to get a twenty-four-hour leave and be with you, but today it appears that they have cancelled all leaves. It may be only a rumor but it may also be true. Since tomorrow, Saturday, you won't manage to come here, wait till you get a letter from me definitely confirming the cancellation of the leaves.

It's a bit odd to sit in the army and just wait for war. To kill and perhaps be killed—instead of being with you. How utterly absurd.

June 5, 1967

(To Tutti)

My love,

Don't be afraid and don't worry too much. We knew a long time ago that war would come, and here we are, a nation at war. And we are a pair of lovers, and that's important.

According to the plans we'd made, we were meant to meet about two hours ago and perhaps go to the seaside. Now I am far from there, waiting —with everything ready to go—lying in a pit on my back and writing. From far away I can hear the thunder of the bombing; God help our tank men who are now under the planes! As a matter of fact, let Him help all of us, it can't hurt.

Under normal circumstances one might say that I'm very comfortable. I'm lying dug into the ground and a couple of feet above me the camouflage net is swaying. It's cool here in the earth, especially with the net hiding the sun. If there was no war going on here, if I didn't have to go out and kill, and if I wasn't alone, without you, it would be nice here.

Except for a thistle, this is the flower nearest me. It will probably crumble away before it reaches you.

I love you.

June 7, 1967

(To his parents)

My beloved,

God knows we didn't want all this! To be at war—so real and yet so impossible to accept. Common sense cries: No, no!

Yesterday I saw Bibi. Was it really only yesterday? An eternity seems to have passed since then. But only yesterday I was laughing in his company. Only yesterday I was home for a few hours, only yesterday I embraced Tutti. Only yesterday!

No one is particularly frightened or excited here. Apart from that, so far we're winning. In the end we will win decisively. I wanted to write you a letter that would calm you and convince you that we are really relaxed and confident, but I'm afraid I'll only frighten you every time I mention battles.

I'm well and healthy. Don't worry if I don't write too often. Also, I don't know when they'll collect our letters. I don't even know when this letter will be sent.

June 7, 1967

Tutti,

I've been through so much that if anything happens to me now it will really be an irony of fate.

I have many plans for the two of us. I love you to the depth of my soul.

Yoni

June 7, 1967

(To Tutti)

My beloved,

That's it. A battle is ended. I'm well and all in one piece. We left the expanses of sand strewn with the bodies of the dead, filled with fire and smoke, and now we are once again in our own country. I am eaten up with worry for you. Perhaps in a few days, when it's all over and we're together again, perhaps then we'll smile. Right now it's a bit hard. When you smile, something inside hurts. Tonight, and maybe tomorrow or the day after tomorrow, we'll be shooting again, and again there'll be dead and wounded. I'll be all right, but I'm sorry for the others.

Toots, I long and I love. Try to find Bibi and tell him everything's okay.

Your
Yoni

Safed
June 12, 1967

Beloved Mother, Father and Iddo,

The war is over! So much joy mingled with sadness overwhelms us all. How good that it's quiet now. It's no fun to run among whizzing bullets and exploding shells, fighting again and again and again. Now I'm listening to soft music with Tutti beside me. I have a bullet wound in my elbow, but don't be frightened. The diagnosis is that it's only an open fracture. They operated on me and the doctor assures me that I'll be a hundred percent okay. The bone was damaged but not the nerve, and I can move my fingers. It's almost like falling from a high rock and breaking a hand. Tutti was notified and she and Bibi arrived the very next day. Tutti is staying here all day—she'll remain in Safed until I go home.

Even Dafu appeared. She was the first of the relatives to arrive. I've finally succeeded in accomplishing what I couldn't do in the three years I've been in the country: I've brought about a "family reunion." Uncle Elisha and Nati came, and today probably all the others will get here. I've received so many "Soldier's Gift" packages that I think I can open a candy store when I leave here.

You mustn't worry about my condition. The main thing is that I came out of the war alive and that I won't be disabled in any way.

And now to another matter. The way things are, after all that's happened, I don't think I'll be able to leave the country in two months. Nor will my hand be healed by then. If you wrote to Harvard for me, Father, and asked them to put off the start of my studies by one semester, I'm sure they'd agree.

What else? This was a "good" war, and it's good that it's over. Had it gone on for a few more days, I'm sure we could have gotten to Cairo and Damascus, but we got what we wanted. You should have seen our men fighting! There's no army like ours! None! It's an army that only wants peace and doesn't look for war, yet when it has to fight, there's no power that can stop it.

On the battles and the circumstances in which I was wounded I'll write some other time. The experiences of war aren't very pleasant.

When I'm recovered, I am planning a trip to Old Jerusalem and the Western Wall, to the Cave of the Machpelah, to Rachel's Tomb, to Jericho, Shechem, Hebron, and many other places.

I'm feeling fine and all smiles.

Haifa
June 15, 1967

Beloved Mother and Father,

I am very happy to tell you that Tutti and I are to be married as soon as I'm better. We've set the wedding date for the middle of August, but as yet have not settled on the exact day.

I would have told you long ago that we were going to get married, but for some months I felt certain that war would break out, and first I wanted to come back alive—before continuing to plan my future.

Interestingly enough, it's easy for me to tell this news to everyone except my parents. To you, certainly to Father, it will no doubt always be too soon.

Previously I considered going to America for a year without Tutti and getting married later. Now I don't see any sense in this. Nor do I believe that I could stay in America for a year and study there with my heart and my thoughts elsewhere.

One of the reasons I want to postpone my studies for one semester is that it seems quite absurd to leave Israel now. I don't know, of course, what sort of arrangements Harvard can make for such a delay. Even if I came now, it would be with Tutti after getting married here. Whatever happens, it's necessary to explore the possibilities as regards living quarters, employment and the like, before the school year begins.

One of the problems involved in my going to the U.S., the one that worries me most of all, is the financial problem. I've no idea how much money two students will need in a country that is almost foreign to me.

Here in Israel I know I can get along, even on my own; in America—I can't. It is quite clear that I'll need your help, Father, and I'm sure you'll gladly try to help me.

A few details about my hand. I was wounded in the left arm by a bullet or fragment which shattered the bone in my elbow. The doctor, Pauker, who operated on me (he is considered one of the best surgeons here, and was brought from Haifa to Safed when the fighting broke out in the north), extracted ten bone splinters from my arm. Luckily, the nerve was not damaged, but to protect it, it was necessary to move it beyond the splintered part. I can move all my fingers easily. In the two end ones— the little finger and the one next to it—I have a dull sort of feeling, as if anesthetic had been injected into them. The doctor says that one nerve was partially damaged and this explains this sensation. Some muscles were torn, too, and that causes pain when I move my middle finger. All this may sound serious, but it isn't. The doctors say it will take a long time for the hand to heal completely, but the main thing is: it will heal.

For me, it's enough to be alive. And I don't say that ironically. When you see death face-to-face; when you know there is every chance you too may die; when you are wounded, and alone, in the midst of a scorched field, surrounded by smoke—mushrooms of smoke from exploding shells, with your arm shattered and burning with a terrible pain; when you're bleeding and want water more than anything else—then life becomes more precious and craved-for than ever. You want to embrace it and go on with it, to escape from all the blood and death, to live, live, even without hands and feet, but breathing, thinking, feeling, seeing and taking in sensation.

It's now seven o'clock in the morning in the Rambam Hospital in Haifa. I'm sitting alone on the veranda. After several days of Khamsin,* a cool wind is blowing from the sea. It's pleasant here.

Everyone insists that you two must be planning to pop over for a quick visit. As far as my arm is concerned there is nothing to fear—it will get well by itself with time, and I believe that unnecessary worrying will only make things worse. Still, I'd be very happy if you were here and we'd be able to talk. There is so much to say.

I love you very much,
Yoni

*An extremely hot, dry wind that blows in the Middle East.

June 22, 1967

(To his parents)
My beloved ones,
I'm out of the hospital. The only thing left is some pain and plaster all over my arm. In any case, I have to come back for tests in three weeks' time; until then I'm free.

I told you that I'm planning to get married before starting my studies. Should it prove impossible to postpone the beginning of my studies till January (for whatever reason, such as my wound, my marriage, or anything else), then I'll begin this coming September. I even thought of delaying a full year, but Tutti and I have finally reached the conclusion that there's no point in doing that. If there's no other way, then I'll start, as I said, in another two and a half months. I gather from a letter you wrote to Bibi that you definitely intend to help us when we get to the U.S. I never had any doubt about that, but it would be helpful if you'd tell me your plans for the near future.

Today I phoned Miri in Jerusalem, and what did she tell me? Iddo is arriving tomorrow! Great!! I'm extremely happy that he's coming. Soon we will all be together for a time.

See you shortly. Kisses.

I love you very much,
Yoni

June 26, 1967

My beloved Mother,
I was so happy to receive your letters and Father's letter. Only yesterday did I receive the letters you sent to the army. I was sure I wouldn't get them at all, but the army seems to have gone out of its way for me and sent them all here—to Jerusalem.

Your letters are marvellous, Mother, and you are wonderful.

I should detail our plans.

First of all, we're getting married not at the beginning of August, but on the 16th or thereabouts. Tutti's exams will continue till August 11th (they were postponed because of the war); and at the beginning of September we'll come to the U.S.

Bibi is wonderful, but Iddo is enchanting. So perfect in everything, very mature and very handsome and full of humor and understanding. Bibi, of course, is well adjusted, and I think Iddo has settled in nicely. He's going to work on a kibbutz at the beginning of July for a short spell, and that will definitely put him on the right course. Right now he's with Tutti and me.

Tomorrow I'll go to the rabbi and he'll no doubt tell me many new things. In the meantime, send me my birth certificate.

Mother dear, write me a lot.

It's a good thing you are resting quietly at home for a bit after all the emotional turmoil of the war.

In my opinion, you both behaved magnificently.

I love you,
Yoni

P.S. I forgot the main thing—we'll try to have our marriage ceremony performed on Mount Scopus.*

July 4, 1967

Beloved Father,

It's hard to tell you how happy I was to receive your encouraging letter from America.†

In about two weeks I'll go to the hospital to have my arm examined; until then I'll stay here in Jerusalem and recuperate. My whole arm is covered in plaster, from the hand to the shoulder, so that I don't feel a thing. Only when I move hastily or carelessly, do I feel a sudden pain, which vanishes immediately. I believe I shall be completely recovered very soon.

Bibi and Iddo are with me and they feel fine. I went with Iddo to the school in Bet Hakerem and to the Gymnasium. They were very nice in both places and I'm sure that Iddo made an excellent impression. But then, how could he not? The problem is that both of these schools are completely full, and special permission is necessary before they can admit students beyond their quota.

Father dear, I'd be very happy if you and Mother could come to Israel a little before the wedding date—say, at the beginning of August. Will you be in America at the start of September or only later? (I think you once wrote me you'd return there on about the 20th of September.) In that case, maybe it would make sense to come to Israel sometime before the wedding and then go back to Spain?

*The newly liberated campus of the Hebrew University in East Jerusalem.
†Yoni's letter was sent to Spain, where his father was doing research in Jewish history.

Since I plan to study very hard at Harvard, and since the first year there is particularly tough, I'll find it hard to start working immediately after my arrival. In any case America has laws that forbid aliens (including students) to work there during the first six months of their stay. The same also applies to Tutti. It's obvious that I'll need your help, especially in the first few months, and possibly in the first year of our stay there. You've already written that you would give us your full assistance, and I'd be glad if we could discuss it before my wedding—and before my coming to America.

My handwriting's a bit untidy because I can't, of course, hold the paper down with my other hand, and it won't stay still.

I miss you very much.

Kisses,
Yoni

July 8, 1967

Beloved Father,

Your plans for the summer are still not clear to me. You'll probably be working in Spain all the time. You postponed the work last summer, so you really ought to get on with it now with all your energy. But I'm worried about Mother's health. She writes that she is not at all well and nearly always in bed. Do tell me, Father, how she is and what she plans to do in the summer months. How is your work coming? I'm sure that as always you sit working day and night and hour after hour without any pause or rest. When I was in the army I noticed that I could endure and persevere, both physically and emotionally, way after everyone else "broke down." It's quite plain to me that I inherited this marvellous gift from you, just as I inherited from you most of my traits.

Now about my health, Father—I am well and strong.

Bibi and Iddo are here a lot. Bibi and I play chess every now and then, and, as usual, the "team spirit" among the three of us is blossoming and flourishing.

July 19, 1967

Beloved Mother,

Honestly I don't know what your plans are. Are you going to join Father in Spain? It appears that you're still in America. How are you, Mother?

I'm really worried about your health. Maybe it would be wiser for you to give up the trip to Spain this time and stay at home and rest? After all, this is an opportunity that may not come again.

Mother, I'll be very angry if I hear that you went to Spain only in order to come to Israel for the wedding. Remember, you'll be seeing us in America only two weeks later.

My arm is getting better all the time. Although it's still in plaster, there's a good chance that the plaster will be off in about a week and a half. I went to the doctor a week ago and he told me to come on the 25th, promising that everything would be okay. Already I hardly feel any pain in my hand and am altogether free in my movements.

I obtained work with Brandeis University. They offer a course in Israel that lasts six months, and I'm responsible for all the extra-curricular activities they plan for their students. As a matter of fact, I do a lot for them, but they pay well and are pleased with my work, so there's no call for complaint. For a change, this is work that requires no effort on my part. All I have to do is organize parties, trips, get-togethers with Israeli students, etc., for the students, who are all Americans.

July 20, 1967

Beloved Mother and Father,

I'm writing to Spain because a long time has passed since I last heard from you, Mother, and I assume that you did decide to come to Israel after all. I hope you're recovered completely. I'm sure that both of you, like me, are waiting most impatiently for the moment when we'll all be together.

All of us feel wonderful. Iddo is brimming with joy. He is tanned and healthy. When he arrived he was all pale and white and now he's much more handsome.

Bibi is already a man in every sense. He gets around everywhere and gets along famously. In thirteen days he'll join the army.

I'm working now at the Hiatt Institute of Brandeis University and have plenty of work—organizing trips and meetings and everything pertaining to all the other social programs that one may think of. Write us about your plans. Perhaps we can still get a letter before you arrive.

HARVARD
AND THE
HEBREW
UNIVERSITY
(1967–1969)

Yoni at Harvard

MOST OF YONI'S LETTERS FROM Harvard were written to his brothers in Israel—Benjamin, who had gone back to serve in the army, and Iddo, who had returned to Jerusalem to go to school. During this period Yoni often saw his parents, who were then living in Philadelphia, where his father was engaged in academic work.

Despite his success as a student at Harvard, Yoni decided to go back to Israel at the end of his first year. This decision he carried out. Upon his return to Israel, he entered the Hebrew University in Jerusalem, but after one term's study, he came to the conclusion that he must go back to the army.

Paris
August 30, 1967

Beloved Mother and Father,
In another few hours we'll* board the plane for New York. Our visit to Paris was even better than we expected.

In the plane coming here we sat next to a Frenchman, a dentist, who for some reason offered to drive us to the hotel. On the way he gave us a comprehensive tour of Paris. He hardly left anything out. Afterwards we went into town on our own, and from then on we haven't stopped exploring the city. This morning we'll visit the Rodin Museum and do some shopping that we postponed until now.

The weather is wonderful and the city is beckoning and smiling at us.

See you soon,
Yoni

*Tutti and Yoni, who had been married two weeks before in Jerusalem.

Cambridge, Massachusetts
September 21, 1967

Dear Bibi,

One more bout of pneumonia and I'll faint with worry. Now don't forget to be a good boy and wear a sweater, and don't get tired, and sleep at least ten hours every night, and don't run around after midnight, and in general—behave the way you should. After all, you're a growing boy and need a lot of rest and sleep and good food.

Seriously, look after yourself.

I'm constantly afraid that something will happen to you. It's rather funny, because when I was in the army, it was obvious to me that nothing would ever happen to me. And in fact that's the way it was (until I came back on reserve duty). But I saw enough accidents and casualties to justify my worrying.

What phase are you in now? Tell me about everything in detail. A little nostalgia won't do me any harm.

Last Monday I started my studies. No sooner had I registered than I was inundated with invitations to join this or that club. It's all very amusing.

We've settled in quite nicely without encountering any special problems. From the point of view of money we're pretty well organized. I told them at Harvard that I'd got married and that it would be hard for me to manage on a scholarship of $700, to which they replied that my marriage was my own business, but that nevertheless they would review my request and maybe something could be done. I explained that I'm not seventeen or eighteen years old and am not prepared to take money from my parents up to the age of twenty-five to finance my undergraduate studies. That was a week ago. A few days later I received a letter informing me that I had been granted an interest-free loan of $1000 and that my scholarship had been increased from $700 to $1600. How about that! I just couldn't believe it! So, with some light work at the library, I can pay my tuition without any trouble.

The house we live in is practically new (four years old). Those who built it thought of everything. Everything functions as it should.

I don't know what the food's like in the army now, but only if it matches the food at The Gondola* can you begin to compare it to the little woman's experiments in our kitchen. It turns out that she's a culinary wizard. We've been here two and a half weeks now and have never eaten

*A well-known Jerusalem restaurant.

the same thing twice. I never knew there were so many kinds of dishes. You're invited to come to supper some time.

We see quite a bit of Elliot.* He has an older brother, Alan, who is twenty-six, married and father of a six-week-old baby daughter. He's a wonderful fellow and his biggest asset is that he likes to run. He lives in the same building we do and every evening we run about six miles. I'm almost as fit as I was before. I feel great (really) and my hand doesn't bother me. Aside from that, Alan likes to play chess. He's now completing his doctorate in nuclear physics at Harvard. His wife is charming. They're a lovely couple to have as neighbors.

October 12, 1967

(To his parents in Philadelphia)

Good evening to you both,

It's now six o'clock on Columbus Day. I've just returned from the library. Since there were no classes today, I studied all morning in my room, and when they opened the library in the afternoon, I went there and have just come back. I still have to work for another hour or two and that will do for today.

Ever since I stopped working at the library, I have lots of time (or so it seems) and can study as much as I need. In addition, I manage to run from time to time a considerable number of miles. That's as essential for me as additional time for study, since running clears the mind and refreshes the body.

Yesterday I received a long letter from Bibi. It's full of "heroes' tales." I think he's a really good soldier. May there be many like him. He's got a few days' leave and is now in Jerusalem helping Iddo with his Hebrew subjects. He must have written to you too.

By the way, Bibi complains that you don't send him letters to his military address. For a soldier whose family is outside the country it's most important to get mail not at his residence, but in the army; there's a big difference between opening a letter in the apartment and opening it in the field when he's sweaty and aching. The letter from home represents, in a way, the fulfillment of the dream of returning home, of rest, of stretching your legs, of good food, of parents. So write to his military

*Elliot Entis, Yoni's friend from "Young Judea," the summer camp where Yoni was a counselor in 1963.

address, okay? But you've no doubt already done so, and he's probably already received your letter.

October 16, 1967

Dear Bibi,

I've been meaning to write you for some time now, but I swear I haven't found a free minute. Believe me, I had more time to write in the army. Here you don't have even a moment's peace. For if you do have such a moment, you may as well think about a physics problem that's not been solved yet, or finish a chapter in math or, for heaven's sake, finish reading Homer, or go over the geology lecture, or write an essay for "Expository Writing." Thank God, there's so much work to do that even if you try your best, you can't manage to finish it all.

Mother and Father were here from Wednesday to Saturday and would have remained for Sunday as well, had I not left on Saturday at 7:00 A.M. for a weekend geology field trip in New York. While they were here they bought us all kinds of things that we'd been putting off buying—a lamp, a new bed, and so on. Bibi, our apartment is really fine, and it's good to sit and read here, or just to be here and look at the pictures.

I'm filled with longing for the army when I read what you write about it. I told you you'd be a good paratrooper and that the only thing that could prevent your becoming one would be—bad luck. So be careful, seriously. In every company there's at least one soldier who gets hurt by a stray bullet or a grenade that accidentally goes off, or some other foolishness. Make sure that it's not you. Remember, there's hardly been a company without someone hurt. Also, be careful where you put your feet; it would be too bad to suffer fractures. You may have already discovered that your feet and your back are your most prized possessions. The back doesn't break so easily, but the feet do.

I forgot: one of the most important things is—topography. Have you already begun to study this subject? I don't suppose you have, but in any case (as you see, I like to give advice) here are some pointers to keep in mind when you do study it:

1. The most basic rule, and the one all too often forgotten, is: Always know where the north is! Always!
2. Wherever you may be, know exactly where you are, according to the map.
3. Never "force" the map—i.e., don't say: this is more or less the way,

and then make some changes on the map. The map is right, don't forget that!

4. Always, always look at your watch before you begin to navigate. Calculate on the map the number of miles you have to go and the time this will require—considering the conditions of the terrain. If you see that in a fixed number of minutes you haven't arrived at the right place—*stop!* Look at the map again.

5. Count the wadis; this is one of the important points. Learn to identify the wadis (even the smallest ones); on a 1:100,000 map, this is sometimes a bit hard to do both on the map *and* in the field. When you're walking in a wadi, count the times it forks off into the mountains.

6. If you want to make sure that the wadi you're about to enter is the right one, fix the north on your map accurately and see if the direction of the wadi's entrance on the map is the same as in the field. If it's identical, fine; if not, think again! On a 1:100,000 map the little curves at the wadi's entrance sometimes appear as a single straight line. Walk inside the wadi about 100–150 yards and see if the direction is correct.

7. Always climb up to a high point and locate the *entire* area on the map. This is very important.

I've got more to tell you on this subject but there's no room left. Still, why not continue in another letter?

Letter No. 2

Bibi, you're probably thinking: Why is he telling me all this? Why, I'm going to learn it all anyway in time, and right now it's of no interest. So let me remind you once again: *A soldier who doesn't know how to orient himself in the field has to rely on others.* He's not independent! They'll teach you a great many other things, but they'll be used in the exercises and then forgotten. The things I'm telling you now—*from experience*— you must never forget. Each of them is a golden rule. Seriously.

Your letter brought me a great deal of pleasure. It's good that you're that kind of soldier. Apparently it runs in the family.

October 31, 1967

Dear Bibi,

Did the rain catch you? What do you think of a "fix" like that? I don't know what kind of rainy season we have in our country, but four out of the five months of my basic training were very wet. The August recruits have a tougher time than any of the others—basic training in winter.

When I was platoon commander I prayed for rain so that I could train with my soldiers in the mud. It's at least twice as hard. Wait till you begin night navigations in the Negev, walking dozens of miles in wet clover that reaches up to your hips. Your entire body actually freezes! At times, when I was a green soldier and we went on long marches in the mud, and everyone was cursing away, I'd feel content and start to laugh. There's a funny side to it.

By the way, did I teach you how to get rid of blisters on your feet? If not, better listen: thread a needle with a coarse thread, pass it through the blister so that the thread remains inside; cut the thread, leaving about half an inch on each side of the blister. During the night the thread will absorb all the fluid. The next day you simply pull it out. I'm sorry I have wasted space if you already know this; if not, try it—you've nothing to lose. Next day you'll be walking as if you'd never had a blister at all.

As to the university—

The "midterms" have started. Today (Tuesday) I had an exam on Homer—the *Iliad* and the *Odyssey*. If you think there are real men among you, just read Homer; it's sure to make you humble. It went okay. I'll tell you the results when I get them. On Friday I have an exam in physics, and next week in math and in geology.

When is jump school? Remember what I told you. How are the guys? Tell me everything. Many times, especially here in America, I miss you *terribly.* Even when I was in Israel I didn't miss anyone at home as much as I missed you. I think the reason may be that you're the only true friend I ever had, and the fact that I think I reached a perfect understanding with you in nearly all areas.

Ten days ago Mom entered the hospital; this Friday she'll be discharged. She underwent surgery to have her gall bladder removed. Now she's all right. Yesterday I phoned the hospital and she sounded fine. She's worried about Iddo's illness; so calm her down—and above all, *make sure that both of you write to her.* The first vacation I have, in two weeks, we'll go to Philadelphia.

November 11, 1967

Dear Iddo,

I haven't written you for a long time, and you're probably waiting for my letter no less eagerly than we're waiting for yours. What's it like to live alone? How is your bronchitis? What is it anyway? Do you see Bibi on his leaves? How is he? I haven't heard from him for such a long time either.

As for me, first of all the exam period is over. I had exams in physics, math and the humanities (i.e., "The Growth of the Greek Classics"). So far I got back only the math results and I got an A, which isn't bad at all for Harvard. I don't suppose I did as well with the physics and the humanities, but I'm sure I didn't fail. I'll get the results next Monday (in two days). Physics still takes up most of my time. No matter how much you study, it's not enough. Although we were about to take an examination, they kept teaching us new material all the time and, as everyone was preparing for the exam, the great majority are now trying to catch up and to understand what the professor's talking about in the lectures.

I feel that I'm finally getting on top of the material and I hope no new problems will come up. Soon (in December) we'll have a new series of exams and after that the finals. I was taking geology, as you know, but I gave it up and transferred to another subject: "History of Ideas in the 18th–19th Centuries." It's much more interesting, but I've got to go over all the lectures that were given until now by myself. I don't think that'll be a problem. The trouble with geology was that it demanded much more time and work than I was able to give it. Also, you've got to go on many field trips—that is, for whole days of "close observation" of rocks and stones, and I didn't want to leave Tutti alone so often. To make it short, it didn't really interest me enough to justify that much dedication. Right now I'm (as usual) in the midst of studying physics. The book is, in fact, open in front of me, but I've decided to stop and write to you. Otherwise I'll never find the time to do it. Since it's Saturday today, I finally did something I've been wanting to do for a long time—I taught Tutti to ride a bike. It took exactly half an hour and now she rides very nicely.

I continue to run even though I don't really have the time. I barely manage to run twice a week. But at least I'm keeping fit and not letting myself go.

Tutti works every day and only gets home at six. During the week we hardly go out in the evenings, mainly because I don't have the time. We generally go to a movie or a play during the weekend. Tomorrow evening we'll visit friends of ours—Israelis who've been here several years. He's a promising physicist and has a charming wife. We haven't bought a television. That's all we need!

In Cambridge the leaves are still falling and the first snow has appeared and vanished. It's a bit cold. This is a lovely season. I wish you were here to see for yourself. When you get back to the U.S. you'll come to visit us and see with your own eyes what a pretty place this is.

December 10, 1967

Dear Mother and Father,

About my hand—don't worry. Although it is not improving at the same pace as it used to, it is not getting worse. The doctor says he doesn't exactly know what its condition had been before the operation (the first X-rays remained in the army; I brought him the ones taken at Rambam Hospital* along with letters from Drs. Steiner and Pauker); it may be that compared with the way the hand was immediately after I was wounded, its condition today is good. In other words, he says there may have been a great improvement. Here, too, I haven't started with intensive physiotherapy (i.e., lifting weights and the like), but with hot baths and ordinary hand movements, which the doctors in Israel permitted me to do.

Even if the hand doesn't straighten out completely, this won't bother me too much. What I want is to be able to use it without worrying that this may damage it, or more precisely—to use it as I do the right hand. I've been promised that—and that's what counts.

Now that I've exhausted all I know on this subject, we can devote less worry to it. It hasn't gotten worse suddenly, so there's no need to worry unnecessarily, or maybe I should say, excessively.

Please write, and send me the letters Bibi and Iddo wrote you. By the way, Iddo's Hebrew has improved remarkably.

Washington
March 31, 1968

Dear Bibi,

Well, I'm in the hospital again.† This time I have a room *to myself* which has everything. Don't ask, it's practically a hotel. I've got nine days of vacation from Harvard, so the timing is excellent. I brought a suitcase full of books with me. I'm reading a great deal, need to read a lot, and plan to read as much as possible while I'm here. On the last exam in

---

*The hospital in Haifa where Yoni underwent a second operation on his arm.
†Walter Reed Hospital in Washington, D.C., to which Yoni was admitted for a third operation on his arm.

philosophy I got an A and I was really glad, but *really* this time. It's very hard to get such a grade, and it's from a professor whom I regard highly. I let Father read the exam, and he praised it very much.

By the way, Mother and Father came for two days; that is, they'll stay here today and tomorrow and go back the day after the operation. Tutti is, of course, in Washington too and will probably return to Boston (to her job) on the day after tomorrow.

This hospital, with all its legless young men, reminds me of all sorts of things, although, I'm glad to say, this passes quickly, without leaving too deep a scar. Still it's a bit hard to fall asleep at night.

You mentioned the Arab houses. Only someone who's seen it with his own eyes can believe it. One may think the houses are made of straw (the granaries of Pharaoh, eh?). It's hard to conceive what 10 lbs. of T.N.T. can do. I saw this first at Samua. The whole ceiling flew up to a height of fifty yards and was shattered into tiny pieces. Even the nicest houses.

Take care of yourself. I always say that, and all I mean can be summed up in the prosaic words: Good combat training. I saw how so many friends were hit only because they did foolish things, lifting their heads too much and the like. This is terribly important, but so many tend to disregard it. They always say that in battle, when you're being shot at, you'll do everything properly. But it doesn't work that way. Quite the contrary. People are either completely scared, tigers turning into birds, or they simply do all kinds of foolish things. Very few remain cool. And the whole idea is to keep cool. But you've been in the army long enough now! Perhaps you've already managed to see many things, good and bad, so that there's nothing for me to teach you. No doubt you can teach me a lot, too.

In the meantime a week and a half has passed since I was operated on. I had every intention of finishing this letter right after the operation, but I was so exhausted that I just couldn't. The surgery took quite a long time, but didn't disturb me at all. How could it? The surgeon worked, I slept. I assume he did his job properly.

Listen, all the talk about the Fatah just annoys me. I get the feeling that the civilian part of Israel despairs of reaching any solution, despairs sometimes even of any military response to acts of terrorism. Obviously this is the only way to fight them! The recruitment of all these little terrorists only strengthens my consciousness as an Israeli. If they come to fight, we—or at least I in the Diaspora—must certainly do so all the more. My national consciousness is no doubt stronger than that of the Arabs, I'm a much better fighter than they are, and so are all Israeli soldiers. Their chances aren't very great (not even small). As I see it, the only thing to do is to return to Israel—and to live there. Now more than ever.

April 9, 1968

Dear Iddo,

Loads of things have piled up in the meantime. But let's take first things first.

I'll start with the operation on my arm. I entered the hospital on Saturday and underwent the operation on Monday. It was a rather long and complicated operation, three and a half hours. I woke up to find my whole arm in a cast with no sensation in my fingers. The sensation returned almost to normal after about three days, and now (a week and a half later) my fingers move freely. The doctors promised that everything would be 100 percent okay—that is, judging by what the surgery was meant to achieve. The nerve is now protected much better, and that's good. My arm, as you know, won't straighten out completely, but that doesn't bother me. I'm now at home, after a week in the hospital, and the arm is still in a plaster cast. This will be removed on Saturday when I go to Washington, and at the same time they'll take out the stitches. I hope I won't have to go there yet again. It's a pity to spend so much money on plane tickets and waste precious time.

The many acts of terror perpetrated in Israel are strengthening my conviction that the sooner I come back, the better—for me personally. It's hard for me to understand the Israelis who sit here for years on end and "agonize" over each new incident. It's a good thing that the papers here (even *The New York Times*) don't write about every occurrence. As if that's possible! At least the Israeli *yordim** are spared nervous breakdowns. We know about all that's going on from Tutti, who works at the Consulate, and, of course, from the Israeli newspapers. In any event, it's obvious to me that I must return to Israel. If the Fatah come to fight, then my responsibility is many times greater. One thing is certain: I'm a better soldier than any of them and my national consciousness is stronger than theirs. If they want war, we have no choice but to fight for our existence.

It's clear to me you would have liked to stay in Israel and finish high school there. But since you haven't written me for so long, I don't know what you intend to do now—or what you've decided. If you have decided to return to the U.S. and finish high school here, you could spend the summer vacation between the junior and senior years in Israel, as Bibi did. But if you've decided otherwise, and I can understand the reasons, of course, you ought to write Father and Mother about it, and me too, so that I can talk to them about it.

Soon, on July 3rd, I'll be in Israel and we'll finally see each other.

*Israelis who left Israel to settle permanently in another country.

April 15, 1968

Dear Bibi,

By mistake you sent your letter to our parents in the envelope you addressed to me, and the letter you wrote me in the envelope addressed to them. That's how they found out that two of your friends were killed. It's a dreadful, horrible thing to lose good friends. In all my time in the army, I had only one really good friend who was hit in basic training. Yet life continues to run its course. Nothing changes. You forget, yet always remember.

Take care of yourself.

The cast has been removed, and you can now see a very long scar on my arm. The fingers are fine, but the arm is beginning to worry me (this is the first time I've been anxious). First, my arm hurts; second—and this is my main worry—the elbow and part of the back of my hand are without any sensation. I can lean my elbow on the table and not feel it at all. I hope it will get better.

After a long time when I didn't run, I began again yesterday. At long last the snows are gone and spring has come. I have to admit that I got short of breath, and six miles demanded quite an effort. I assume that within a week I'll be back in shape. It's raining hard again today so that running is out of the question. I'm still a little weak after the operation and it won't hurt me to rest another day or two.

I'm pleased that you're pleased that Tutti and I are pleased. Truly, we feel good together, and it's a good thing we're spending our first year by ourselves, away from everyone. So you may begin to be optimistic on this subject. I'm pleased also for another reason. You'll finally get "some status and self-confidence," as you once said in a light mood, when Micki starts adding a little more weight on her shoulders.* These bars† place more of a burden on you, more responsibility, more work, "more" of everything. Perhaps not in Training Center # 12,‡ but certainly in the paratroops and where you are. You're no longer responsible for yourself alone, but for your platoon as well, and yet you're much freer—and there's much more room for individual initiative (again, not in Training Center # 12). It's much more interesting and worthwhile. Give Micki our greetings. It's worth her while to stay on as an instructor at the Women's Officers' School.

Harvard continues to be marvellous, even though I'm impatient to return. I have to return! I want to return. And I hope with all my heart

*Benjamin's girl friend who graduated from Women's Officers' School.
†Officers' insignia.
‡Women's training base.

that my hand will improve enough for me to be able to go back to reserve duty. It's important because that is the duty of every good Jew—or at least, of every good Israeli, since the Jews are losing their links with Israel. This is the Jewish tragedy. All the talk about the "unity of the Jews" is just nonsense. The Jews are like every other people and, as Father showed in his book, whether under duress or of their own will, they become assimilated. The awakening of the Jews on the eve of the war and immediately after shows that we are (still) a nation and not just a rabble. But it seems to me that if the war had broken out fifty years from now, instead of in June 1967, so close to the Holocaust and what's remembered of it, the Jewish people would not have become aroused as they did last summer. Deep in their hearts they know that Israel is the only haven they can escape to—poor wretches!

The more I talk with Father the more I value him as a thinker and as an educator. He is a great man with enormous capacities in many, many areas.

I wrote Iddo a letter about a week ago and I'm anxiously awaiting his reply. Tell him to write. Or better not tell him. He's probably written by now.

April 20, 1968

(To his parents)

My dears,

Now that my initial enthusiasm over Rabin's autograph* has simmered down, I don't see any point in taking the photograph from you. First of all, it's yours. Secondly, I'll never hang it on the wall and it'll just get lost among all the papers and photographs.

On the spot where the surgery was performed, especially in the back of the elbow, the nerves are still numb, but my fingers are now in good shape and all motion is fully restored. For the time being I'm satisfied. If sensation doesn't return by next week, I'll phone the surgeon to talk about it. They did tell me it would take time because they stretched the nerve during the operation, and that causes a loss of feeling.

As to our last discussion, Father, about counter-terror tactics in enemy

*Tutti, who visited the Israeli embassy in Washington, asked Yitzhak Rabin, then Israel's ambassador to the United States, to autograph a photograph of him with Yoni at the graduation from Officers' School. Rabin did so.

territory, and using helicopters to chase down terrorists inside their own territory—it seems to me a pretty effective method. In any case, the wave of terrorist killings has stopped recently. We haven't really started yet. Let them continue with their activities, and they'll discover that the Ten Plagues of Egypt can befall them all at once.

June 20, 1968

Dearest Father, Mother, Bibi and Iddo,*

Good news, and not so good. Let me begin with the latter.

On the eighth day of our trip in Canada, as I was driving in a leisurely fashion down the street in Charlottetown, Prince Edward Island, a car came out of a side street speeding madly and crashed into us. First, let me assure you both of us are all right; second, the car didn't suffer any serious damage; third, I called the insurance company at once and they took care of everything; now the car looks new and beautiful as always.

We've been to almost all the places we wanted to see in Canada, except for the cities of Quebec and Montreal. But I didn't want to go on with the trip, preferring to go back home to fix the car and take care of the insurance. Anyway, we were both beginning to tire of the Canadian scenery, which despite its great beauty is rather monotonous—water, trees and again trees. Still, we enjoyed the trip immensely.

Now for the good news. When I left Boston the results of the exams were not yet out, but now when we got back I went to the university and saw the grades. They exceeded my expectations. My average for the year is nearly A so that naturally I'm on the Honor List and in the top 10 percent of the class. I parted from the university people in a good and friendly spirit.

On Saturday we'll go to Philadelphia,† rest a bit and get ourselves organized, and in less than two weeks we'll leave for Israel. We're leaving on July 2nd and arriving the next day. I hope Bibi and Iddo will manage to get to the airport. Perhaps you could also stay on for a few more days so that we may see each other?

---

*Yoni's parents had gone to Israel to visit his brothers.

†Elkins Park near Philadelphia, where Yoni's parents lived at the time.

Philadelphia
June 28, 1968
Dear Mother,
The garden is blooming and lovely. Today a boy came to cut the lawn. We ate a lot of berries—don't you regret leaving them and the flowers?

We spent three days with Tutti's elderly aunt in Pittsburgh, who is very lovely and very young in spirit, and now—a few days in the house here that were really delightful. It's a bit sad to leave the house. I'm toying with the vain hope that we'll see each other in Israel after all.

Two days remain until our departure for Israel—and already I'm impatient.

Jerusalem
July 7, 1968
(To Spain)
Dear Father,
I hoped so much to see you in Israel. When we didn't meet at the airport on our arrival I consoled myself with the hope that at least we would meet at Lod the next day, but that didn't materialize either. Really, it's too bad. In the meantime we've adjusted here and have started to look for an apartment. Before I go into that I want to tell you about other things.

First, I got from the Ministry of Defense about I£430 which accumulated in my account during the year; this money is a grant for disabled veterans. In addition, I've found out that as a disabled veteran I am entitled to have my tuition fees at the Hebrew University (to the end of my undergraduate studies) paid by the government of Israel. I've also begun to work for Brandeis University again. It's good and pleasant work, not tied to office hours and no doubt requires far less hours than an office employee has to give. Best of all, I'm my own boss.

This morning I went over to Dr. Stock, who's in charge of this program, intending to ask him for a salary of I£600 a month, which is considered very nice. To my surprise, when I asked him how much he was thinking of paying me, he offered me I£750. What do you think of that? Most important of all, five of the six months I'll be working there coincide with my vacation period. So most of the time I'll be able to devote all my attention to my studies.

July 22, 1968

(To Spain)

Dear Father,

Tutti and I feel wonderful and enjoy every minute we're here. Now that I'm in Israel, I realize how much I missed that part of myself whose origin and place is in Israel. When I was in America, I missed it and I knew that my place was here, but not until I got back did I know how right I was.

It seems to me that we are facing another war. Not a day passes without an act of sabotage, mining or murder. Everything is reminiscent of the situation that led to the Sinai War in 1956 and to the last war in 1967. We must, we are obliged, to cling to our country with our fingernails, with our bodies and with all our strength. Only if we do that, if we give all we have for the well-being of our country, will Israel remain the State of the Jews. Only then will they not write in the history books that once indeed the Jews roused themselves to action and held on to their land for two decades, but then were overwhelmed and became once more homeless wanderers.

I belong to Israel, Father, the way Israel belongs to me and to you and to every other Jew. I belong to Israel now, at this moment, when everything points to a new explosion (although I fervently hope it will not come to pass), at this moment when every citizen who has served in Zahal is being called up for two and three months of reserve duty, when the whole House of Israel is united in its desire to continue its independent life, and in its conviction that this life is ours by right and depends on our will and our readiness to sacrifice our all for its sake. That is why I have to be here —now. It would be intolerable for me to be in Boston at this time. I can go back there a few years from now, when everything calms down, but not now.

You gave many more years than I to Israel, and no doubt you feel and grasp with your intellect and your knowledge many things that I only sense. That's why it seems odd for me to preach Zionism to you of all people, in order to explain my attitude toward our country. I've fought for our right to live in it more than once or twice. It was somehow unreal for me, even a kind of nightmare, to leave Israel after the Six-Day War.

July 31, 1968

(To Spain)

Dear Father,

I got in touch with a Bible teacher for Iddo as you asked me to do. Dr. Breiman sent me to someone who's going to be teaching Bible at the

Hebrew Gymnasium next year. I went with Iddo to see him and he made a good impression. Iddo has already had one lesson with him and is very pleased.

Iddo visits us often. We spend at least two hours together every day. He's really delightful—bright and handsome. It's a pleasure to be in his company.

Bibi comes to Jerusalem very rarely. We hardly see each other. But he may come this Saturday. Each visit of his turns into a holiday, and the three of us enjoy being together.

What else shall I tell you, Father? The mood in Israel is as usual. It's hard to define it. It's a mood of sadness, anger and helplessness against a primitive foe who's after blood and vengeance, whose behavior is guided not by logic or reason but by the dark whims and emotions of a bloodthirsty barbarian. It's difficult to believe that this type of people is seeking to destroy us and that we have to fight them again and again in self-defense and for lack of choice.

In addition to the hijacking of the El-Al plane, there are daily acts of terror in Israel. Yesterday, for example, a button mine was found in Ben Maimon Street in the Rehavia section of Jerusalem. Unbelievable. Each day our casualties mount. The day before yesterday, the commander of my paratroop brigade, a colonel, was killed in pursuit of terrorists. How long can we remain silent?

In the face of these acts of murder and the proclamations of the Arab leaders, it appears to me that the day isn't far off when we'll have to fight a fourth war with the Arabs. It may happen in a year, or perhaps in three years, but I'm convinced that we're in a cul-de-sac at whose end there is only war.

July 31, 1968

(To the U.S.)

Dear Mother,

This evening I'll go before the medical committee at the Rehabilitation unit of the Defense Ministry, where they'll determine my disability level (resulting from my wound). My arm is in excellent condition, strong, and doesn't hinder me from doing anything.

Only after we got here did we realize how much we missed Israel. In America I felt bad, not because of my studies, but because of the void that my absence from Israel created within me.

HARVARD AND THE HEBREW UNIVERSITY, 1967–1969

August 11, 1968

Dear Mother and Father,

It appears we've got the most wonderful luck. After the war, they decided to settle the area between Mount Scopus and Jerusalem, or rather the prewar Jerusalem. A tender was announced for acquiring lots in Hamivtar Hill, which is located about three hundred yards from the Pagi quarter. This hill is not surrounded by Arab neighborhoods and the main road leads directly to downtown. There was a very heavy response, so they required that anyone interested in a plot put down a deposit of I£1600 as down payment. Yonah and Micky* did this for us while we were abroad, but at the time we didn't take the matter seriously as our chances seemed very slim. Lots were cast among the applicants, and then among the disabled war veterans, and it turns out that I'm one of the winners.

August 17, 1968

Dear Mother and Father,

Today is our first wedding anniversary, Tutti's and mine.

So much has happened since that day on Mount Scopus, a month after my discharge from the hospital, a month and a half after the end of the war. All unbidden, the old reflections about the war come up and occupy my mind once more: It would be so good if we could say now that "the war is over." How simple things would be if this had been "a war that was," merely a part of the distant past. But it isn't so. I've managed to do so much since June 1967: I got married, traveled to America, studied at Harvard, toured in Canada and before that, on the way to the U.S., visited Paris, and afterward came back to Israel, and I've already been working here and seeing the country and have got myself organized. And yet it wasn't the war that was a "passing stage," but everything that came in its wake.

A kind of sadness has overtaken me which doesn't leave me. It does not control me or direct my actions, but it is inside me, it exists, sunk in a well-hidden corner deep in my being. This isn't exactly an emptiness, but something with a very heavy deposit—a sort of "heavy emptiness." Perhaps this feeling does not exist only in me. There are times when I sense the cry and the depth of this sadness in others, in all of those friends who came through the war with their bodies intact. I think we all came out

*Tutti's father and sister.

of it wounded, changed, more sensitive, more "caring," and much, much older. That harmony that characterizes a young man's world is not part of me any more. Although I'm still young, still strong and confident of myself and my ability, I can't ignore the fact that a sense of old age has taken hold of me. I've never been old, not in years, and I therefore don't know whether the feeling I have is the same that comes with advanced age; but it is a form of old age no doubt—an old age particular to young men.

When I try to understand why this is so, and why this feeling has grown within me, I reach the conclusion that not only the war, the killing, the deaths, the wounds and disabilities are to blame—these can be overcome. Their imprint may perhaps be dulled by time. The real cause is the sense of helplessness in the face of a war that has no end. For the war has not ended, and it seems to me that it will go on and on. The June war was only one campaign. It's continuing right now, today, yesterday and tomorrow. It continues with every mine and killing and murder, with every explosion in Jerusalem and every shot in the north or the south. This is the "quiet" before the next storm. I've no doubt that war will come. Nor do I doubt that we will win. But for how long? Until when? We can't wipe out the Arab people; they are too many and have too much support. Of course we shall go on striking them, again and again and again, and we shall be fully justified in delivering a more powerful blow each time. Knowing this makes us feel good, but the good feeling is mingled with sadness. We're young, and we were not born for wars alone. I intend to go on with my studies; I want to do so and I'm interested in doing so. But I can no longer see this as my main mission in life. Even if studying is the right thing—right for me and right for Israel—this isn't the important matter at this time. Deep within my being I'm convinced of this. Hence the sadness I referred to earlier, the sadness of young men destined for endless war.

I wanted you to know what I'm thinking about so that you may know me better, as I should like to know my own son. I realize that I've been impatient many times, and I'll probably stay that way. This doesn't indicate any resentment toward you or anyone else. It's the child, who has always been inside me and who will perhaps disappear with the passing of time.

September 12, 1968

Dearest Mother and Father,

It's a long time since I wrote you last, and since then I've received quite a few letters from you. In the meantime we've managed to rent an apartment. It's located at the entrance to Kiryat Yovel—in fact, in the first house of the neighborhood. There's a bus that stops right by the house, so transportation is quite convenient.

The owners of the apartment left us excellent furniture. Some small pieces of oak, two large cupboards, a fine bed, a huge desk (even Father would want one like it), a brand-new refrigerator, and, of course, a gas range, a bookcase, etc. It sounds like a lot, but is just enough. We added Tutti's sofa and the rocking chair from her home, as well as the black armchair that I took from the storeroom at our house.

A week ago I went again to Haportzim Street, and I must say the house is in very good shape. The garden is delightful. But the storeroom is something else. Whoever put the furniture there is really a "criminal." I've never seen such careless, irresponsible packing. Furniture laid upside down, broken glass, sofas without covers, and much more. It offended my professional porter's pride. In any event, I carried some of the furniture outside, cleaned it, swept out the storeroom, and packed everything properly. Since I was working alone (Iddo was doing his homework, so I didn't want to disturb him), I didn't do the best job possible, but I did put in four hours of work there and improved the situation considerably.

I went to the Medical Committee of the Defense Ministry to have them establish the degree of my disability, and they left it at 20 percent. My arm, in fact, has become much stronger and scarcely bothers me at all; I've almost forgotten that it was injured.

I see Bibi only rarely. Iddo appears every now and then and he's quite pleased with his lot. Both are delightful and we're happy to be together. Hey, congratulations! I'm sending this letter to Denver. How is the place and the apartment? Please write.

September 28, 1968

Dear Mother and Father,

I plead guilty! Not only because I haven't written to you for a long time, but also because I think I lost a letter that Bibi gave me to mail to you.

What's happening in Israel is well known to you. It's plain enough that the war that broke out a year and a half ago didn't end but simply took on a different form. Not only has the number of killed not decreased; it has actually increased. Shooting and mines on *all the borders* have become so routine that they're mentioned by the press unobtrusively. Far graver things claim central attention.

Life goes on in its usual way as though nothing had changed. Yet everything appears to be rather pointless, or, to put it more accurately, our routine life seems to me to be based on a bit of deceit. For me at least it has secondary importance, and I find it hard to concentrate on everyday matters. In general, if I wanted to be philosophical, I could prove that we (the whole world) are marching toward destruction. People have not changed. Day in and day out thousands are killed in local wars: minor eruptions preceding the great cataclysm.

In Jerusalem the first signs of autumn are visible. The air is saturated with moisture. It seems to have absorbed from the earth, the flowers and the butterflies a somewhat intoxicating flavor of its own. The breeze caresses, cools, calms. The skies are blue and deep, and everything is in blossom. It's delightful in Jerusalem, in the mountains. Such a lovely season! Too bad you're not here.

Now that we live outside the city proper, I find lots of time and space for trips in the Judean Mountains. They contain many bubbling fountains, caverns hewn deep into the heart of the mountain, into the source of the water, and many little pools that channel water into them. It's beautiful here!

Lots of kisses to you both.

Your loving
Yoni

November 2, 1968

Dear, beloved Mother and Father,

A week ago I began my studies at the university, and here briefly are my first impressions. I'm continuing more or less along the same line I chose for myself at Harvard—mathematics and philosophy. In philosophy I'm taking the following subject: "The History of Ancient Philosophy" from Thales to Aristotle. The instructor is Dr. J.B. who, I'm glad to note, presents the material in an interesting manner, and I enjoy his lectures. This course will last one semester. In the second semester I'll take "The History of Modern Philosophy" from Descartes to Kant. Another course in philosophy is "Introduction to Logic." I haven't yet been to a lecture in this course and don't know how good it is. I didn't and don't expect the same level of philosophy lectures that I got used to at Harvard, and that may be why I'm not disappointed. In any case, for the time being I'm rather enjoying the lectures; and even if it turns out that most of the teachers are mediocre, or even poor, the subject itself is too interesting for me to become really bored.

But the main subject is mathematics. This faculty is reputed to be the best at the university and one of the best in the world. The professors are internationally famous and, what is more, they present the material well. The subject matter is divided into three parts: calculus, algebra and set theory. I've never studied this material before, except for a small part and very superficially. It's well known that over 50 percent of the math students give up and leave the field. I believe I won't fail, but I must admit that I have to make an effort. That, very briefly, about the university. As of this moment, I'm pleased with my studies.

December 23, 1968

Dear Father,

Mother is with us, and it's nice and pleasant when the four of us meet. What a pity you're not with us! Mother looked a little tired when she arrived, but now she's much better. Bibi had many leaves, and since Mother is also staying at Palgi's,* they get together often.

The university courses are now in full gear. A few days ago I finished the job I'd been working at these past six months. The Americans I was guiding returned to the U.S. last Wednesday and now I feel like a free man. At last I can devote all my time to my studies.

I'm quite pleased with the university. All the mathematics lectures (fourteen hours a week) maintain a really high standard. The work and effort that this subject demands hardly leave time for anything else. The standard of the philosophy courses is not, of course, that high. I did have an excellent professor (J.B.) who taught the "History of Ancient Philosophy" (Plato mainly), but unfortunately he's no longer teaching us. It seems he's one of the rare pearls of this department. Still, I'm also taking a course in "Introduction to Logic." This course involves mathematical logic, and all it needs is perseverance and sound thinking.

*The family from whom Benjamin was renting a room.

January 11, 1969

Beloved Mother and Father,

The year 1969 has started, and it looks as though it won't bring peace and quiet. The situation in the country is perfectly clear to anyone with eyes in his head. We are marching toward another war. The tension is far greater than it was a few months before the war of June '67. Sometimes it seems to me that that war was merely a hard battle in which we stabilized our borders and strengthened our positions for the next round. Meanwhile the fighting continues every day. We're surrounded by enemies, and it looks as if we can rely only on ourselves. If only we could fight without being obliged to get help from the great powers. But that isn't realistic. The great powers can play with us like a wind-tossed leaf if they reach an agreement among themselves. It's an unpleasant feeling, this business of being everybody's football. I have no faith at all in the judgment of the United States. Hope my misgivings are wrong. After de Gaulle's actions,* we're in a bad position which is likely to get progressively worse, for France was our chief arms supplier, and it's doubtful whether America will be willing to fulfill the role the French played without imposing conditions that we shall perforce have to accept. As I've said, if we could depend solely on ourselves, I'd be much happier, for I believe in our ability and our will with all my heart.

I find it hard to concentrate on studying. Not only to me, but to many of my friends, the university seems divorced from reality. When the day-to-day realities are hitting me in the face every minute, I can't lose myself in Plato's philosophy of ideas, in the essence of good and bad, in "being," in Socrates' theory of definitions, and the like. All these things are far removed from me now, and I can no longer treat them as earnestly as I would like to. For when I study philosophy or mathematics, I'm doing so purely out of intellectual curiosity. I study philosophy not to get a profession but to acquire knowledge, to develop my thinking, to learn from the mistakes and wisdom of others. Today I'm simply unable to read even a page of this material. To study these subjects demands peace of mind, and that's just what I lack, what we all lack at this moment. This also applies to mathematics, though in a slightly different way. Here you've got to forget everything and only apply logic; this too is hard, and for me almost impossible at present. I keep trying, but the periods in which I can forget all that's happening around us and concentrate on the material are brief and sometimes unproductive. I haven't worked for

*The French arms embargo on Israel.

weeks now, and I sincerely desire not to let myself go. But you mustn't worry; I won't neglect my studies or exchange them for some job. That would be surrender on my part, and I don't believe it would solve anything. I'm just writing you some of my inner thoughts.

This Saturday Bibi came home. Badly in need of sleep, but in great spirits. He keeps asking how you left, Mother, and whether you were very disappointed that he couldn't come to the airport. Iddo is marvellous as ever. In about an hour the three of us will meet in Rehavia.

Those were six good weeks when you were here, Mother. I hope, Father, that you, too, will be able to be with us very soon.

January 17, 1969

Dear Mother and Father,

First I received the books you sent, Father. They're exactly the ones I wanted. The edition of Aristotle's works is excellent, and I'm enjoying it immensely. You probably took a lot of time to search for these books, so I appreciate the gift even more.

Lately I've done a lot of thinking about our situation, and I'd like to share my thoughts with you and hear your opinions.

We're sitting on a powder keg that can explode at any moment. The fuse that will ignite the keg is already burning and getting shorter all the time. A sensible person won't wait until the keg goes off but will hasten to take steps to defend himself, knowing that the explosion is inevitable.

The analogy is clear. We're heading toward war—gradually and irreversibly. The Arab world won't agree to let us live in its midst. Two countries, Syria and Iraq, have already stated explicitly that the only solution to the "Palestinian Problem" is the expulsion of the Jews from Israel. The other countries want the same solution, although they haven't announced this publicly.

Let me analyze the situation as I see it. On the southern front, huge Egyptian forces are concentrated along the Canal. In the light of Nasser's declarations, and in view of the type and size of force amassed there, it's plain that he's planning to attack. His forces have been put in offensive positions, and they're likely to attack soon. Obviously, he's waiting for help from the Russians. He may not expect actual military aid, but he will certainly get the support of the UN. For example, Nasser will capture the Canal and the UN will immediately announce a cease-fire, thus establishing a fact: Suez belongs to Nasser. And don't think that this is impossible.

The Canal is very long, and even if we wanted to, we couldn't prevent his forces from breaking through in several places. Such an act would obviously lead to war, for we shall always try not only to repel him, but to carry the war over into enemy territory, i.e., to the western side of the Canal. Russian intervention is also possible—naval bombardments or perhaps stationing Russian forces to block our advance. The Russians may not believe that we'd dare attack their forces if they stand in our way, but to me it's clear that if we have no other choice we'll do just that. It's also not at all clear to me whether America would intervene physically on the battlefield if the Russians stepped in.

On the Jordanian front, battles are going on nonstop. News about most of these doesn't even find its way to the newspapers. Jordan is receiving military equipment all the time, including war planes from the U.S., some of which have already arrived. From the point of view of equipment, Jordan is the most inferior of the Arab states. Hussein is trying to maintain his pro-Western posture, but with less and less success. He hardly has any control over what is happening on the Israeli front. He keeps his loyal Bedouin forces next to him, while the pro-Egyptian officers are at the front, and, of course, the Iraqi expeditionary force is stationed at the border.

As for Syria, it's well known that it wants one thing: war. Not much is known of its activities. It's obvious that it serves as the main base for the terrorist forces and that it's preparing very energetically for acts of aggression.

Lebanon has unequivocally joined the chorus of incitement for war against Israel. The declarations from there were once a lot milder. Even before Zahal's operation in Beirut, the terrorist forces in Lebanon were shelling our northern settlements heavily, causing serious damage to our civilian population there. Here, too, as in Jordan, the Palestinian Arabs exercise almost autonomous rule and are not subject to any authority. Lebanon is, of course, the least of our worries. At this stage its military strength is nil. But if it gets military assistance from the Arab countries (such as Iraq) or from France, then the situation along this border will also deteriorate.

This is more or less the situation on the different borders. Very few countries have fought like us, on so many fronts at one time. The problem of Al Fatah and the other terrorist forces is well known, so there's no point in analyzing again the situation they've created.

The atmosphere here is tense, just as it was before the war. No one misses a single newscast, lest, God forbid . . . Look, I know for certain that we're moving toward a new war. It won't be a war that we'll begin, but one that the Arabs will. Perhaps the word "know" may be too much, for I can bring no definite proof, but everything points in this direction. I know this just as I knew that the Six-Day War was going to break out. Then, too, I was sure beyond a shadow of a doubt. It's painful to tell you this, but that's the way I see things.

In the light of all this it's not surprising that I find civilian life almost intolerable. When I live my life as I'm doing now, I resemble the man who ignores the keg of explosives in the hope that it won't go off, thereby sealing his fate. It's hard for me to bear the thought that I'm alive thanks to others who protect me with their own bodies while I'm left to play the role, so to speak, of the civilian. And this is indeed merely playing a role, for I'm unable to live like this in times such as these. There's a war on *right now*. At this minute, throughout today and tomorrow. I'm seriously considering returning to the army for a stretch of time. Although I haven't yet made a final decision and I'm waiting to hear what you think about it, I feel that you should know my reasons when you come to express your opinion.

So the primary reason, above all else, is the grave security situation and my firm conviction that I, as a son of this people and this country, am obliged to do everything in my power at this time. Although it's important to be a good citizen in Israel, at this crucial moment it's not the most important thing. Of course, it would be good if I completed my studies and specialized in some field—and I haven't the slightest intention of not returning to school; but, as I've said, the time is pressing.

In addition, I'm at present unable to concentrate on my studies, even for a minute. Every time I look into a textbook I find myself staring into space and thinking, or dropping into an armchair to read the daily press. It's not as if I've despaired of school or have lost the ability to concentrate. You know very well that's not the case. I fully appreciate the importance of education and recognize my abilities as a student, and it's just for this reason that I'm having so many doubts.

My main problem about going back to the army is not leaving school, but leaving home. I find it difficult to part from Tutti so frequently and for such long periods; but again—I don't plan to do so on a permanent basis. I feel that I'm being called on to perform a deed that I know to be essential. You, too, Father, gave up your private life and for years devoted yourself fully to the struggle for the state. And the fact that at the time you already had an academic degree makes no difference. For I'm convinced that had your studies stood in the way of the political struggle you were then waging, you'd have given them up, too. You knew what you had to do, and what's more, you *believed* you had to do it, and for this reason you acted as you did.

By the way, physically I'm entirely fit for military service. My arm is no obstacle. I even parachuted three days ago when I was called up for two days of parachuting refresher course.

These are my reasons, or at least some of them, and as I've said, I haven't yet acted or made a final decision. I'd like to know your opinion.

January 29, 1969

Beloved Father and Mother,

To say that we're worried about you would be an understatement. We haven't received a single letter since Mother left Israel more than three weeks ago. We don't even know whether she arrived safely. And Mother wasn't well when she left. Did she get sick? Or is Father ill? Please write, good news or bad. Don't delay!

In the past week the elements have turned topsy-turvy. The weather has gone mad. Israel hasn't seen such torrential rains for a long time. Galilee is almost cut off. Haifa cannot be entered from the north. Many villages have been cut off for days. The ancient quarter of Acre is in danger of collapsing. Snow is falling in many parts of the country. Jerusalem has been covered with snow for two days now. There's danger of flooding even in the Judean Mountains. The Sea of Galilee has risen to a level never reached since they started keeping records (about forty years ago). All the rivers, including the Jordan, are overflowing and flooding entire regions. In Nahariya and other settlements in the north, the roads have vanished and the houses are standing in water.

I received your book, Father, a few days ago. I'm so happy. It's time I became more familiar with the field in which you work. By not taking time to delve into your work, I wrong not only you, but myself as well— and mainly. You've given us a lot of joy by sending us the book. Congratulations!

Getting the book eased our minds somewhat, because if something really untoward happened, you wouldn't have had the time to mail it. Still, we're worried. It's not like you not to write or answer our letters for such a long time.

February 16, 1969

Beloved Mother and Father,

It seems to me, Father, that you misjudged the chances of war in the near future. The error isn't based on any incorrect political analysis, but on the physical distance that separates you from the spot where events are actually taking place. Although the Israeli papers probably reach you, I don't suppose you get them every day, and what is more, you don't hear the Israeli newscasts every hour. As a result, you don't hear about many acts of terror, sabotage and murder. I'm convinced that the analogy I used —that of a powder keg—is absolutely correct; and I may also know more facts which indicate that conditions on the borders are as bad as they can be. We are sliding steadily toward war and the chances of preventing it, I'm sorry to say, are very small (even though they do exist, of course).

But that is not the main point. I am not at all reconciled to being a civilian. Not only am I restless, but I feel that by continuing with my present way of life I'm being untrue to myself. I have been torn between my desire to go on with my present life, and my conviction that my duty to my country, to my people, and above all to myself dictates that I go back to serve in the army. It would be an evasion in the full sense of the word if I went on with my current way of life, an evasion well camouflaged by all kinds of considerations and arguments. Not that these considerations and arguments are groundless. They may have a solid enough foundation, but to me they don't constitute sufficient reason not to rejoin Zahal. I won't be faithful to myself, and I will betray that inner summons that calls me forward, if I fail to do so. Your argument, Father, that if they needed me they'd call me is wrong. You have no idea how badly Zahal *needs* good officers now. Things have come to such a pass that in the newspapers and even in the cinema newsreels appeals are made for young men to reenlist for active service.

When I talk about this with friends, they all agree that we ought to enlist, but most don't do so. How can I also say that, and yet not do anything about it?!

I'm thinking of signing up for two years of service, the minimum time for which you can join. In these years we will be able to see much more clearly what we have to face. The present situation can't go on much longer. I don't delude myself into expecting peace; may I prove mistaken in this. As I've said, a new war is possible, and it's also possible that peace will come in its wake after the fall of the present Arab regimes, although this, too, seems to me a vain hope. There's also another possibility—

there'll be war, and afterward the situation will return to what it is today, repeating the whole cycle. Obviously there's also the possibility that we lose the war, if not the next one, then the one after it. This doesn't seem likely. Zahal is capable of resisting and defeating the Arab armies with their Russian advisers and latest arms. But Zahal is the *only thing* that stands between ourselves and the slaughter of our people as in days gone by. Our state exists and will go on existing as long as we can defend ourselves. I feel that I must lend a hand in this defense *by force* against the Arab states. In two years I'll know which way to turn. I hope with all my heart that I'll be able to resume my studies. Perhaps there won't be any need for me to stay in the army. It is essential for us to have educated people in all spheres, and in the future they'll be the ones who will determine the direction of our country; but at this moment, now, the problem is far more fateful. It's a question of life or death, and I opt for life!

I hope you'll understand me. I'm not listing all the reasons that have brought me to this decision. I deliberated hard for months before reaching the conclusion that I must return to the army. It will be hard for you to imagine the sense of relief that came over me when I finally arrived at this decision. I know I'm doing the right thing!

ZAHAL AGAIN:
IN AN ELITE UNIT
(1969–1973)

Company Commander at a march in Jerusalem

YONI'S DECISION IN JULY 1969 TO RE-
turn to the army came at a time when Isreal was facing mounting pressure
at home and abroad.

The Arab states, recovered from their defeat in the Six-Day War and
massively resupplied with arms, began mounting new campaigns against
Israel. Nasser embarked on his war of attrition along the Suez Canal,
which was meant to inflict unbearable casualties on Israel. By 1970, as a
result of Israel's military response, Egypt was forced to seek a cease-fire.

But the campaign of Arab terror, which over the next decade was to
change the face of international politics, was gathering momentum. In
Europe, Asia and the Middle East, Israeli—and Western—targets were
indiscriminately attacked, airplanes were hijacked and blown up, hostages
taken, children and tourists massacred. Most of the terrorist activity in
those years, however, was concentrated along Israel's borders, where Arab
terrorists were launching raids from neighboring Jordan and Lebanon.

Along the Jordan Valley, the Golan Heights and the Lebanese border,
the Israeli army organized to intercept terrorist attacks. Time after time,
its special units struck deep inside Arab territory to destroy the bases of
terrorist activity.

This was the work Yoni was now engaged in. In 1970 he served as
company commander in the "Haruv" reconnaissance unit, defending the
Jordan Valley from terrorist infiltration. Later he assumed increasingly
important positions in other special anti-terror units.

A former soldier of his recalled his first meeting with Yoni from that
period:

"I remember the day he arrived. He came to our camp, dressed very
informally—I don't think he wore his rank insignia. He sat down on a tree
trunk, and the word spread that our own commanding officer had arrived.
We gathered around him just to see what was happening.

"He started talking to us informally. I don't remember exactly what he
said, but I remember the spirit: 'Let's do it together, and do it the best
way we can, because it must be done . . . ' It was a special spirit, I can't
even express it, but I still feel it. He was not merely a commanding officer
but an educator—a great educator, I believe. We became very attached
to him . . . "

Not once in his letters from this period does Yoni mention any of the
many military operations in which he took part. Most of these operations

cannot as yet be made public. Of those that have been revealed, the most famous is the raid on the terrorist PLO headquarters in Beirut in 1972. Yoni was among the small team that landed in Beirut, made their way in rented cars and killed, among others, three leading members of the PLO's high command. He also commanded the Israeli force that seized a clutch of Syrian generals on the Lebanese border to exchange them later for Israeli pilots in Syrian jails.

By 1972 he had risen to the rank of major and had completed his term as second-in-command of one of Zahal's crack units. In June 1973 he took a leave of absence for two months. After a brief tour of South America, he enrolled in Harvard summer school, where he successfully completed a full semester's course. He came back to Israel a few weeks before the outbreak of the Yom Kippur War.

February 26, 1969

(To Tutti)

My darling,

Well, where am I? Still at the recruitment office, waiting for the results of the medical tests. In five minutes I'll be driving back to the unit. Guess I'll finish this letter there.

Back at the unit. On the way here I heard the news of Eshkol's death. Of course, everybody's beginning to speculate about the future. The idea that Eshkol is no longer Prime Minister is a bit hard to take in.

Yesterday when I was taking a walk in the fields, I discovered millions of flowers. All the protected and rare species are here in abundance. In all the places where visitors are few, everything grows and blossoms. Maybe when we find a little time, we'll go for a walk here.

How hot it is today! Good thing it's cool at home. In the winter we grumbled about the chill, but maybe now, in summer, we'll be grateful for it. Actually, it's not summer yet; we will still have rains and cold spells. But it's good to feel the spring for a few days.

Did you find the note I stuck on the mirror? Everything written there is absolutely true.

I love you very much.

Yoni

March 17, 1969

Dear Father and Mother,

I have just read your letter, Father, and all I can say is that we are lucky to have been blessed with such a pair of parents. I'm overjoyed you agree with my decision to return to the army. I've already taken steps in that direction. They accepted me as an officer in B's unit.

Tutti is also in complete agreement with my decision. Needless to say, it's hard for us. Tutti fully understands me and my reasons, and since I'm blessed with a wonderful wife, we'll be able to overcome this difficulty.

In another week I'll be twenty-three. Time flies, doesn't it? My years bear down on me with all their weight. Not as a load or a burden, but as the sum of all the long and short moments that have gone into them. On me, on us, the young men of Israel, rests the duty of keeping our country safe. This is a heavy responsibility, which matures us early. It seems that the young Israeli belongs to a special breed of men. It's hard to explain this, but it can be felt. All those wonderful pilots of ours, all our paratroops and commandos, are Israelis of my age or younger, who grew up and were educated in Israel. Men of the moshav, the kibbutz and the city, united by something that is above and beyond political outlook. What unites them produces a feeling of brotherhood, of mutual responsibility, a recognition of the value of man and his life, a strong and sincere desire for peace, a readiness to stand in the breach, and much more. In another week I'll be twenty-three, and I do not regret what I have done and what I'm about to do. I'm convinced that what I am doing is right. I believe in myself, in my country and in my future. I also believe in my family. That's a great deal for a man of my age who has already managed to feel very young and very old.

As regards the latest incidents, I really must praise the Jewish people of Israel. The cool-headedness, the lack of hysteria, the immediate control of every situation, are really surprising. You don't find here the raging mob quality that is rather typical of hard times. This is a special people, and it's good to belong to it.

April 9, 1969

Beloved Mother and Father,

I am writing now from Beersheba, in the midst of a whole week's leave. Tutti and I are on our way back from Eilat, and we stopped for a while at the home of Micky (Tutti's sister) who's been living here since she started work at the Institute for the Study of the Negev in Beersheba. We got very suntanned in Eilat, actually even a bit burned. But it was nice to feel the sun.

During our second night there the Jordanians began to shell Eilat from Aqaba. They started shooting at about 4:00 in the morning, and we could see clearly how the shells hit the center of Eilat. Just like that, without any provocation, they shelled a peaceful city and wounded a considerable number of civilians. After about half an hour the shelling stopped. Our response came at about five o'clock. As usual, it was quick and effective. Two planes swooped down over Aqaba, and when they climbed up a few seconds later, Aqaba's police station was sliced in half.

All the Jordanian announcements about scores of civilian casualties are sheer nonsense. I saw the bombing quite clearly. Our aircraft stayed well away from the town (the police station is outside it); but if we didn't bomb the place this time, that doesn't mean we won't do so if they shell Eilat again. The following day the Chief of Staff declared that Aqaba is more vulnerable than Eilat, and the Jordanians know very well what this kind of declaration means. It's true that the shells were fired by the Fatah, but even a child could see where the shelling came from, and the Jordanian authorities could easily have prevented it, if they only wanted to.

Meanwhile the Egyptians keep firing across the Canal. A real war is being waged there. They are receiving mortal blows, but they seem to have decided that they have nothing to lose. The "flourishing" towns along the Suez Canal are in ruins. Terrorists continue to cross the border and continue to be killed or caught—the Jordanian border is well sealed. The "Palestine Liberation Front" is having some success, but only on a small scale, and they are caught very fast. What is most disturbing is the political situation (as you, Father, have noted more than once). It's hard to predict what the results of the Four-Power talks will be. It's plain to me that we will oppose any agreement that does not suit us, but this is liable to cause us much damage. In view of all this—the repeated shellings (like the one at Eilat, which occur almost daily in the north of Israel, in and around the town of Beth-Shean), the acts of terror and sabotage all over the country and the general political situation—the whole country is seething in a quiet way, without fear or hysteria, but seething just the same. We are definitely heading toward some climax. To me it seems inevitable that sooner or later another war will break out.

April 16, 1969

Tutti my love,

I'm lying on a field cot in a bunker, trying to thaw out my frozen limbs. A couple of guys are sitting around discussing card games, though it turns out the only game they know is beggar-my-neighbor, and even that they only played as kids, and then not much. As they're all kibbutzniks, their verdict is: "It's really against all the values we've been taught." "Primitive people! Let them pass their time playing chess, or drinking coffee, or reading the paper. But cards—hooey!" In short, really nice kids, and Mama's boys to a man.

A long time has passed since I started this letter. I keep falling into all sorts of thoughts, such as: What's my Tutti doing at this moment, Wednesday, at exactly 8:15? What is she thinking about? And lots more. I'd like to describe my whereabouts to you, but that's forbidden. I'm buried in a small bunker, lit only by a storm lantern; at least it breaks the wind, which is howling outside. I don't yet know how I'll post this letter; we'll see in the morning. If I can't send it tomorrow, I'll go on with it every free moment.

May 5, 1969

Beloved Mother and Father,

Really a long time has passed since I wrote you. I've been very busy, and on top of that had to adjust to the pace all over again. I have finally found a free hour, an opportunity I'm not going to miss.

Just now we're all depressed. A good friend of ours, Shemarya Dobkin, was killed in a traffic accident in Jerusalem the day before yesterday. All of us, his friends, are looking after the family as best we can. But this is a situation of utter helplessness. The funeral will take place today.

In the country things are as usual—local wars continue with considerable casualties. Not a day goes by without someone getting hit. The Suez Canal front is especially hot, and the other fronts are not much cooler. The truth is it's rather tiring to live so long in a state of war—a war whose end can be foreseen only in the distant future. You need much perseverance and patience to overcome all the crises we're facing now and those we'll face in the future.

Iddo has decided to take his studies seriously and is really sticking to his decision and doing well. In a few weeks he'll finish the year and be able to join you in the U.S. Maybe you'll manage to visit Israel for a while before he comes to you? At least you, Father, maybe you can make it? We hope so. The truth is, Bibi and I will be able to get very few leaves during these hectic days.

Bibi wrote you about his decision to go to Officers' School. I didn't try to influence him one way or the other. It's his own decision. You needn't worry about us. We take good care of ourselves.

May 12, 1969

(To Tutti)

Beloved,

The day after tomorrow you will be twenty-three. Happy birthday! When I get home we'll celebrate. Even this letter will probably arrive late. Never mind. Just remember that I'm thinking of you all the time.

Without lingering on the paradox, I must admit that I enjoy my work with the army. It interests me and at this time it's important for us. I'm writing this to preempt the thought that may come to your mind: "So why the separation?" Because otherwise we wouldn't be so happy together. Otherwise I'd have been strained, feeling I was evading that summons deep inside myself. Not that we'd have loved each other less, as that's inconceivable, but I'd have been "nervy." I realize now that both of us are nervy when we're *not* together (I write "nervy" because I don't know how else to define this restlessness), and that it's very, very hard for you. But, darling, at least when we're together everything is fine.

I really am very much in love with you. My wife, my beauty, my beloved has entered her twenty-fourth year. *Mazal tov!*

May 19, 1969

Beloved Father and Mother,

What's this we hear? You underwent surgery, Mom, and didn't even tell us! Only now we've found out! So this explains your long silence! It's good to know that everything is all right now and that you are already at home, recovering.

I'm glad you agree with Bibi's decision. I can imagine the difficulty that has been your lot—to have two sons in the army at one and the same time. A pity you aren't here. At least we'd be able to see each other on our leaves. Iddo is now studying so hard that I'm almost afraid he's overdoing it.

During a break in training, 1972

May 30, 1969

(To Tutti)

My beloved,

Now that I know the meaning of "being married," I've tried to picture to myself how I'd like my wife to be, to behave, to look, to love, etc. I've tried to be objective, to dissociate myself from my love for you; but the image I formed in my mind of the ideal wife was always like that of my Tutti. Exactly as you are, no other, no different.

It breaks my heart when I hear that it's so hard for you, that you are "broken up" by the whole thing. You cannot imagine what a mood I get into after I talk to you in your moments of depression. That is not to say that you ought not to tell me what you think and feel. God help us if it came to that. You must tell me everything, and I you. Otherwise we won't have between us what we have. Otherwise the union between us will not be complete. Never will any shadow pass between you and me. I am in love with you, my wife.

I am in the grip of a serious conflict. On the one hand there's you (and you outweigh all else), while on the other hand I am doing what I believe in and what I enjoy doing. Years ago I told you that what is needed is "to live and let live." But that doesn't seem possible in the kind of world we live in, not so long as we are built the way we are; but I wish it were possible.

June 7, 1969

My beloved Father and Mother,

It was so good to get your letters, Father, but why doesn't Mother write? Mom, are you really all right? It isn't like you not to write for so long. We have to know if anything is wrong. Please write us because I am really worried about Mother. I hope the surgery you underwent passed without complications. But how are we to know what the true situation is if we hear nothing more about it?

Perhaps one of the reasons for my failure to write is the strenuous work I'm so deep in—all of me. Not that I don't think of you very often, but I simply don't manage to write. The work itself is most interesting and demands all my time. I now realize how important my work is, and, of course, I still think that the step I took was 100 percent right.

Wars continue to be waged here on a small scale, and sometimes on a large scale as well. It is truly shocking to realize how far things have gone:

when we hit them, and only one of us is killed, we sigh with relief—
"Lucky it's only that." In the final analysis, no one in Israel doubts our
ability to defeat the Arab states in these little wars as well—but it's a
nerve-racking business all the same. People are called up for reserve duty
very frequently, despite the fact that the period of regular compulsory
service was lengthened long ago to three years in order to make things
easier for the reserves. There is scarcely a person in Israel who is not doing
his share in the general effort on behalf of Israel's existence. Of course,
it wouldn't be true to say that we're all pioneers and saints, as it depends
on the person (there are also shirkers, but very few), on the unit in which
one serves, and on many other factors.

By the way, what's your opinion of our new Prime Minister?* Here in
Israel, she has, surprisingly enough, emerged as a new star. I, too, am one
of her advocates. She is far more resolute and down-to-earth than the late
Eshkol. She doesn't hesitate to make decisions and conducts the affairs
of state with a much firmer hand than her predecessor did.

The building of the house on Givat Hamivtar is progressing very slowly,
but is bound to be finished eventually. Like everything else in this country,
the plan has to pass through committee after committee—of the Ministry
of Housing, the Municipality, etc. Each committee contradicts the previous committee, and the upshot is endless delays. On the one hand, they
are anxious to expedite matters, and on the other, they delay as much as
they can. They haven't yet learned the meaning of efficiency. Why didn't
they concentrate the whole matter in the hands of one committee—and
be done with it? Maddening!

June 22, 1969

Beloved Mother and Father,

By the time this letter reaches you, Iddo will probably be with you
already. I couldn't get away on Tuesday to see him off, but Bibi was with
him at the airport.

Iddo is still deliberating whether to continue his education in the U.S.
or not. His decision will depend, of course, on his impressions of Denver,
its schools, etc. I sense an inclination on his part to remain with you, but
he'll surely be able to tell you better than I will what he intends to do.

Tutti is about to take her finals. She finds it rather hard to concentrate

*Golda Meir.

on her studies—and no wonder. She is alone at home, always waiting for me to phone or come, and unfortunately that doesn't happen very often. Poor thing, it is really tough on her and nerve-racking to sit at home and wait for the soldier-husband. I try to make it easier for her as much as I can, but things always end up the same as they were, with me back in the army and she alone at home. Don't get the idea that it is insufferable or that I regret what I've done. On the contrary, the more I work, the more certain I am that I did the right thing. It was the only road I could take.

July 30, 1969

Dearest Mother, Father and Iddo,

I've been putting off writing this letter until I had a quiet moment, but quiet moments are few and far between. I've been busy twenty-four hours a day lately. Really busy. Both the borders and the interior have been "heating up" more and more. Recently we have been hitting them pretty hard, and in the end they'll learn their lesson. I believe that within a few weeks, we'll quiet down the Egyptian border considerably. Despite all the lies of Egyptian propaganda, it is difficult to assume that their soldiers, sitting in the front line, believe a word of it. They are taking a pounding right and left and lately, following our air force operations, they've even started to abandon their positions and flee.

It is hard for me to tell you how sorry we were to learn of Uncle Matti's death. Although we knew he was ill, we didn't imagine the end was so near. We saw him about a year ago, and then he seemed healthy and looked wonderful. It's hard to absorb this. We heard of it only three days ago. Tutti and I went to Savyon to visit Grandma and Miri, and Luzzi, who was home, told us the bitter news. I assume, of course, that Grandma doesn't know and won't be told. We didn't see her as she had gone to Jerusalem with the Margolins just before we arrived.

August 10, 1969

(To Tutti)

My lovely,

I'm writing this in a moving truck, so I imagine the letter and the handwriting will be all bumpy.

What did I want to say? Ah, yes—I still haven't seen you in the skirt my mother sent you; perhaps when I come home?

We are now leaving Hadera and turning toward Afula. Soon we'll be in Wadi 'Ara. It's a beautiful country we've got. Every time I come to a place in Israel I've never been to before (like today), I'm filled with anticipation and curiosity. That's one of the reasons why I enjoy navigation: to walk and discover spots of beauty.

What a mad world we live in! In the twentieth century man has reached the moon and is out for more. The twentieth century has seen Hitler and his mass murders, as well as the terrible First World War— and still all this hasn't cured us. We watch as a whole people is being starved to death,* and no one in this ugly world is moved by it sufficiently to do something. Everybody is preoccupied by his own wars (including Israel, including me), and no state goes in there with its army to put an end to the whole thing. But of course not! No one wants to get involved. Men are such strange animals. I prophesy a brilliant future for us as ugly particles floating in space after the big bomb that is bound to come.

I'm in a mood of being "sick of it," mixed with cynicism and considerable helplessness. I can push back the end for us—for Israel—and do something for our country—i.e., for ourselves. But how do I do it? Again by learning war, by a whole week of training in street combat, etc., instead of spending the week with my wife at the Sachneh.†

I raise my eyes from the paper and see the Valley of Jezreel, Mount Tabor and Givat Hamoreh.

Oh, well, such is life!

August 27, 1969

Beloved Mother, Father and Iddo,

The country is like a pot boiling over. It is really appalling to hear the news on the "Voice of Israel." *Every day* brings its toll of dead and wounded, acts of murder and mine-laying, exchanges of fire along the front lines, and shelling of settlements. Yesterday they fired three Katyusha rockets into Jerusalem—at Katamon and Talpiot; four days ago two small explosive charges went off in Kiryat Yovel, and two children were injured. Incidents like this have been Israel's lot for many days now. I don't think we have ever before been under such pressure—even the

*In Biafra.
†Recreation area in the Jezreel Valley.

pre-state riots* didn't occur with such frequency. The difference is that now we are in a position of strength and capable of returning two blows for one; and we are not standing by. Despite all we are doing, it's still not enough; for facing us are not real armies (with these we can settle accounts very well), but a mixed lot of barbarians fighting for "freedom and progress," etc. But never fear; this little Jewish nation is holding its own nicely.

September 18, 1969

Dearest Father, Mother and Iddo,

I enclose a snapshot of Bibi and me taken a few months ago on an army trip to Sinai. In the background you can see the "fjord," which is located some twenty miles south of Eilat, in an area that used to belong to Egypt. This is an enchanting spot—beautiful and utterly serene.

Happy New Year to all of you! This is the first day of the New Year. What a mad year has just ended for the people of Israel! It's a bit odd to mention the war in every letter (and who wants that), but there seems to be no way to get around it. This was a year that began with war, and continued with war to its very end. The enemy strikes, and we strike back with greater force. The best of our sons are killed, and the void they leave behind is hard to fill. It is only pushed aside a little by the deaths of others, who again leave a fresh, new void behind.

And the world goes on as usual!

In order to be objective: We are actually but a drop in the ocean of wars and calamities. Why, at this very moment an entire people is being destroyed in Biafra, and no one utters a peep of protest. And if anyone does, no one lifts a finger. A crazy world. That is, I don't understand the world, but I don't expect it to intervene on our behalf either.

Tutti and I have moved to a new place in Rehavia, smaller than the previous one but in a much more convenient location. It is easy to come and go without a car, and that's an enormous advantage. We don't have to wait hours for a bus, because everything is within walking distance. Before I forget, our address is: 25 Abarbanel Street, Jerusalem.

Construction has started on our house in Givat Hamivtar. The foundations are being dug, and soon, I hope, we shall lay the cornerstone.

*Outbreaks of violence and organized attacks by Arabs on the Jewish population of Palestine under the British Mandate (1921–1948), before the establishment of the State of Israel.

October 26, 1969
Dearest Mother, Father and Iddo,
Father, I find you are sending me too much money every month. For the time being I am earning enough, and it's a pity for you not to invest the money. Truly, at the moment I don't need assistance. Both Tutti and I earn enough for our needs and lack nothing. I think you should instruct the bank to stop for the present these monthly transfers.

November 9, 1969
Beloved Mother, Father and Iddo,
Bibi completed the Officers' Training Course as outstanding cadet (of course!). Today he is starting on another course of the Corps, which will last two months, and then he'll return to his unit. He's in high spirits and looks marvellous.

Winter has begun. Sun and rain are still intermingled. Fascinating, astonishing weather: one day—torrents of rain, the next—birds chirping away.

We have already settled down in our new apartment, and Tutti has turned it into a lovely spot. It's good to be home!

I hope you are not too worried about the situation here. There is room for great sorrow over the loss of life and the permanent strain put on the country—but there is no room for excessive concern. The Arabs are Arabs (for better or for worse, depending on one's approach), and it's not they or their like who can uproot us from our land.

November 19, 1969
Dearest Mother, Father and Iddo,
I work a lot, but the work is gratifying. This is a difficult life. The days are very long, extending into the nights. At home things are more wearying. It is very hard for Tutti; she spends most of her days alone. It's good that classes at the university resumed two weeks ago; now there is something to keep her busy. I generally come home every Saturday. When I occasionally come on a weekday as well, it's like a little holiday. It's pretty hard for both of us, but especially, as I said, for Tutti. After all, I'm doing something I want to do and believe in, and I brought the present situation on myself of my own free will. I can always stop serving in the army, if

I so choose. For the moment, though, I intend to carry on for a while. I'm doing very important work. I can say important not only within the limited confines of one military unit, but very important for the whole army and for the welfare of the State.

Again they are reporting on the radio about the American astronauts. A tremendous operation! It's good to hear something encouraging and not just news of wars and killing. The news broadcasts here are full of them. Always the same refrain: "There was loss of life" or "There was no loss of life," but it's always referred to. I still believe that what I'm doing is right, but I do it with a heavy heart. A strange army the Jewish state has; perhaps the best of its kind in the world; perhaps the youngest in the age of its soldiers and commanders, but at the same time perhaps the most heavy-hearted and the oldest in spirit.

December 7, 1969

(To Tutti)

My beloved,

I am always filled with joy and anticipation on a day when I plan to come home in the evening. Even if in the end I fail to get there, as long as it's not certain, I make every effort to get home. At the moment, I'm trying to organize a schedule that will make it possible for me to leave the unit in the evening and arrive home before ten at night. Tomorrow I'll have to leave Jerusalem at about five in the morning. A navigational exercise of about thirteen miles is planned for tomorrow, and only if I manage to explain all the material to the soldiers and get everything organized for tomorrow and get a car, and if, and if—I'll come. What's sure is—I'll make it.

January 14, 1970

Beloved Father, Mother and Iddo,

I know that I write very little, but there's not much I can do about it. The brief time required to write a letter is always at the expense of something else I have to do.

It's hard for me to write to you about my state of mind. This is my private domain, and it's hard for me to talk about it. Life in the army fills me and gives me interest and satisfaction. Yet long ago I ceased to be young. Not so much in age as in feeling. It seems to me that all the young people in the army who are daily engaged in guarding our borders are seized by a feeling of depression. This is a special kind of depression. It comes from the great burden laid on our shoulders. A depression you cannot shake off, so that it is part and parcel of you all the time you go on with your military activities. This depression leads to melancholy. It's odd to point to somebody young and say: there goes a sad man. That is our lot.

One of the things that weighs me down most is that it's forbidden to speak of this sadness outside the limits of the army. In fact, I'm forbidden to share it with anyone. The main reason is the secrecy that surrounds everything that has to do with the military.

In order to explain the depression, you have to talk about its origins, and that's prohibited, of course. Another reason is that it's almost impossible to explain the nature of this sadness to anyone who doesn't know it; the sadness will always be interpreted as something else. Within the army itself it's not mentioned—it exists, but for each man separately. It is never discussed. Thus another factor comes into the picture—loneliness.

But loneliness, sadness and depression are the lot of great masses of people in this world. Well, then, what kind of God-forsaken world are we living in? It contains so much beauty, so much grandeur and nobility—but men destroy everything that is beautiful in the world. It seems, indeed, that from time immemorial we have been forgotten by the gods.

March 2, 1970

Beloved Father, Mother and Iddo,

Yesterday, March 1, 1970, I was promoted in rank; I am now a captain. This came as a complete surprise. As a rule the rank is awarded after three years' service as lieutenant, but they do take into account 50 percent of the reserve duty done. In other words, the two years I served in the reserves count for one year of regular service. So by this reckoning I have been made a captain after two years' service. That's quite unusual and quite cheering. With the promotion in rank comes an increase in pay, which is always useful.

March 18, 1970

Beloved Father, Mother and Iddo,

I'll just dash off a few hasty words, as time will permit. I received your letter, Father, and it made me very happy. A few days ago we received one from you, too, Iddo; and your letter, Mother, to Tutti arrived as well. It was good to hear from all of you.

Don't be surprised if we're not writing very much. I guess even Bibi writes less than he used to. We're both up to our necks in work—twenty-four hours a day, and hardly have a moment to spare.

I have some sad news to tell you. Yael Barmeir was badly injured yesterday in an automobile accident. She's in the Beersheba Hospital, and I don't as yet know what her condition is. As soon as I can get away, I'll of course go to see her, and then I'll write you right away. I'm so sorry for the whole family.

To pass on to a different matter—Tutti and I contacted another contractor about building the house. Let's hope we get some results at last.

I must end as I have a full day's workload ahead of me and I must get started (or rather, end the short break I took to write this letter).

My work in the army continues to be very interesting—and very important. Bibi too has found in the army an opportunity to give full expression to his abilities. Perhaps the term "full" is not the right one in this case, since there are many spheres in which Bibi's great gifts cannot be best expressed here. But there's no doubt that he derives great pleasure from his work, his soldiers and the heavy responsibility resting on him, and he's doing extremely well.

Micky, Tutti's sister, is getting married on April 19th. Her husband-to-be is a very nice fellow—a hydraulic engineer who came here from Australia.

I have no more news, sad or glad. I'm so sorry for the Barmeirs.

March 30, 1970

(To Tutti)

My beauty,

Again I'm leaving you for a full week. I do it with such a heavy heart —it's so unfair to you.

We love each other so much, we're so much married—and here we are removed from each other by a distance of some 150 miles. Would that it always remain just a physical distance and never anything worse.

What I mean by "worse" is, of course, not a separation, but that I'm sometimes afraid it may lead us further and further apart. We won't let that happen to us, will we, my wife?

I'm off in a few hours to the Arad region, and from there with map and compass to the Craters. I love these navigational exercises—roaming about the country with gun and ammo, boots heavy on your feet, over hills and mountains, feeling your breath getting a bit short and your legs a bit tired, and arriving at last at some magnificent mountain peak, one of many —some of which I've seen and some I have yet to see.

I've got to do this by myself because it can't be done any other way. That's on the one hand. On the other—my going off for a week means that my wife will spend a whole week without me, and I without her.

There is always this conflict within me—between wanting to stay with you and wanting to do the other things that I can do only in the army.

And I come back to the old theme—that I believe with all my heart that it's extremely important that I be in the army now. And not just I personally, but many others as well. Anyone who has something to contribute at present ought to do it. I believe that the Jewish people's survival depends largely upon Israel—and more than that: that Israel's survival depends on us—on our capabilities and staying power. It's enough to read just once all the war slogans of our tens of millions of neighbors, to note their hatred and desire to annihilate us (including you, my wife), to get an extra boost and encouragement for my staying on in the army.

Tutti mine—this is an old subject and a bit outworn. But what's to be done?

May 3, 1970

Beloved Father, Mother and Iddo,

You ask, Father, what my plans are. Well, as for the distant future I haven't yet formed a definite opinion, but a certain direction is beginning to emerge.

At this stage I'm signed up for more than another year. When this period ends, my present job in the army will end as well. Until then, it's clear to me that I'll go on serving in the army. After that, the future is a bit foggy. It depends, of course, on how the situation in the country develops; it may change for the better (I'm pessimistic on this point— insofar as the date we have in mind is concerned), or it may get still worse (as if that's possible). It's hard for me to judge today how I'll decide when the time comes, even though I can guess that I might stay on in the army. At the same time, resuming my studies appeals to me very much, especially at Harvard, and I would like to go back there. When? In about eighteen months, I hope, but, of course, this isn't clear. The truth is that the army offers many of the things I should like to find in my work—the kind of people I like, who have initiative and energy, who break conventions when they have to; who don't cling to fixed ideas but are always searching for new ways and new answers. The army offers a wide scope for developing and testing ideas. What's more, you don't find there all the helplessness, the hypocrisy (sometimes), the bureaucracy and the indifference that you encounter outside it. Perhaps the very words "outside it" explain it all. In this country, at this moment, to be in the army is to be *inside*—doing, believing, knowing that, after all, my work does bring peace closer or, at least, saves lives and pushes back the threat of war from our gates.

May 12, 1970

Beloved Father, Mother and Iddo,

When we visited the Barmeirs last week they told us you had phoned them—that was a nice thing to do! Yesterday we saw them again. Yael is improving, but she's still far from recovered.

The time of your arrival is fast approaching. I do hope, Father, that you too will manage to come right at the beginning of the holiday. I suppose you won't be able to stay here for your whole vacation, but you will be here for a few weeks, won't you?

Our house is actually getting built at last. They've already dug the foundations and are beginning to put up the walls. We've engaged Jewish contractors, and so far everything's fine. As I wrote to you before, we'll most probably need your help to complete the building. Things, however, haven't yet reached that point, and I'll tell you more about it when the time comes.

June 3, 1970

Dearest Father, Mother and Iddo,

I can imagine how worried you are about us and about the situation in general. In view of the latest developments, there's certainly some justification for this. Indeed, even the optimists among us are hard put to say that the situation is encouraging. Nevertheless, you mustn't despair or be depressed; it's not as bad as that.

Things don't look encouraging on any one of the fronts. In Jordan, Syria and Lebanon it's not the Arab armies but the terrorists who do the damage. The military there is on the whole fairly quiet. Although the terrorists have increased their activity, they don't constitute, in my judgment, the main problem. At this stage they're a nuisance, and no more. On those fronts we have known worse times: in Judea and Samaria there's relative quiet, although every now and then grenades are tossed in the streets of the larger towns (Shechem, Hebron). As for the support the terrorists receive in these areas, they have no serious foothold there and are forced to base their operations in the Arab states. In the Gaza Strip the situation is different. Here a grenade explodes almost daily, generally hurting local residents rather than our forces; there are almost no cases of direct harm to Jews.

The problem is Egypt. And more than Egypt—Russia. We've coped with the Arab states in the past and we'll cope with them in the future, in peace or in war. But with the Russians—I don't know. I do not say with certainty what the outcome will be because I really don't know. Although it probably seems obvious to you that we'll lose in the case of Soviet military intervention, I'm not convinced of this at all. Things aren't as simple as they appear at first glance. A lot depends, of course, on what the U.S. will do. I know they won't intervene militarily. It's possible they won't even present the Russians with an ultimatum, and even if they did, I personally believe that it will be an empty ultimatum. It is, I think, more likely that they'll give us all the arms and ammunition we ask for. That, of course, at a later stage. Meanwhile, in their foolishness, they are giving us a bare trickle. But there's no doubt that this will change for the better. I fully believe that if they give us what we ask for, we shall be able to stand fast.

And don't forget for one minute: regardless of Russian interference, we are the strongest power in the region. How sad that we cannot achieve peace! For that is all we all want in the end. But the simple fact is that we have no one to talk to. Not one of the Arab states will agree to have peace talks with us.

June 14, 1970

(To his parents)

My dear ones,

I still don't know when exactly you're coming and hope that this letter will reach you before you leave the U.S. I assume that at least you,

Father, will stay behind for a while owing to your work.

We feel fine and our thoughts turn mostly to you. How good it'll be when we're all together. The truth is that Bibi and I will have very little time to visit you—far less than I had on your last visit when I was serving in the paratroops. Just the same, though, I'm sure we'll manage to steal some hours and come home as often as possible. I say "hours" and not "days," because our work will not permit that under any circumstances.

Tutti's mother is very ill. She's got leukemia and has been in the hospital for two weeks now; she'll stay for quite a while longer. She doesn't know exactly what her illness is and that makes it easier for her.

February 5, 1971

Dearest Father and Mother,

This is the first day of the renewed cease-fire. We're all glad that fighting didn't resume. Waging war is a most demanding "business," entailing physical and mental effort, not to mention the great danger involved. After such a long period of fighting, it's good to breathe easy again, even if only for a limited time.

True, this is a narrow, confined view, and the future must be looked at in a more sober light. But all the same, it's a fact that I've felt relieved ever since I heard that, as of today, I'm no longer in a state of active warfare. I have no desire to sink into a sea of flame once more, and from a personal point of view, this quiet is, of course, comfortable. But if I were sure that we were going to fight a total war with Egypt (rather than merely exchanging shots), I'd say it would be better to fight such a war now than later on.

Iddo is already a full-fledged paratrooper, with wings and a red beret. He looks great and has adjusted well to the army.* Bibi, as usual, is also A-okay.

Work on our house is progressing, and we're already starting on the carpentry—windows and doors. The walls are up, including all the partitions, and the house looks wonderful. It's a pleasure to see it take shape. When you come on your next visit, I hope you'll find a place with us for rest and relaxation.

As for me, I enjoy every minute—both at work and at home.

*Iddo returned to Israel in the summer of 1970, joined the army and volunteered for the paratroops.

March 25, 1971

Beloved Mother and Father,

First, thanks for the lovely present you sent for my twenty-fifth birthday. For that alone it was worth hauling my weight for twenty-five years. It is, of course, a very practical gift and will be put to good use at once.

It's a bit sad to hear that neither of you is feeling tiptop, and particularly that Mother is again troubled by the pains in her leg. I hope it isn't a chronic condition, and that you both smile every now and then.

I'm now sitting inside a tent in the Jordan Valley, a few miles to the north of the Dead Sea. It's hot! The sun is blazing and the summer is at its height. The surprising thing is that only a week ago snow fell in Jerusalem, shrouding all the streets and cars in a layer of white.

As to the situation on the political front, it is quite clear that we are getting deeper and deeper into the lion's jaws. And the lion is in greater part—the Americans. I hope we'll have enough sense not to take the final step and be swallowed by those jaws. I assume this won't happen. At the same time, I think, we may have to give up territories in return for certain guarantees from the United States. Of course the only guarantee that would mean anything in this part of the world is an *Israeli-American defense treaty,* which could leave no room for doubt as to the Americans' readiness to act on our side if the need arose. It should also guarantee regular arms shipments to Israel like those of the last few months. The quantity they've sent us surpassed our demands, even our dreams.

Needless to say, things are far from simple and cannot be summed up in the two words "defense treaty." But insofar as we are moving in that direction (and I think the prospects of it are good), perhaps we won't sink in the mud.

Don't worry about us. Things are quiet in Israel, and everything is as it should be.

May 1, 1971

Dearest Father and Mother,

My day begins at two or three in the morning and ends at almost the same time the next day. In another month I'll be going back to my former unit. I think you know that these past few months I've been serving as company commander in one of Zahal's reconnaissance forces.

Iddo looks marvellous. Simply great. Tanned and tall and handsome. He feels fine and enjoys the army.

Bibi, as always, is tops. At the same time he's beginning to think seriously about his studies, and it's absolutely certain that only one of your sons will stay on in the regular army.* At least, in the coming year, as far as I'm concerned.

The house is coming along fine. They've finished building the frame, apart from a few finishing jobs. The carpentry is nearly done too, and soon we'll bring in plasterers and tilers. Although it'll take a few more months before we can move in, it already looks beautiful and inviting and attractive. I really believe that on your next visit you'll be able to stay with us in perfect comfort.

After fierce rainstorms, the like of which Israel has not known for years, the sun has come out at last, and with it came the first Khamsin.† The road linking Ein Gedi with Ein Fashkha has been opened to traffic; now it's just a short hop to get there. The road is magnificent—winding along the Dead Sea and passing through flourishing oases in the midst of the blazing desert wilderness.

I won't discuss what's happening on the international scene. The situation is bad, and the Americans are pressuring us relentlessly. Still, the supply of arms from the U.S. continues in an orderly fashion, and in fact is actually increasing. At least, there's some comfort on this score.

May 20, 1971

Beloved Mother and Father,

Lately you've flooded us with letters, and we're all very happy. First, because of the letters themselves which are wonderful; second, because of the good news that you're moving to Cornell; I hope that now, Father, you'll at last have the opportunity to devote yourself to your work without being bothered by trifles; third, because both of you feel your health has improved. It's too bad that Mother still limps a little, but I hope this will pass soon; and fourth, Ithaca is closer to Israel than Denver, so perhaps you'll both come soon; the very move brings you halfway here.

Mother, how did you work out from a telephone conversation lasting only a few minutes that Tutti is pregnant? Remarkable! We'd deliberately held off telling you about it because we wanted to make sure that this time it would come off successfully, and we wanted to avoid upsetting you needlessly.

*Consisting of volunteers who sign up for a given time.
†A warm, dry desert wind that blows in the Middle East.

Tutti is in her fourth month now. Although she's following all the doctor's instructions and taking care of herself, all is not completely well, and last week she had to go into the hospital for several days. But the chances are good that this pregnancy will not be marred by complications.

This is the last day of my service in the paratroop unit* in which I've been serving for the past few months. Tomorrow I'm going back to my previous unit in a higher position of command.

July 23, 1971

Beloved Mother and Father,

I haven't written you for a long time because Tutti again had problems with her pregnancy, and we wanted to know the outcome first.

To my great sorrow, Tutti miscarried again a few days ago, in about the middle of the sixth month. The baby girl was born and lived a few days. Last Friday (two days ago) she died. Of course, she didn't stand a chance right from the start, and we both knew it. But just the same—it's very sad.

A short while ago we bought a German shepherd puppy. I know that Father doesn't like dogs because of their uncleanliness, but you should see this one—really marvellous. I've always wanted a dog, and since we'll soon be moving into the new house at Ramot Eshkol (yes, yes!), we decided to bring along a grown dog, not a puppy. The speed of a dog's growth is really amazing. Week by week we see her developing. When you see her, you'll love her too.

As to the house: well, we're laying the floors. The plastering is finished. The sinks and toilet bowls are being put in, all the frames for doors and windows have been installed, the plumbing and electrical work is nearly completed, and we really are approaching the end. My guess is that in four months we'll move in.

September 5, 1971

Dearest Mother and Father,

We received the suitcase you sent and found many useful things in it. Next Saturday, when Iddo gets here, we'll divide the loot.

Congratulations on the move to Cornell. Tell us what it's like there, and how you've made out.

*"Haruv" reconnaissance unit.

Ilona's* condition is very bad. She's been in the hospital for a long time. Tutti is at her bedside *all the time,* literally day and night.

Mother, congratulations on your birthday! Lots of good wishes and kisses. Maybe next year we'll be able to celebrate it more properly, with the family united in one place. It was nice that you phoned. Too bad I wasn't around to talk to you.

Tutti sends lots of thanks for all the nice things you sent us.

December 30, 1971

Dearest Father and Mother,

I haven't written for a long time, and it really was very hard to write. So many misfortunes and catastrophes have befallen us that before we recovered from one, another arrived. I am hoping that in the next few months Tutti and I will have a quieter spell that will enable us to return to a normal way of life. On the surface everything seems to be all right, but the truth is that it's a bit hard to adjust to things (even the death of our dog affected us deeply).

The house is in its final stages. Although it won't be finished by the time you arrive, it'll certainly be *almost* finished. I know I said that about five months ago too, but this time it's different. They're already painting the walls, the carpentry is almost done, and today the glazier was called in—in short, we're finishing. We'll still need to do the landscaping and gardening job, which will require more time, but we've already started on that, too. Nearly the whole street has been built up, and the neighborhood is developing beautifully.

Bibi is seriously planning for his studies after discharge. From what he says, he's sure he'll leave the army for good. He's been doing extremely well in the army—he's truly an excellent officer, and from the point of view of the army, his discharge will certainly be a loss. But his mind is firmly made up.

Iddo is a very good soldier. He has a good deal of psychological toughness which helps him a lot. I knew he had excellent qualities, but everyone always said, "Iddo isn't like Yoni and Bibi." This is true in a way—it seems to me he is more mature and more critical than we were at his age. In all other matters he falls short of his brothers in nothing.

*Tutti's mother, who died two weeks later.

With his dog Lara

March 9, 1972

Dear Father and Mother,

It's a bit disconcerting that you worry so much about us. It would be natural for you to worry a little, but there's no call for excessive concern.

First of all, nothing extraordinary is happening. All we did was to go into Lebanon to make some order. This operation was directed primarily against the Fatah and not against the Lebanese army. The Fatah almost never fight (firing off Katyushas from deep inside Lebanon into Israeli kibbutzim, or using prewired bazookas to ambush civilian cars, cannot be called "fighting"), and the Lebanese army is certainly not combating us. If we were to launch a campaign against Egypt, it would be a different story; but Lebanon—that's almost a friendly little stroll. Really, it's high time you stopped worrying so much. If anything special happens, we'll make sure to bring you up-to-date. Until then, take every piece of news presented on television as largely blown up and exaggerated.

March 29, 1972

Dear Mother and Father,

I was surprised to hear that you haven't received any letters from me lately. Right after our telephone conversation, I wrote you a detailed letter. True, some time has gone by since then, enough for at least one additional letter, but it was difficult for me to write.

Tutti and I have separated. It's hard for me to analyze the reasons for our split, especially as they are not entirely clear to me. Perhaps they are well founded in logic, but the separation is hard on both of us nonetheless. For the time being we've decided on a trial parting only. I hope it won't deteriorate into a conclusive act.

There are many reasons. There's no doubt that my serving in the army is a contributing factor, because it prevents us from having a regular family life. Another is perhaps a certain degree of incompatibility, and possibly also the fact that we married so young.

We decided to have the trial separation now, because later, with children and the burden of added years, it will be that much harder and perhaps even impossible.

Don't jump to any far-fetched conclusions. It's happened so recently (about two weeks ago) that I myself am still unable to reach any conclusions, far less see what the end will be.

In the meantime I've grown a year older and so have you, Father.*
Here's wishing you, a bit tardily, the best of everything and much joy and
pleasure, and above all—many years of fruitful and creative work.

April 18, 1972

Dear Mother and Father,

I haven't yet received your reply to my last letter. But you must have
already heard that Tutti and I have separated, for Bibi told me that he
also wrote to you. I don't come to Jerusalem very often, but stay in Nir
Zvi most of the time. It's a delightful place—with an abundance of lawns
and chirping birds.

After four and a half years of married life, it's hard to get used to living
alone without the woman one loves; but it seems that one can get used
to anything. It's more difficult to reconcile yourself to the separation as
a reality. It's hard for both of us, and I hope it will all end in the best way
—whatever that may be.

Tomorrow is the eve of our Independence Day. Spring is in leaf, and
everything is coming to life and blossoming. The borders have been quiet
for a number of weeks now—the feeling of tension has almost disappeared
in the civilian population (and the army as well). A proper Independence
Day.

But there's a catch in all this. When the Jews don't have trouble to
unite them, they immediately start fighting each other. Waves of strikes
are sweeping the country—in the ports, at Lydda airport, in factories, in
government firms. Everyone is warning of inflation (as though it hasn't
already come) and of another recession to follow, after which, of course,
there'll be greater bitterness and new demonstrations. I grow pessimistic
about our ability to hold out—and to improve the State in the long term
with a population like this. If we're not destroyed from without (a hypo-
thetical assumption, of course, as I'm 100 percent certain it won't happen), we'll be destroyed from within.

One of the few bodies in the country that does function efficiently, and
to a large extent is free from the evils of bureaucracy, and in which things
are judged by results (and not merely by the professed intentions), is, of
course, Zahal. True, this is an army of all the people, but the trouble is
that our people look on it as a baby to admire and boast about, and not

*Yoni's birthday preceded his father's by three days.

as a body that can serve as a model for their own behavior. I may be wrong, but it seems to me that at the moment the best thing I can do to help the situation is to be in the army, and thereby contribute toward the security of us all.

Bibi is about to get his discharge and go abroad to study. Iddo continues to enchant everyone as usual. Mature, very intelligent, and with a wonderful sense of humor. All in all, both of my brothers are terrific guys. You are lucky to have such sons. There's no doubt that to a very large extent you have made us what we are.

Elliot Entis (my good friend from Harvard) came to Israel a little while ago for the Passover vacation. We went to Eilat together, and it was good to be in his company. His brother, who's got a doctorate in nuclear physics, came to settle in Israel about six months ago with his wife and two small children. He soon came up against an impenetrable wall* and is still trying to break through it and begin a normal life. I can't offer him much comfort, but he is beginning to "find himself," and I hope they'll stay in Israel.

May 3, 1972

Dear Mother and Father,

I received a letter from each of you and was happy with both. I'm glad that you are not overly troubled over what is happening on my domestic front. There is really no need for that. Whatever form the separation between Tutti and me takes, in the long run it will be for the better. Both of us—it seems to me—are slowly adjusting to the situation.

It would be nice if I could come to America for a few weeks, but at the moment it is impossible. I can't leave my work at this stage. It may very well be that I'll come on a visit in another year's time. But I hope that you will be here before then.

June 18, 1972

Dearest Mother and Father,

I assume you were very anxious following the tragedy at Lod† which looked like a promise (so far unfulfilled) of a new wave of violence. It was

---

*Of red tape.
†The Lod Airport massacre, in which dozens of people, mostly Christian pilgrims from Puerto Rico, were murdered by several Japanese terrorists operating on behalf of the PLO.

indeed a terrible tragedy. Meanwhile our air force has brought down two Egyptian MiGs—not at all a bad thing for us: first, that's two planes less for the neighboring air force; second, and this is much more important, we've reminded the Egyptians that there's a vast difference between firing on innocent civilians and waging war on a mechanized army.

These past weeks I've been working day and night. In the three weeks just ended there were at least five whole nights I didn't sleep at all, and on each of the other nights I didn't sleep more than three hours. This Saturday I had a proper rest, and I think that from now on the pace will slacken somewhat and allow me more free time.

I intend to exchange the house I rented in Nir Zvi for an apartment closer to the base. It's rather difficult for me to look after the large garden, and I hate to see it run to seed.

July 8, 1972

Dear Mother and Father,

Now that Bibi is coming to the States,* it will probably be much easier for you. In the days before he left he overflowed with efficiency, taking care of all the things that had been neglected because neither of us attended to them. You really need to be a civilian to have time to get things done.

Tutti and I have decided to be divorced, and we're now in the final stages of the proceedings. Don't be too upset. It's the way of the world. In any case, I'm completely reconciled to this decision (both rationally and emotionally) and have no doubt that it's for the best.

August 3, 1972

Dear Mother and Father,

Something must have happened to justify such a long silence. I wrote about two weeks ago to Cornell University because I forgot your home address; I hope the letter reached you.

I now understand your worry whenever we didn't write over a long period. We, of course, knew that we were all right, but you didn't, and so you were worried. I hope it's the same in this case—that you

*After five years' service in the Israel Defense Forces, Benjamin went to study at M.I.T. in Cambridge, Massachusetts.

are all right and that my apprehensions are unfounded.

Bibi must have arrived by now. I hope that at least he will write.

Everything's fine with Iddo and me. Iddo has decided not to go to Officers' School, and I didn't urge him. To tell the truth, I was even a bit glad; we've had enough army in our family. Although one gets a great deal out of serving as an officer, the commitment is long and rather arduous. Anyhow, I didn't want to push him in either direction, and he decided as he thought best.

August 28, 1972

Beloved Father and Mother,

I see that a really good year has begun. Congratulations on your son's* wedding. We were really happy to learn that they finally decided to get married. I don't have Bibi and Micki's address, so I can't write to them. Please send our best wishes ("our" meaning the remaining two brothers) to the young couple.

September 16, 1972

Dear Father and Mother,

I'm writing this while traveling to my unit, so the handwriting will be a bit "jumpy."

It's six-thirty in the morning. October is here already. The mornings are a bit chilly, and the sun no longer blinds you even when you drive eastward.

On a normal working day I get up at six o'clock in the morning and my driver comes for me half an hour later (which explains how I can write during the drive); or, if I want to keep the car, I pick him up on the way to the unit. The length of my working day depends on the circumstances. On an ordinary day I get home between nine and eleven at night (although this is up to me and sometimes I come home earlier). On busier days there's no end to the hours, and one can easily work around the clock and then continue the following day.

*Benjamin's.

I work quite hard, but hard work never bothered me. Since I'm among people much like myself, I enjoy their company as well as what I do. On Saturdays (which are generally free), I enjoy the total absence of work; we still go to the beach, pick berries, and catch up on lost sleep.

Mother lavishes endless praises on you, Father. I'm glad to hear that you manage to concentrate on your writing and you're feeling so well. Keep it up!

October 2, 1972

Bibi and Micki, hello!

It needs getting used to, writing to the two of you together. My warmest and best wishes! It's high time!

I am a bit envious of you, carefree students in Boston town. The place arouses my nostalgia. I spent the first year of my marriage there. Don't follow our example.

Don't think I've suddenly become a bum just because I've time to write letters. It's six-thirty in the morning now—I'm at the unit (in my office) and have just finished writing a letter to Father and Mother. The drivers didn't show up for work on time yesterday (i.e., A. routed them out of their beds at 8:30), so I decided that this morning all of them would report at 06:00 for a roll call and that A. and B. would inspect them. I also decided to inspect the inspectors—and appeared at the unit at 05:45. Needless to say, the drivers did *not* get up on time, and A. and B., too, didn't appear until 06:30 (because of a flat tire). All of them were scared stiff when they saw me at the unit (surprise!). Now there will be some follow-up treatment. In any case, at 06:45 they all have a barracks inspection. I intend to keep this up for a few days, until things shape up. On Saturday all the drivers will be confined to the base.

Don't think I'm all bad. Last night I went to the wedding of one of the drivers. I stayed about half an hour (even wore my best uniform, in deference to the parents and in line with good manners). It wasn't right that the rest of the staff didn't show up.

Now, to the point: Tutti and I are getting divorced on Sunday (October 10, 1972), unless God (or one of us) wills it otherwise. Since I don't expect surprises in this matter, I guess we can consider the matter closed. It's a little sad, and still hurts. And it's even strange.

October 3, 1972

Beloved Mother and Father,

In your letters, Mother, you expressed concern for my condition as a result of the separation from Tutti. I can't say it was easy. On the contrary, I still find it hard to accept the fact that this has actually happened to me. The most difficult moments are long past, and yet . . .

But never mind. The truth is that everything is all right. Next Sunday we'll be divorced—barring surprises. By surprises I merely mean military operations, etc., not a change of mind. There's no need to worry about me. I've long since passed the age in which one needs "protection," and I manage very well on my own. But it's still good and important for me to know that in case I do need assistance, there'd be someone who would understand and help.

I'm having no second thoughts about being in the army—at least, not at the moment. Sometime in the next few years, I'll certainly complete the studies that I dropped. But now I'm not too disturbed that I dropped them. I realize the importance of my work and enjoy doing it.

November 1, 1972

Dear Father and Mother,

I bought a supply of aerogrammes, which I use for writing letters on every long journey, when I'm not busy with military paperwork (like today's trip to the Meron-Safed region). We've just pulled up beside Mount Meron at a little roadside restaurant, and I'll try to finish my letter there.

I don't remember whether I've already told you that Tutti and I are actually divorced. About two weeks ago we went to the Rabbinate—for the last time—and it was all over.

Last night I met Iddo, and since we both had a few free minutes, we popped into town for a bite. It's a pity we never see each other long enough to have more than a snatched conversation. Iddo intends to study at Cornell after finishing his military service. At last you will have children nearby. Really, I must say that as parents you are experiencing very difficult years. It's a good thing that the period of your sons' military service is drawing to a close. With only one son in the army, you can breathe a bit easier.

November 17, 1972
Dear Mother and Father,
It's too bad you won't be able to come to Israel in January, Father. At least, I can promise you, Mother, that we'll do our best to make your visit here enjoyable. To be sure, it'll be hard to find free time, but both Iddo and I will do all we can to get it. I don't think there's anything special I need, Mother, but if you manage to think of something, bring it—it's always nice to get presents.

November 19, 1972
Two days have passed. Since most of my letters—like this one—are written on the road, I stop writing when I get to my destination.
If my plans work out, I'll be able to take leave around July and hop over to visit you. I even miss America, and a real rest won't do me any harm.
I still enjoy my work, still work hard, still wait for letters. Did I tell you that I rented a house with Bari and Dani Litani? I don't get there very often, but it's good to see them every now and then.

November 18, 1972
(To Benjamin)
Bibon,
Two of D.'s fellows (he's a remarkable man—sends you his regards) struck a mine; one lost an eye and a hand, the other was slightly wounded in the face. The following day S.'s command car collided with a truck and two of his soldiers (I. N. and A. C.) were killed, while two others escaped with relatively minor injuries. S., who was suffering from a leadership crisis and was convinced that he wasn't fit to serve as an officer, sank into an even worse state of mind after the accident. Two days ago we buried them . . . When will it stop! . . . I'm sick and tired of these outrages which cost us human life. Write S. a few words, and it won't hurt if you add some encouraging remarks about his ability as an officer.

November 30, 1972

Dear parents,

I've been thinking about my schedule for the next few years. Between June and August '73 I'll conclude my present assignments. About April '75 I'm due to take command of the unit in which I'm serving, and I'll have to be there about February '75 to complete the necessary preparations. It follows that I'm going to have some eighteen–twenty months at my disposal between assignments. There are, of course, many possibilities within the army, and there are already many who are jumping at the chance of "acquiring" me for the said period.

I've been considering the use of this interval for studying. I expect that in two years' time I could complete my studies either at the Hebrew University or at Harvard. But since I don't *have* two full years (and that's irrevocable), I think I could get through three terms plus a few summer courses at Harvard and get almost as far as a B.A. Of course, it still depends on a number of things. First, on the army, which must consent to my studying abroad; second, on the university, i.e., whether they'll accept me for said period; third, on whatever other options I'll have by then.

Going to Harvard appeals to me. I'd be glad if you would find out a few things I must know before I can reach a decision:

1. When do the university terms start and end?
2. What courses are available in the summer?
3. Would they be prepared at all to consider me as a student?

When you make your inquiries at the university, you might point out that by the time I arrive there I'll be a major. I'll be promoted on April 1st.

Should they require recommendations from the army, I'll be able, of course, to obtain them. If necessary, I think Israel's military attaché in Washington would be glad to intercede on my behalf (provided the army okays my studying in the U.S.).

I've already sent in my proposal to the army and am waiting for their answer. But still it's important for me to hear from you if the whole thing's feasible.

Please let me know soon; it's fairly urgent.

Nothing much is new otherwise. I'm working very hard—at a really mad pace. Even this letter, which is very important to me, was written with five interruptions.

December 24, 1972

Dear Mother and Father,
I'm still attracted by the possibility of continuing my studies at Harvard, but everything hasn't been settled with the army yet. I have to check to see if this is really possible. At the moment it looks feasible, but apparently I'll know for sure only at the end of January.

In the meantime, I'll carry on as though it were settled that I'll be resuming my studies. Maybe it's worth waiting until Mother gets here so she could help me word the letter to Harvard? If there's no rush, it's probably worthwhile. Tell me what you both think. In the meantime I'll prepare a draft, just in case.

Does the summer course really start at the beginning of July? I have to know this to plan my schedule here.

If Harvard counts the accumulated credits for five years only after the interruption of one's studies, that's, of course, one more reason to study now, and not in a few years' time. Anyhow, my strongest argument for studying next year is that it won't impede my military advancement. I want it to be clear that I plan to stay in the army in the coming few years —or at least for two years after completing my studies, and maybe even longer. After that we'll see. In the meantime I find my work very interesting and see no reason to stop.

A few days of leave have come to an end today. It's been so long since I had any vacation that I'd forgotten how it felt. It turned out that I needed it badly. It's so good to rest and make up for gaps in sleep, reading, going places, etc. Tomorrow—back to work. Since I've been under this pressure for several years, it'll be good to take a break and go away to school.

December 31, 1972

To Bibi and Micki, greetings from the Holy Land!
I had a few days' leave, and herewith declare it's just "far out." It was so long since I'd rested properly that I'd forgotten what rest was. Such peace—it's wild. It lasted less than a week and made me hungry for more.

About studying—I can't quite decide what's preferable: to stay in the army and go over to armor or skip over to Boston. From the army's point of view, the right thing would be for me to stake myself a place in armor, and not begin to fill command posts (like battalion commander) after commanding the unit. But from my own personal point of view, it would be better to finish my studies now and not put them off until God knows when. In short, I haven't yet decided.

Meanwhile—how are you two? You don't write a thing about yourselves, and I'm cross. Correction: I'm embittered (à la "embittered officer")! Kindly supply information. In every letter I give precise instructions on what to write, but—no reaction (see previous letters).

I work very hard and wonder how long I'll be able to stand this murderous pace. Soon it will be four years since I returned to the army—a long time for an officer in my unit. At any rate, it's interesting.

January 28, 1973

Dear Father,

Mother's been with us for several weeks now. Unfortunately we don't see each other every day, mainly because of my work load, but both Iddo and I try hard not to let days go to waste. It's only a pity you're not here. Your presence is missed very much both by Mother and by us. Mother checks the mailbox every day to see if there's a letter from you. And indeed, one letter from you cheers her up for days. Mother's busy arranging the house, bank affairs and all the rest, and her only worry is that she won't have time to finish everything before she leaves. We try to persuade her that she ought to rest a little, but you can't change a person's nature just by talking.

I still haven't received the army's reply about my going abroad. I hope to get it by the end of the month and then I'll know where I stand.

It will be interesting to see what the future brings us in the wake of the Vietnam peace agreement. I still cannot see peace in the offing in the Far East, of course. Quite the contrary, I foresee bloody wars there and possibly a Communist victory. But this, apparently, will not prevent the Americans from moving on with a loud fanfare of victory to the Middle East to make "peace" here.

Don't misunderstand me. I want peace very much; I don't like to live by the sword—a life of killing and trying not to be killed. I believe that it will be very hard to force peace terms on us that are repugnant to us, and I hope the Americans will have enough sense not to try to do so. But I'm pessimistic about the chances of a lasting peace between the Arabs and ourselves, although a respite of an additional ten years would also satisfy me. Right now we're in a favorable position, and we've no reason to change it except against very good terms.

Father, please write to us. We're all impatient to see you.

March 23, 1973

(To his parents)

A big hello to you both!

I received both your letters with your good wishes for my birthday and your many suggestions as to how I should behave now that I've reached this ripe old age. It was nice to get such warm letters. You, too, Father, have warm good wishes coming to you. Time does fly, and what a pity that we spend so little of it together. I'm glad you're managing to concentrate on your very important work. Perhaps I'll manage to glean something from your knowledge when we're together. Would that it be so!

Last night (Friday) I got to Jerusalem and found Iddo here. We went to a restaurant together for a late dinner. Afterwards I stayed home to finish some work and to study (army matters), and Iddo took the car and went out. I'm really dazzled by him. Such a marvellous and gifted fellow. He is really very special and quite out of the ordinary. You gave me two wonderful brothers.

April 16, 1973

(To his parents)

Happy holiday!

Tonight's the Seder. Saadiah and Phirah invited us, and since neither Iddo nor I had any definite plans, we decided to accept. Incidentally, Saadiah was very nice. Before he went abroad, I talked to him about selling the house, and as soon as he got back a few weeks ago he went and discussed the matter with Erwin,* then took the trouble to track me down (no easy matter) and advise me. Actually it was too late because by then I had already sold the house, but it was very kind of him anyhow.

I've bought a flat that Rassco is building in Ramat Hasharon. Construction has only just begun and will take over a year, but Rassco generally keeps to schedule. It's a luxury apartment house in the private homes section of Ramat Hasharon. I imagine our high rise is an eyesore to the villa owners, but not to me. The more villas around, the better.

Concerning my studies, I must tell you that I still don't know the army's position. There's no point in pushing too much either, since it'll become clear before long and anyway there's nothing that requires immediate action. I wrote to Harvard some time ago, asking for a scholarship. Iddo and I drafted the letter, and I must say Iddo's English is far better than

*The late Erwin Shimron, then the family lawyer.

mine. I'm now waiting for their answer. It might be a good idea for you to call them and make sure there are no special problems about my registration for summer courses and the coming school year. If there are any, it isn't too late to meet their requirements.

Your loving
Yoni

May 7, 1973

Dear Mother and Father,

Today is the eve of Independence Day. Twenty-five years for the State of Israel. So little, and yet so much.

By the way, two days ago I was promoted to major!

My plans are still not entirely clear. It seems that even if I don't come to Harvard for a full year, I'll still come for the summer; whatever happens, I do want to take the summer course at the university.

Could you make sure there won't be any problems on this score?

Forgive this hasty note. Just terribly busy.

May 21, 1973

Bibi and Micki, Hi,

Well, still no response from the parents re the Harvard summer course. I plan to leave Israel on June 3rd, and to arrive on the 5th or 6th to arrange matters at the university. After the summer course, I'll have to return here for the Command-and-Staff course (October to August). Following that I'll be able to go back to Harvard for another semester before having to rejoin my unit (C&S includes a school year at Tel Aviv University). It's not as good as continuous study at Harvard, but things won't work out any other way.

Incidentally, a little over two weeks ago I was made a major. It was quite interesting and unexpected. This year Zahal suspended all shortening of MPT's (Minimum Promotion Time) on the ground that there's no genuine criterion for knowing who is really good and deserves the shortcut. The issue is still under discussion, and they still haven't made up their mind as to how to give out shortened MPT's. I was already resigned to getting my majority only next year. In short, in some forum or other it was decided to promote G. and myself anyway, without counting it in this year's quota of shortened MPT's.

What else is new? A. has finished his conterm with me and has begun to work. I think he'll do well. A gifted fellow. I was still working last night, but this morning (after a debriefing session) I'll be all through and start pulling up stakes. Hope I'll keep to schedule.

Cambridge, Mass.
June 13, 1973
Sweet Dorit,
Tonight I fly to South America.
Before I leave I hope to find living quarters at Harvard for the summer. It turns out to be a pretty expensive business, but I hope to manage it all right.
America is as I remembered it. A country that moves you to pity on the one hand and honest admiration on the other. Pity because young people here are caught up in the toils of endless frustration and seem unable to progress beyond the infantile stage. On the main streets of Cambridge (where my university is located) one sees young people sitting on the sidewalks barefoot, half-naked and dirty, begging alms and strumming guitars or toying with Indian beads, or distributing religious propaganda ("Jesus Saves!"—this is the latest thing). Of course, not all of them are as extreme as that, but they're all brought up to be anti-Establishment and they all sling mud at the U.S. government. It seems that people here stopped being objective long ago.
You feel sorry for America; these lunatics will destroy her.
On the other hand, there's no end to my admiration. This country is colossal! Just so—in technology, achievement, efficiency, courtesy, order, convenience and such they are ten times better than the rest of the world (and fifty times better than Israel).
I think of you often.

Yours,
Yoni

June 20, 1973
Dorit mine,
I've been abroad for two weeks now, and I've already visited three countries. I stayed nearly a week in the U.S. (hope you got my letter) and now I'm writing from Brazil, which I reached via Argentina.

I miss you quite a bit, but since I'm busy time passes quickly—and that helps.

Buenos Aires (Argentina) is an interesting city—and even an odd one, full of contrasts. In one way, A. was probably right when he said that it reminds one of Europe at the beginning of the century, but in another way it reminds one of the Arabs of Israel. On the one hand, everybody wears suits and ties and they are wonderfully polite and don't push in queues, but on the other hand, they are all politically hysterical, chalking and painting slogans on every wall, sidewalk and street, conducting endless demonstrations, and never getting to work on time. All in all, they're full of contrasts. They drive like lunatics, and where there isn't a free parking space, they simply push aside any car in their way without giving it a second thought. They talk nonstop and make promises all the time (which they never keep). Maybe the most curious custom of the Argentinians is that they don't sleep at night. People come out of a movie at 2:00 A.M. and spend another two hours at a restaurant, where they eat an enormous meat dinner, and this every day—not just on weekends. This city boasts the widest street and also the longest one in the world, and just to keep it that way they're prepared to pull down whole neighborhoods, to enlarge the avenues.

After five days in Buenos Aires my interest in this city evaporated (and my time was up, too), and now I'm in Rio de Janeiro, Brazil.

Rio is perhaps the most beautiful city in the world. It's certainly the most beautiful I've seen so far. The people are delightful. No one's in a hurry. They take everything lightly and with a smile, they never get into fights, and money means nothing to them (though there are desperately poor people here). A cab driver may tell you that you don't really need to pay him today, it's not important. And a guy who's been tipped five cruzeiros (about 3 Israeli pounds) will first of all go and get his shoes shined (they love to shine their shoes), then spend what's left on a beer, and feel happy for the next two days. Everything makes them laugh, and they dance all the time. You can't help loving them.

September 9, 1973

Dear Father and Mother,

Nearly two weeks have already passed since I returned to Israel. I've been busy with arrangements all this time and I'm not quite through yet.

I've arranged to take, while attending the C&S, additional courses at

Tel Aviv University, which will be relevant to my studies in the U.S. C&S starts in a week—on the 16th.

I am still in a glow from the months I spent at Harvard. There's no question that the summer gave me a lot personally. It was a wonderful opportunity to widen horizons and to deal with subjects I hadn't delved into for years. Above all, shedding responsibility for a few months gave me a sense of freedom and lightness and allowed me to enter new domains; a new curiosity, a new interest, a different world, unfamiliar books, interesting conversations, staying in your company—and all in one summer! Without any doubt, I'll return to complete my studies. For now, it's good to be back in the army despite everything and to work as usual.

(September 1973)
(To Yoni's former commanding officer and his wife on leave in California)
Dear E. and N.,*

I can see already that this is going to be a long letter. So that's it—I'm back from the Diaspora! I'm sorry I couldn't get hold of your address, though I kept asking for it in the unit. Funny, but in Israel nobody can understand how "provincials" like us didn't meet in America even once in all those months (in the morning, no doubt, on our way to the grocery for buns). ·

I'm only just back from the States, so there isn't much I can tell you about the unit yet. I sat in on an officers' meeting today (just to refresh my memory), and it all seemed very familiar—one more installment of the same everlasting meeting that never ends. The same old "problems," and precious few new solutions (I've been hearing almost the same story in slight variations for the past five years). No doubt some things have changed, and many others will, as indeed they should with a change of command and the injection of new blood, with new ideas and different priorities—but on a first superficial survey it all looked and sounded very familiar. G. and A. are working hard, and it seems they're well on top of things.

I imagine you are already past the settling-in stage,† and are beginning to fall into a regular routine. It's a rather drastic transition, and not always

*This letter was found among Yoni's papers. Apparently, it was not mailed due to the outbreak of the Yom Kippur War.
†E. had gone to study for his M.A. degree.

easy—hope you made it swimmingly all the way without taking any dives.

After my tour of South America—three charming and refreshing weeks —I came back to Harvard and started to take things seriously. In the two months I was there I managed to complete a full semester. Besides moving a step nearer to my B.A., I must admit that I got much more than I expected out of my stay abroad.

Over the last few years I'd been letting myself unconsciously sink into a very narrow furrow of interests, restricted to a few themes. I suppose it was inevitable in the kind of work we were doing. Personally, of course, I don't regret a moment of it, and that goes both for the past and for the future. But it was only when I got to Harvard, free from the pressure of responsibility, only when I could sit down with a pile of books for weeks on end until three in the morning and read at will without having to think about the consequences of anything I did (sounds familiar?), only when I became my own master—that I began to open up to the big world outside.

This summer I concentrated mainly on international relations, in particular on the Middle East from the political and economic points of view and the implications for U.S. policy in the region. I had several excellent teachers, and I can humbly say that I had much to learn, and more important—every book I opened led me to open three more and to want to open yet another three. The only problem was perpetual lack of time —eight weeks is really very little. It was a bit like the thirst you have on a tough navigational exercise, without water in your canteen to slake it.

Anyhow, I've come back completely revived, and ready to plunge back in. It's a bit difficult to be so near the unit and yet so far from it.

C&S is due to start in ten days—hope it won't be a waste of time.

So much for me (and at length too). I imagine you went through the same experience of release and opening up. Even more drastic in your case, I'd say, as the transition from one world to the other was much more extreme for you. I'm glad the two of you got this chance to be together at last (despite all the pressure of your studies, Europe must have been a dream), and I hope you're managing to ignore the decadent, naïve and destructive American society around you long enough to see the other side —the democracy, the technology and the efficiency of this great country. As far as I'm concerned, I left America with mixed feelings—on the one hand, the tremendous achievements, which inspire admiration, and on the other, I got the impression that this whole colossal creation is subject to the self-destructiveness of a crumbling society that shows no signs of recovery. I wonder what it's like at your end in the Far West? Do write.

I want to turn to an entirely different matter.

They said so many good things about you at the summing-up that it's hardly necessary for me to start singing your praises. Actually the best summary of everything you gave the unit was made, as usual, by yourself in your "credo" at the change-of-command ceremony.

All the same, a few personal words—

You can't imagine how much I enjoyed working with you. I view these last years as a great privilege and a real *personal* gain. More than once, when I thought I already knew you, you'd suddenly surprise me with something new and open another window to get a fresh view of things. During the time you were in charge of the unit, you weren't just an exemplary commander, you also taught us efficiency at our jobs and readiness to accept responsibility. You taught us to distinguish between the important and the trivial, and to concentrate on the important. You were flexible and generous enough to retreat from a stated opinion (e.g., when you realized you were wrong), yet you were firm and unswervingly resolute when that was appropriate.

You not only introduced working habits and ways of thinking on an entirely new scale into the unit, you also made the army at large recognize our capabilities (and this may well be the most significant of all your achievements). It's not for nothing that D. said that he considered you the best commander the unit ever had. He was right, of course. Only I realized that nearly two years before he did.

On top of all this you surprised me by the great tact you showed in working with both officers and men in the unit, and by your genuine understanding and concern for them. And not just because you thought it *expedient* tactically (that's obvious), but also because that's the way one *should* act, for it's more humane, more ethical.

I'm absolutely certain that if you'd had more time you'd have gone into all those matters you didn't manage to go into, and you would certainly have contributed much to the unit's development in many diverse areas. I'm aware of the reasons that made you choose the path you have followed, and I'm convinced that your choice was the right one.

I don't want to go into *all* the many things they said about you in your presence (tactical insight, clarity of thought, etc., you'd start blushing!). Only this, then, in closing: I always enjoyed being in command and working independently, and I always disliked the idea of being restricted by being under the direct command of anyone. I have to confess that you succeeded in doing something that I'd thought was impossible for me— you made me enjoy being second-in-command of the unit. The fact that my views on the substance and style of managing the unit coincided with yours, and the absolute trust and independence of action I knew I had, no doubt have much to do with the fact that I consider my years working with you as a most enjoyable and fruitful experience.

I see I have run to so many pages that this letter could be published as a book.

(Don't set standards by the length of this letter—it's only just this once —but don't forget either that there's someone here who'll be glad to hear from you.)

FROM THE YOM KIPPUR WAR TO OPERATION JONATHAN

(1973–1976)

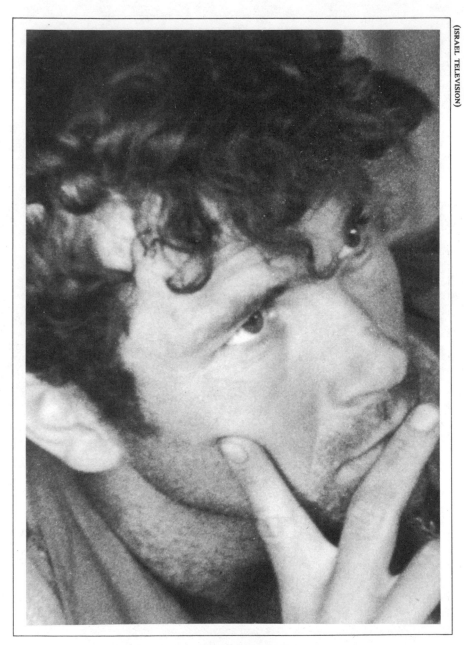

During a briefing, 1973

O N YOM KIPPUR, OCTOBER 6, 1973 —the holiest day of the Jewish year—Egypt and Syria simultaneously initiated a surprise attack on Israel. Caught completely off guard, Israel faced the gravest threat to her survival since 1948. Troops in the Golan and Sinai, heavily outnumbered in men and material, succeeded at great cost in holding the line against the invading Arab armies. As Israel mobilized her reserves and rushed reinforcements to the fronts, the tide of battle first stabilized and then turned the other way.

At the outbreak of the war Yoni was in command of part of his unit in the Golan Heights. The following description has been given of the battle in which Yoni and his men took part on the second day of the war:

"We spotted a landing of Syrian commandos near Nafah (H.Q. of Zahal in the Golan Heights) and were informed that we were in fact the last force to defend the place. We moved fast to that location. We were standing on the road looking for the enemy when suddenly heavy fire was opened on us, killing one of our officers. The Syrians caught us very conveniently, with themselves behind cover, while we were exposed in the field. At this point somebody had to start giving clear orders; otherwise the situation there could have been grim. There wasn't much firing after that first barrage, and there was a kind of feeling that you were waiting for somebody to do something. I personally remember that I began to be frightened. I was very frightened. What I saw then was a picture I'll remember all my life: suddenly I saw Yoni stand up quite calmly, as if nothing had happened. With hand movements he signaled to the men to get up. They were all lying down behind cover, and he began to go forward as if it were a fire exercise. He walked upright, giving out orders right and left. I remember my thoughts then as his soldier: Hell, if he can do it, so can I! I got up and started to fight." (From the reminiscences of an officer)

Yoni's second-in-command in this battle, and later his deputy at Entebbe, recalled:

"As soon as they opened fire on us, Yoni conducted a battle the likes of which I've not come across even in the books.

"I remember we stormed in two groups, Yoni's on one side and mine on the other. When I reached the top of the hill, I saw a kind of crevice farther ahead where one or two Syrians were firing at us. I shouted to Yoni to cover us so that we could attack the position, but before I could move,

Yoni had already taken his men and in a matter of seconds stormed the place. I had nothing left to do but give him cover. And the picture I always remember is that of Yoni running ahead of eight men and destroying the enemy force. When I reached the crevice I saw some ten Syrian commandos there. They were all dead.

"This was a classic example of leadership under fire with relatively small losses."

The battle ended with the annihilation of the Syrian commando force, which numbered about forty-five men. Yoni's force of about thirty men suffered two casualties.

After the Syrian assault had been checked, the Israeli army went over to counterattack. The unit commanded by Yoni was attached to the attacking tank battalions, as a reconnaissance and protective force. At night, when the weary tank crews, who had been fighting all day, were in night encampments, Yoni's force would protect them from sudden attack. One night Yoni's force wiped out a group of enemy tank-hunters. On other nights Yoni went reconnoitering behind the Syrian lines and carried out successful ambushes on enemy supply lines.

In the last assault by the Israeli forces on Tel Shams, the last point of Syrian resistance, Yoni heard over the communications network that the tank commander Yosi Ben-Hanan had been left seriously wounded in enemy territory. The area was covered by Syrian machine-gun fire. Previous rescue attempts had failed, and it was only a question of time before the Syrians sent their forces in to evacuate their own wounded. Yoni volunteered to get Yosi out—and did. For this action he was decorated in 1974.

Another operation in which Yoni played an important role was the deployment of Zahal's 175mm cannons to firing positions on the outskirts of Damascus. The brigade commander in the northern Golan Heights, Lieutenant Colonel Avigdor Ben-Gal ("Yanosh"), entrusted Yoni with the task of leading artillery forces by night in difficult terrain between the Israeli and Syrian lines, so that the artillery could fire on the enemy capital. Yoni's navigation was precise and successful, and he led the forces back to Israeli lines toward dawn.

At the end of the war Zahal prepared to recapture the Israeli army outpost on Mount Hermon, which had fallen earlier into the hands of Syrian commandos. Yoni and his men penetrated enemy territory, climbed to one of the summits of Mount Hermon, and for several nights observed the activities of the enemy in the outpost. Yoni supplied intelligence information that was vital for the launching of Zahal's attack, which ended in the capture of the outpost. Yoni and his men were also ordered to block any reinforcements that might come to the aid of the Syrians on Mount Hermon, and when the outpost fell into Israeli hands, they fought some of the retreating enemy soldiers and took dozens prisoner.

Wednesday,
November 11, 1973

Dear Shula,*

Every evening I realize that another day has passed and I still haven't been to see you. I want you to know that it isn't due to thoughtlessness but to real pressure of work. I won't even manage to get to the memorial meeting on Thursday.

It's strange to think of ourselves without Amitai, without the proud upright walk and the hearty laugh, without his moral integrity and passionate caring, without the efficiency and the air of confidence he'd inspire in those about him, without the drive with which he'd tackle any task he'd undertaken, without his familiarity with every beauty spot in the country and without his stories about Vered.

But none of this really conveys what I'm trying to say. For above all, Amitai was the essence of the sound, whole, living person.

For years now we've been trying to inure ourselves to the price we must pay so that we—and others—can live in this country of ours, on this soil. We've tried to build a defensive wall around us that might help us resign ourselves to the gaping holes that have been created around us, to the fact that there are people we will call by name no more, friends who will no longer walk by our side.

And now, with this sudden void opening up with Amitai's death, this defense mechanism, which we took so much trouble to erect, has been shattered—and nothing remains but the pain.

It's hard to talk of Amitai in the past tense. He is still among us, with us, part of us all.

Yours,
Yoni

*The widow of Captain Amitai Nahmani, Yoni's fellow officer who was killed in the Yom Kippur War.

November 17, 1973

Dear Mother and Father,

This is my first letter after the fighting has ended. Nobody here talks of the end of this war yet, or even of the next one, only of the continuation of this one (if it starts up again, of course). The mood here is still of a nation at war. All our reserves are still mobilized, and the effect on the economy is very apparent. It's easy to notice this in the streets of the towns in which you see many women, children and old people, but very few men. What now? I have a definite idea on what ought to be done, but I'm not sure the present government is quite clear about where we're going. The war has finally brought a change of mind to a large section of the public, and this shift in thinking is all to the good. How far it has spread to the nation at large is hard to say, but we'll soon know—elections at the end of December. In any case, I see with sorrow and great anger how a part of the people still clings to hopes of reaching a peaceful settlement with the Arabs. Common sense tells them, too, that the Arabs haven't abandoned their basic aim of destroying the State; but the self-delusion and self-deception that have always plagued the Jews are at work again. It's our great misfortune. They want to believe, so they believe. They want not to see, so they shut their eyes. They want not to learn from thousands of years of history, so they distort it. They want to bring about a sacrifice, and they do indeed. It would be comic, if it wasn't so tragic. What a saddening and irritating lot this Jewish people is!

And yet, how strong and how great is the nation at moments of crisis. You can't imagine how the fingers tighten into an iron fist when the threat of violent days approaches. The entire people—young soldiers, lawyers, doctors, clerks, laborers—all turn into tankmen and infantrymen, pilots and sailors. They aren't reserves who've come from "another world," but an integral part of a strong and united army. Amazing how we succeeded in establishing this fact, of the whole people being an army.

This, no doubt, has been the hardest war we've known. At least, it was more intense, more frightening (not for me personally, but for those who are less "experienced"), more costly in dead and wounded, more marked with failures and successes, than any of the wars and battles I have known. But it's precisely because of those initial blunders (which I won't go into now—I mean the failures in military judgment, in interpreting intelligence data, in military doctrine, in political assessments and, of course, in the whole nation's complacency) that the victory achieved was so great. The army is strong and sound and has proved its ability beyond all doubt. And again when I say "the army," I don't mean just the regular forces, but the whole people. The regulars managed, at heavy cost, to hold the enemy. But it was the people who won the war. What a pity they're now starting "The Wars of the Jews" (among ourselves) even before the fighting at the fronts is over, while the whole nation is still on the borders. "The Wars of the Jews" are always the ugliest and hardest of all. These are wars of apologetics and futile bickering, suppression or distortion of facts, and procrastination in making decisions. There is no doubt that what's called for is a new leadership, a more correct perception of the realities, a sound recognition of the enemy's aims, and clear, definitive strategic-political planning. There must be no fumbling in the dark and no mere tactical expedients, for these will get us nowhere. If we don't have a well-defined, realistic objective, we won't have to fight the Arabs for our survival. The Arabs won't need to fight. The Jews, as usual, will destroy themselves.

I said before that I feel our people are sobering up—and I only hope I'm not wrong. Maybe, maybe this time! Actually I'm a little pessimistic. I don't doubt that we have the ability, the power and the will to stick it out here long enough to turn ourselves into an accomplished fact. Nor do I doubt that the Arabs do not and will not have the ability to move us even an inch. But I do doubt the nation's readiness to go on making sacrifices over the long run; not its readiness to fight minor battles from time to time, but its will to enter upon yet another long and drawn-out war with heavy casualties, which requires perseverance. In the main, the people, as a body, lacks perseverance while it abounds in political and military blindness. But I repeat, maybe this time we'll sober up.

Give my love to Micki and Bibi, and don't worry too much. Things will work out. Don't forget: *strength, justice and staunch resolution are on our side, and that's a great deal.*

November 1973
(From a eulogy to Shai Shaham of Kibbutz Kabri, who froze to death on Mount Hermon after the Yom Kippur War)

The war has demanded of us heavy sacrifices. There is hardly a family in Israel that does not mourn, hardly a home without its dead. And just as we thought we had gained a respite, when we hoped that the end might come—more tragedy struck.

Shai fell. Perhaps I should say, *our* Shai fell.

On Thursday night the group to which you belonged attempted to scale new heights.

*October 1973, during a briefing by General Rafael Eitan
on the Golan Heights*

A detachment of our soldiers had stayed behind at the top of Mount Hermon under difficult conditions, with no possibility of extricating themselves. The bad weather made us fear gravely for their safety, and we decided to send a detachment of our men to show them the way down, to rescue them.

Bad conditions, unfamiliar heights and freezing temperatures took their toll. It was only much later—when you began to stumble—that your comrades found out how hard it was for you. Maybe you had already been in trouble long before, but you preferred to keep silent and struggle on. That's the way you always were. And so, until the last moment, you didn't let us notice your struggle and share in your suffering. And when we found out—it was too late. You died shortly before the arrival of the force that was moving to reach you.

I remember you as a young recruit. A thin, slightly built boy, tousled, your shirt always hanging out and something always unbuttoned. Something about you made one smile.

And I remember you a few weeks later—my first meeting with you in the field. We marched in the same squad on a long, twelve-hour navigational maneuver. I remember I was surprised by your physical stamina and moral strength. You were marching in torn boots, and yet you kept forcing the pace, pulling the others with you, demanding the utmost of yourself and them. I was impressed by your pertinacity, your readiness to carry on without a word, and your endless vitality. That night you won my heart.

But there was much more than that in you.

You were a unifying and guiding force in bad as well as good times. You were liked and loved by all, always wise and clearheaded—

How terrible it is to say, you *were*.

Rachel and Shaul, and all the house of Kabri—how can we comfort you when we cannot even comfort ourselves?

December 2, 1973

Dear Bibi and Micki,

I'm glad you're together again.*

December is much in evidence here, both in the weather and in the overall drabness of Israeli public life.

The war atmosphere is at a pitch, and I can only hope they're not going to disturb your peace again. We're preparing for war, and it's hard to know what to expect.

What I'm positive of is that there will be a next round, and others after that.

But I would rather opt for living here in continual battle than for becoming part of the wandering Jewish people. Any compromise will simply hasten the end. As I don't intend to tell my grandchildren about the Jewish State in the twentieth century as a mere brief and transient episode in thousands of years of wandering, I intend to hold on here with all my might.

I'm about to carry out my plans of transferring to armor.

December 9, 1973

Dear Father and Mother,

Work in the army is in full swing. We in our unit are used to the pace from prewar days, but now it's the same throughout the army, and things are really picking up—there's something to work against on the opposing side.

On the whole I'm keeping my spirits up, working hard and getting lots of fresh air. That's one thing the war hasn't spoiled—the air. On the contrary, it's grown tastier, clearer, cooler, and one swallows it in deep, thirsty gulps.

There's nothing to worry about, I hope. We're going through one more stage in the Wars of Israel, and we shall win the next round too. That's almost certainly unavoidable; and if so, let's take it as a matter of course and be duly prepared.

---

*Benjamin came back to Israel at the outbreak of the Yom Kippur War and joined his army unit. Both he and Iddo took part in the war. At the end of the fighting Benjamin returned to the United States.

December 12, 1973

(To Lieutenant Colonel Nathan of Army Personnel)

To Nathan, greetings!

With our present jobs in the army being what they are, it's unlikely we will meet and work together for some time.

That being the case, I can afford to say a few words in your praise without being suspected of flattery, or of an attempt to gain something for myself.

I've greatly appreciated your deep concern and devotion to the affairs of the unit in general, and to the matter of my placement in Zahal in particular.

Things are measured by results, and these you've achieved in full— without fail. One could almost think you had only one unit in your care, though we obviously were the smallest and least problematic of them all.

I have no doubt that, in the more distant future, we'll meet again in some common framework. Insofar as it will depend on me, I shall always be very happy to work with you.

So long,
Yoni

December 22, 1973

Dear Micki and Bibi,

Some time ago I sent you a letter via the parents. I assume you got it, and I view your lack of response as a grave insult to the product of my pen.

My transfer to armor, which should have taken place a week ago, was put off until tomorrow, giving me a few days off. On one of the nights I joined a raid exercise led by one of the officers. It went off okay. My little holiday was a reminder of how comfortable life outside the army is. I've got the time to read again (just now I'm in the middle of *Nuclear War and Nuclear Peace*), sit in an armchair and smoke a pipe leisurely, and run about town.

The fact that I enjoy civilian life shouldn't make you jump to any conclusions. The tone of what I said was nostalgic, to be sure, but it didn't indicate a desire for any change of status. I enjoy my stay in the army and don't have any dark thoughts of quitting. I wrote what I did mainly to tell you, Bibi, that you for your part are acting wisely. It's good that you've resumed your studies and didn't lose any time unnecessarily.

In spite of Geneva,* I'm worried chiefly by the Jews, not by the Arabs, and not even by the superpowers, though they're quite a nasty thorn in our side. The dissension within is what will bring us to grief—unless we can overcome it. It's true some things have changed, but not much. We said this, however, even before the war, so there's nothing much new. We've not sobered up.

January 9, 1974

Dearest Father and Mother,

The year 1974 has started ominously for us. I believe that another war is inevitable. Sooner or later we shall have to take up arms. And if so, better now when Zahal is at the height of its strength and all the reserves are mobilized. It seems, nevertheless, that the war will be delayed and start again under less favorable circumstances.

Incidentally, I was surprised by the election results. It seems that the public was repelled by the Mapai† scandals, and it's a good thing the Ma'arakh‡ was shaken up. I hope they'll be sensible enough to realize that it wasn't just a reaction to their political approach, but also a protest against the way they run the state—educationally, culturally and economically. I doubt they will, though: our political parties are extremely slow to learn from experience. Still, the potential alternative to the Ma'arakh is pretty ineffectual, and we are stuck in the middle—on the one hand we want a change, and on the other we don't see the body that can bring it about.

I've received your latest letters along with the newspaper report containing your assessments, Father. That's exactly how the regional problem should be presented to the world. The report was badly done, of course, and it was obvious to me that (as you said) it offered only a faint echo of your words. Yet if one ignores the poor style, one can't help paying attention to the things said there—and trying to contend with them. It will be difficult, I believe, to refute these arguments.

I am now enrolled in a transfer course to armor. The course is very interesting, and I must say I'm getting to know an entirely new field— a world unto its own.

*The Geneva Four-Power talks on the Middle East.
†The Israel Labor Party that formed every government from 1949 to 1977.
‡The labor coalition.

January 21, 1974

Beloved Mother and Father,

I have free time this evening—and what better way to use it than for writing?

Just now I'm in the middle of the great sandy desert, getting ready to go to sleep. Oddly enough, it rained today, and the tent over my head is dripping. Strong winds blow, which can raise blinding clouds of sand (driven with such force that the grains of sand have blotted out the license plate numbers of a car parked nearby). These sandstorms are followed by rain that damps down the dust for a while, then the wind rises again forming a new sandstorm, and the whole cycle is repeated.

Outside my tent there's a meeting going on: someone from the university has come to talk to a group of reservists. The present situation is certainly tough on mobilized students, not to mention the self-employed; some of the latter are seeing their whole life's work going to pieces— whether it's a business, a factory, or a farm. The problem of the reserves is really severe, and the solutions to date are only partial.

I don't feel like going into political speculations at the moment. But just to put your mind at rest, I'll say that, *militarily* speaking, we weren't hurt too much by the Disengagement Agreement.* Our position is far from perfect, of course, but it isn't all bad either. The value of the agreement depends largely on factors unknown to the public, such as whether we've reached an understanding with the Americans about the next stage of negotiations, and whether this understanding is linked to an unequivocal agreement between them and us, and also on the conditions for future supplies of American arms. I fear we didn't get definite commitments from the Americans on these matters, and I only hope I'm wrong. We might have gotten a better deal from the Egyptians if we'd toughened our stance at the negotiations, but I don't believe that's the decisive point. As a barrier between the two armies, I'd say the present lines are better than what I feared the government would settle for.

Some ten days ago Iddo and I and our girl friends (Daphna and Miri) had dinner together at the Dolphin restaurant. Iddo is really great—such charm and common sense. His Daphna is a truly nice girl, and they seem happy together.

I forgot to tell you that I wrote to Mr. Marquand of Harvard and got a very warm and gracious reply, saying in effect that I can resume my

---

*The first Israeli-Egyptian agreement on Israeli withdrawal to new lines in the aftermath of the Yom Kippur War.

studies at Harvard whenever I want. I only need to let them know four to six weeks in advance. I'm keeping the letter with my other papers.

February 28, 1974

Dear Mother and Father,

In another two weeks I'll be twenty-eight. I just mention it because I suddenly noticed it as I wrote the date at the top of the page. The year 1974 is in full swing.

I'm still in my transfer course to armor. In spite of the limitations shown by armor (especially the tanks) in the last war, there's no doubt that armor is still the major ground force, with great power and potential. What really counts here is the human factor—the men operating the machines, their levelheadedness and sound judgment under fire, their common sense, which must dictate their tactical moves. And there lies our strength—the human factor!

I expect to stay in armor for about a year and a half, and then return to take command of my former unit. At present it seems to me that I *will* return to the unit, but ultimately it will depend only on my decision, and it may be that other considerations will make me decide differently —for example, to stay in armor.

My desire to study hasn't slackened a bit—on the contrary, it has grown stronger, and I do believe that some day I'll find the time for it. Today, of course, it's out of the question—not when everyone is out to get us, "friends" and foes alike. We've only got one country, and we must work hard to keep it ours—so I'm putting off my study plans for the time being.

Incidentally, I feel fine. It's good to be young and to be in our country —living in it and seeing its sights. Last Saturday I had a wonderful walk about Jerusalem—round the city walls in the Jewish Quarter (splendidly restored), the Temple Mount, the City of David, the Antonia citadel, and the ancient wells.

March 1, 1974

(To Bibi and Micki)

Brothers in misery—unite!

I hope you can afford to take some time off from your studies and other pressing affairs to read this letter. To give you the illusion that it's businesslike, I shall proceed to divide it up under headings.

FROM THE YOM KIPPUR WAR

1. (section no. 1) *Wedding*
   a. (sub-section a.) Iddo and Daphna are getting married in a week's time (March 11, 1974), and I'm very glad. Prospects for success—very good, and it's a pleasure to see them together. I've never seen Iddo so open and so happy, and that in itself is a credit to Daphna.
   b. No kidding—she's a delight.
   c. Complaint: How do my brothers manage to find themselves wives like that, while I myself am still on the rove? (More on this subject in section 2, sub-section b.)
   d. In short—they make a *very good* impression together.
   e. The bride is not pregnant (apparently there are still people who fall in love in this day and age. Well, well, and I thought our youth was going to the dogs).

2. *Personal*
   a. I'm apartment-hunting again (this time I'll take a room with a closet).
   b. From this you can gather that I'm still "married to the law."
   c. I'm fine, and well pleased with life (what's left of it—why not?).

3. *Military*
   a. Have finished transfer course—outstanding cadet.
   b. Going to be a company commander for a few months, after which I expect I'll get a battalion. At least, that's what Yanosh and Raful told me explicitly when I saw them last (Yanosh was C.O. of the 7th Brigade in the north; was promoted to Brigadier a short time ago, and made second-in-command of a division in the North. A truly creative spirit).
   c. I assume I'll be serving in the north, but you never know till the last moment (as usual in Zahal).

4. *The Unit*
   Everything's okay, barring the usual complaints. I visit often (when there's time) to get updated.

5. *Miscellaneous* How are you two? Tell me about your studies, about your public activity, about everything.
Much love to the parents.

Yours,
Yoni

Golan Heights
April 3, 1974

Sweet Miri,

Time flies. You look up and it's April already. I haven't been home for nearly four weeks (well, maybe less), and the way things are, it looks as if it'll take some more time before I can come south.

All in all, being here is quite instructive. It turns out that a minor gun and tank war is going on here. Endless shelling and a constant state of alert. Doron has left the area at last (yesterday), and now I breathe alone the dust of tank tracks in this charming country. It is really charming— lots of water, lots of tels, and lots of green. Too bad that above it all there are also lots of shells. We take off our shoes for two hours a day, and shower once in two weeks. But it could be worse.

A strange war, but a war all the same.

Just now a shell dropped in our section (a long, loud boom), and in a minute I'll have to get everybody into the tanks. There goes another boom. Actually, today is comparatively quiet, and there's even time to write a letter (fact!).

The committee's report,* the Chief of Staff, Pompidou, the kidnapping of the two U.N. officers (less than a mile from my company's position) and the other tidbits are all very interesting (we even remember to listen to the news when there's time); but I don't have the strength to go over all that, and you may not feel like reading my thoughts on the subject (oops—another boom). I wonder if people really know what sort of war started up here three weeks ago. A strange business. My biggest worry is that one day a shell will drop on top of the tent that serves as our mess, with everyone inside. For lack of bunkers to sit in and watch TV, everyone sits in the tanks.

Now this boom was a close one. Time to stop and take care of the boys.

Do write, it'll be nice to hear something from home. A month has passed since I received any letter, and this is the first letter I'm sending from here (I attach my military P.O.B.); although I'm used to not getting any mail, it would be nice to get a smile from the big city.

So long,
Yours,
Yoni

*Committee of inquiry into the circumstances of the Yom Kippur War.

April 12, 1974

Dear Tutti,

I'm utterly content just now. A sort of complete self-satisfaction. A precious moment of peace on a late Friday afternoon at half past five in the evening.

It's still light outside, and I'm sitting here on a chair outside the tent, with my tanks in a row in front of me. Behind me there's music coming from the tent, and in my hand a book that I'm idly keeping open with two fingers, without reading it.

The day has passed without serious shelling, and there was even time for a wash under the field-shower. Yesterday a shell dropped right on the mess and razed it to the ground, along with the kitchen shed.

My second-in-command passed me just now with a blissful smile on his face—"Sabbath, ahhh!"

These are moments you'd like to preserve, and I felt the urge to write you a letter.

Soon I'll get on a jeep and set off for home. Exactly a month has passed since I took over the company, and I've only been home once, for twenty-four hours. It's interesting that I don't even feel any urge to get away, and the truth is that I don't quite know where to go. A pity, that. It wouldn't hurt if I had someone to come back to.

Most of the time a rather real war is going on here. Not quite like the wars we've known, but still one can easily do something foolish and pay dearly for it. The company's deployed at a rather critical spot and is doing a very good job.

A few days ago I thought of you for a long time, and felt a stab of pain. It strikes me that whenever I think of you, I remember the times when I gave you sorrow and pain. And again I regret them, and my lack of understanding. Not that I'd be any more understanding today, but things take on a different significance in perspective.

Regards to Avner.*

Yours,
Yoni

*Tutti's second husband.

April 13, 1974

My dear Father and Mother,

On leave today. I'm staying with the new couple in the family, and in a while we're going out to celebrate our meeting with dinner in one of Jerusalem's restaurants.

Iddo and Daphna are very happy, and so am I—happy in their happiness. I'm convinced you'll like Daphna. She's a bright and warmhearted girl, who complements Iddo and is just right for him. I think the prospects are excellent that all will be well in the future.

How about me? Well, nothing new—I have no real girl friend at the moment. My last romance is over, and as I don't have time to run around anyway, it looks as if I'll remain on my own for the time being (all this in response to your request, Mother, to tell you something about my private life). On the whole, I've nothing to complain of. I'm up to my neck in my army work, and during leaves I move about a lot in our lovely land.

The whole world marvels at the Inca and Aztec civilizations and such —and they do indeed deserve admiration. Nevertheless almost all of these came into being after the start of the Christian Era (not that this detracts from their value), whereas here it seems that the cradle of world civilization is all around us, everything dating back thousands and thousands of years. A few Saturdays ago I visited the Biblical Gibeon, and saw the remarkable ancient pool there (I'll take you to see it when you come). It's this pool that's mentioned in II Samuel in connection with Abner ben Ner and Joab ben Zeruiah, who "met together by the pool of Gibeon" and let "the young men arise and play before them." And the country is all like that!

April 19, 1974

Dear Father and Mother,

I am trying to write from time to time. Last Saturday when I was in Jerusalem at Iddo and Daphna's I wrote from there, and even took a few aerogrammes back with me. I hope that a letter going out through the army mail (like this one) won't get held up too long.

The work is hard and tiring. I'm used to these sorts of difficulties, and I've been through much tougher wars. The younger soldiers are learning what shell fire and a minor war mean. It's not so terrible, on the whole. All it needs is a little vigilance. It's clear that the Syrians can't make us budge, and if they should start a war (which they may), they'll be dealt a crushing blow. To be sure, it won't be a walk-over, and we may expect a hard struggle (particularly in the initial stages), but they don't stand a chance.

Meanwhile Israel's government, as you know, has been reshuffled and at last there's hope for some change on the political scene—and any change will be welcome. The public is waking up too, and that's good. It's hard for me to predict what changes will occur, but what counts above all is the shock Mapai got, as well as the fact that new elements like Rabin have taken significant positions in that party.

As I see it, the Labor Party isn't going to hold out much longer.

The army has recovered from the war and gained strength. Armor (where I'm serving now) is undergoing a process of consolidation and reinforcement, and we're stronger now than we were before the last war.

I'm being urged to finish this letter as the outgoing car has already been held up long enough (they're not actually urging me, of course; but I must finish).

I'm waiting eagerly for your arrival here. Even if you come for a brief stay, it will be wonderful. We meet so very rarely that every family gathering is a festive and wonderful event. Besides, you ought to congratulate Iddo and Daphna in person—I'm writing all this as if it's necessary to persuade you to come, when it's perfectly clear that you want to come no less than we want to see you.

April 24, 1974

(To Bibi and Micki)

"Hello Folks!"

How are you? It's ages since I wrote to my family in the Diaspora.

Not a bad war is going on here. The tanks are well, thank God. On the desk in my tent (in the middle of nowhere) a ten-inch splinter is lying. It hit the wood full blast and got stuck fast there (an inch from where I always lean when I'm working). Lucky thing I got up from my chair a minute before. Shellings are common and one gets used to them (that is, as long as nobody's hit, and here everything's still all right, thank God). Two weeks ago a shell dropped right in the middle of my company mess, scattering it in twenty directions. I'm writing this to give you an idea of the kind of war we have here. There's no telling when the next shell will come, and you ought to expect one any moment. As a result, it's a dog's life. My boys live in the tanks—work, sleep and eat in them.

I'm sitting near one of the tels at the southeastern end of the enclave* and breathing the smell of cordite. Now and then our tanks fire, and to good effect as a rule. Mount Hermon is in our hands—and that's very important.

Don't get the idea that all this is depressing. All in all, it's a minor war, and the Syrians will not change a thing by it. It calls for a lot of patience, perseverance and steady nerves—and nothing else.

May 4, 1974

(To Benjamin)

Hi!

This will be a hasty letter. I'm in a great hurry—writing from the Old City on my way up north (Saturday!).

Two weeks ago my Brigade C.O. offered me the command of a battalion in his brigade at the next change of command (in about five months), which rather pleased me. I told him that if a battalion in some other brigade became available before that and was offered to me, I'd probably take it. I talked to D. as well, and he said that even if I do get a battalion in October, the command of the unit will still be kept for me.

In short, yesterday I was called to the Division C.O. and was given the appointed battalion C.O. as of today at 12:00 (that's why I'm in a rush to get up north). The battalion is stationed in the enclave.

May 27, 1974

Dear Bibi and Micki,

I've been battalion commander for nearly a month now. I've carried out a real palace revolution here. When I got the battalion it was falling apart and pretty decrepit (you had to be on the inside to know how bad it was). Anyhow, there are three battalions in this brigade, and mine was fourth in place, slipping into fifth.

To be brief, all of a sudden people got down to it and started working at a normal pace (that is, my pace), and things are looking up. I'm certain they are going to become an excellent battalion, and I don't expect any

*The Israeli enclave deep inside Syria that was captured at the end of the Yom Kippur War.

particular difficulties. In any case, it's an interesting job and, for a change, I'm entirely independent. I'm working hard—with a long-term plan, intermediate aims and immediate objectives. It's the only way to make progress—knowing precisely what you want to achieve. Otherwise you get bogged down in routine and forget what you're really after.

Meanwhile the wars go on here nonstop. (Kirschner, a paratroop battalion C.O., was killed a few days ago in a shelling. Know him? A really nice and decent guy.)

I have no information about Maalot.* I should meet the guys and find out the precise plan of execution and the pre-briefings. But I'm too busy to do it.

May 27, 1974

Beloved Father and Mother,

Some weeks ago I received the command of a tank battalion. A battalion is a sizable force and offers me much greater opportunities to give direction and exert influence. It's rather a flattering appointment, actu-ally. It wouldn't have been so surprising if it had been in infantry, because I'm known there. Armor, however, is an entirely new area for me, and I've had to learn from scratch. The fact that they thought I deserved a battalion pleases me. I still haven't given up the option of returning to my old unit as C.O. (in another year). When it comes to it the decision will be mine alone, and it's clear to me that if I want the job, I'll get it. I'll decide in a few months, when things become concrete. They're trying to press me to give my answer now, but I don't intend to cross bridges before I come to them. After all, the decision depends on a combination of factors, not all of which are yet known to me. I'm in no hurry.

Meanwhile the war goes on here, even though we're on the verge of a disengagement agreement. That's what it looks like, anyway. Today there's still shooting and people are hit. A daily occurrence.

Though it may not be popular at your end, I personally don't view the disengagement on the Golan as a great disaster. At least, not from the *military* point of view. The territory we're giving up is territory that we can afford to give up, and the army needs time to reorganize. True, the Syrians need the time, too, but they lost less in the war (relative to their

---

*The massacre at Maalot, in northern Galilee, of twenty-seven young boys and girls taken hostage, with many others, by PLO terrorists. The massacre took place during a rescue operation by the Israeli army.

manpower). Politically speaking we do lose a lot. But you can't separate one thing from the other and concentrate on one aspect alone. On the whole, this disengagement isn't so bad.

August 27, 1974

(To Colonel Yosi Ben-Hanan* and his wife)

Dear Yosi and Nati,

I felt a sudden urge to drop in on you tonight and say hello—a sure sign you've already been gone a long time.

Hope you've managed to get acclimatized to greater America, and have found that normal people live there too, besides all the usual nuts.

We here are busy, as always, preparing for the next round. Training intensively and getting results that aren't bad at all.

The battalion is fast becoming number 1 in the brigade. The fact is, the competition isn't very tough—which is a pity. Anyhow, I'm very happy with the battalion. It's getting better from week to week. But there's still plenty to do. As a result of the war and its aftermath, and particularly the very incompetent leadership of my predecessor on the job, I wasn't even at square one when I started. But we've long since closed the gap and moved on.

Nothing much has changed in the brigade, as you can probably imagine. You know the people there better than I do. Too bad you aren't here.

There isn't much "civilian" news. Girls come and go and there's nothing steady in sight, but as I don't intend to get married so young (the way you two did), it doesn't bother me. Actually, even if it *did* bother me, it wouldn't help as I haven't a moment to call my own. Hard life.

It'd be nice to hear from you occasionally.

Yours,
Yoni

October 26, 1974

Dear Father and Mother,

It's already six months since I got this armored battalion, and I feel as if I hadn't even started to work. We've reached a point where the battalion is universally recognized as number one in the brigade, and perhaps

*The wounded tank officer whom Yoni rescued in the Yom Kippur War.

even the best in the whole Golan Heights. But from there to the goals I have set for myself as regards the quality of men and training, the distance is still great.

The Israeli government goes on as before, committing follies and dabbling in party politics and in scandals (chasing off settlers, etc.), while time is running out and things should be corrected before everything's ruined and it's too late to do anything about it.

Iddo has pepped up also in the political sphere, and it's a pleasure to be in his and Daphna's company. I went with them to see the demonstration against Kissinger that was held in Jerusalem—and I really became encouraged. A crowd of thousands (20,000 in my estimate) gathered before the Prime Minister's Office Building. It was a respectable, serious and intelligent group of people. The reporters, of course, tried to minimize the crowd's number, but to no avail. There was a similar public gathering, which I didn't see, in Tel Aviv, and there too many came. There are people here to work with—that's certain—but they must be led properly.

November 3, 1974

My very dear Bibi and Micki,

I feel profoundly apprehensive about the future of the Jewish State. Shedding illusions, I see that the process aimed at annihilating us is gathering momentum and the noose is tightening. It won't be a rapid process, though our strength will diminish from one war to the next. There's a chance (just a chance) that we may come out of it whole, if we can manage to drag it out for a few additional decades.

Meanwhile I'm in the army, and fairly convinced that—at least for the present—I'm doing the most I can to lengthen our thread of life, or prevent its premature severance.

A tank battalion is a very serious business. As time goes on, I discover more and more the awesome power and maneuverability a tank force possesses. From the army's point of view, I'm doing very well. This battalion is now recognized as number one in the brigade, and according to many, in the Golan Heights. This is just the beginning. I still have six months to improve matters, and there's a lot to be done.

From a personal point of view—i.e., girls—not much has changed. A. I've no time. B.? In fact, there is no B.

Just now I'm going out with a nice girl, but as I've only just got to know her, there's no telling how things will develop.

November 11, 1974

(To Bruria)

Did you really telephone me yesterday, or is it just my imagination? I woke up this morning with a feeling of having talked to you, and yet—I'm not sure. I remember the conversation in detail, but I don't remember if it actually took place. It's unusual for me, for generally I remember things as they are.

I miss you.

Found me a nice time to love a woman! Tough.

The weather is still good—looks as if winter is reluctant to come. At night the trees outside my room go wild and seem to whistle in the wind.

November 17, 1974

(To Bruria)

My faraway girl,

This will be a brief little note, because it's very late and I'm tired, and tomorrow (today, actually) I have to get up at five in the morning.

Z.'s bunch worry and annoy me. They don't work the way I want, and the results are unsatisfactory. That, and a lot of other things, make me feel like giving them a good jolt that might force them to shape up—and it's the same in nearly every area of the battalion's activity.

In the last analysis, it's all to the good, because as a result of all this, everyone will buckle down to work. Not that they don't work now, but—

Wow! A flash of lightning just lit up the whole room, followed by thunder and more rain. I'm lying in bed with my notebook propped up against a book. I miss you very much.

How are you? I forgot—had a letter from you today, and I'm keeping it for another reading before I drift into sleep.

Golan Heights
November 11, 1974

(To Bruria)

Half past six on this Friday evening. Outside, the usual marvellous wind storming through the trees nearby, and me relaxing alone in my room, sitting on the bed with my back to the wall—and writing. The radio is playing beautiful music, and I'm smoking an awful cigar that I bought on the way up here, and I'm wearing a track suit and enjoying life—alone in the room, yet not alone.

The wind outside—I can never have enough of it! I love to walk hunched up into the wind, pulling hard against it; or stride with growing speed and feel my ballooning jacket blast at my back. It stirs contradictory emotions in me, such as the pleasure of being snug in a room with the wind whistling outside, and just the opposite—a sense of adventure, danger and storm. It also reminds me of things gone by, which I did during my previous stint in the army.

You wrote about *American Graffiti* and the thoughts this film aroused in you. I believe that in every generation people fall back on the past. It's not because the past was more peaceful, more serene, but because time makes us forget things and allows us to view them through rose-colored glasses, so that everything looks rosy and doesn't hurt the eyes.

The Last Picture Show doesn't hark back to a better time either. On the contrary, they deliberately chose a difficult period—a time of scarcity, violence, world war—and in the context of that period a number of special people were chosen, with an inner beauty and special souls. These people are the whole point of the film. I'm not moved or impressed by the period it portrays, but rather by the people who rose above their surroundings.

When I was young I used to like William Saroyan's books (I still do). A wonderful, simple writer, who loves people and shows them in a special light. In one of his books *(The Human Comedy)* he describes a boy called Homer to whom I was especially drawn. A fascinating boy, inquisitive, intelligent, fearless, whose childish eyes can see through the adult world. Aware and still unaware of the suffering in the world, he sees the bad in it but isn't scarred himself and matures together with the world. There, too, the world is at war, and the town, Ithaca, loses the best of its sons and goes on living with the same inner rhythm it always had, and the world outside only serves to light up the town in all its beauty. The contrast between the characters and the world around them is essential to make us see them in all their strength and uniqueness.

Beyond all this, it is true: we are all searching for "a different place—a beautiful and glowing place—a place worth waking up in." Maybe that's why I'm so fond of those lines. I love to walk in the streets watching the children, to whistle down sidewalks and gaze at mountain scenes or sprawling lawns. The world is truly full of beauty, and the ugliness in it only highlights the beauty. If it weren't for what is ugly, we might not notice the good and the beautiful. But that's a philosophical reflection and oversimplified at that. Maybe we shouldn't look for meanings beyond ourselves. I believe that the force that propels our lives also embodies their purpose. Anyone who believes there's another purpose is welcome to it —the main thing is not to live aimlessly. Those who have nothing to hold on to are always discontented, always find idols for themselves and always abandon them for new ones. They're lucky in having an idol when they do, and unlucky in not having "long-term satisfaction"—something that idols cannot provide.

I started writing this morning, and suddenly I see it's time for the reconnaissance patrol I've scheduled. It's still morning, and all the officers are outside with their vehicles waiting—and it's too bad because I wanted to go on. Maybe later.

November 23, 1974

(To Yosi Ben-Hanan and his wife)
To the Ben-Hanans, Greetings!

Things are acting up here in Israel. Actually you don't need a "Voice from Jerusalem" to tell you that. As far as I remember, it's the other way round. From the outside things always look worse than they are.

The military side of it doesn't worry me—as far as that goes, we'll beat them soundly. We've achieved a good, in parts even a very good, operational level. Much work has been done on inter-force and inter-branch coordination, and there are good results. We've applied many of the lessons of the war, which have been well absorbed by the soldiers. All in all we're on the right track. What does worry me is the economic and political situation, which is going from bad to worse. It doesn't look as if anyone here sees a way out of the mess we're in. They live from day to day, from one fund-raising campaign to another, from one Kissinger visit to the next. But enough of that.

I was glad to get your letter. I put it aside to answer as soon as I had a free moment—and as always happens, free moments keep getting put off.

Although I have a good battalion with a high level of performance, and officers and men I can rely on, there's still plenty of work before us (it never ends, in fact). As usual, I display dissatisfaction and continue to apply pressure, even though there's no more competition. We've left the others behind—but that's not what counts. We are still a long way from the ultimate standard, and many things need improvement. The more intermediate objectives the battalion achieves, the greater the demands made on it.

Write something about yourselves. What does the Diaspora look like? Above all, I'm curious about the American army—how professional is it? Which of its methods can we adopt for our own use? How prepared is it for military intervention in the world? What is their thinking about the Middle East? In short—write!

So long,
Yoni

December 7, 1974

(To Bruria)
Hello!

Yesterday I fell asleep early. It's morning now—raining, and everything has slowed down. I've no patience with this rain; I need another two weeks of sun. Z. is making good progress and his boys are becoming men after my own heart—but we need more time to get into really good shape. On top of that we have to finish attending to the tanks—we started off well, and then, for lack of choice, I had to slacken the pace. Work goes on, but with constraints. What else? The camp isn't finished yet—they've started tarring roads; no stoves and no electricity—and the work that was begun has stopped.

I've noticed that when my officers come to me with problems resulting from rain, I announce firmly: "Tomorrow it won't rain!" And I mean it too, as if the matter can be determined by sheer will power. When I realized this I started to laugh inside—because that's just what Joshua said: "Sun, stand thou still upon Gibeon, and thou, Moon, in the valley of Ajalon." I suppose he too meant it—that Nature obey him. Ah well, if you can't change the weather, at least you can fight it, or at any rate adapt to it and do your best.

I can hardly bear it when people stay inside in their (cold) rooms when there's work to be done—even when it's pouring outside. I got Z. out on an exercise in driving rain and heavy fog, because I consider it of vital importance, and an opening for interesting possibilities; at the same time I wanted to knock out of him and his men this pampered behavior so typical of our soldier: "It's raining and there's no visibility." I slogged along with him in the rain for three hours, and I hope that, apart from the lessons of the exercise, they also got the "de-pampering" message. I have the impression they did.

As a battalion commander in the Armored Corps, 1975

(To Bruria)

Hello,

This morning I gave Laor and Lior the "Carmel"* to go to Haifa with Yosi,† and on the way they had an accident. Laor is all right, but Lior is injured (slightly) and in the hospital—by the way, he's an excellent Intelligence officer; Yosi is bruised all over, but he's back here, and as for the "Carmel"—it's curtains. This battalion C.O. isn't lucky with "Carmels"; but never mind—I've already gotten used to jeeps.

Yosi showed up pale and upset to explain how it happened (in fact, the accident wasn't his fault). To cut it short, I calmed him down, and reminded him I'd always said that in the final analysis only the jeep is important. I told him to take a week off. He can hardly move, and I'm sorry he feels so bad about it.

It's raining on and off here, and there's a thick fog. Today I was driving about twenty yards behind another car's taillights (at high noon), and only after half a mile did I discover that I was following a bus. This murk turns day into night—something like the "fog and filthy air" of Shakespeare's three witches.

Since the Beth-Shean incident‡ I've been positively bitter—that's bad, of course, but it really exasperates me. On the one hand, you have the naïve Israelis who refuse to see things as they are and to accept the fact that war is apparently unavoidable; and on the other hand, you have a bunch of hotheads with a mob mentality who put on a lynch act and show the ugly side, some of which has apparently stuck to all of us. When it comes down to it, they represent me, too; they are part of the same body to which I belong. So how can I help feeling bitter?

This is such a choppy letter that there's hardly any connection between one paragraph and the next. Actually each of them is like a new letter, because I've been constantly interrupted in my writing.

---

*C.O.'s car.
†Yoni's driver.
‡After a terrorist attack on Beth-Shean, in which four Jewish civilians were brutally murdered, some local residents burnt the bodies of the terrorists killed by an Israeli army unit.

December 16, 1974

Brur my own,

I still can't let myself go in letters. Nor face to face either, actually. But I want you to know that when I say "I love you" I am expressing my whole self.

Don't lend too much weight to words when it comes to conveying emotions—at least not as far as I'm concerned. Perhaps it will come with time.

No doubt there has been a significant change in my ability to open up to another person. It amazes me and, viewed dispassionately, intrigues and even charms me; and I love you (I was going to add parenthetically: "no connection with the preceding sentence," but of course that isn't true—everything's connected).

You wrote that I love in another way—different, you meant—and I wonder if you know that for sure. Maybe I only express my love in a different way. It's true there are degrees of love—but how do you know where each of us stands on the scale? I don't. I do know that I love you very, very much.

Last night I worked till dawn, slept a bit and at 06:30 conducted a meeting. Now it's 08:00 and I'm going up the Hermon. The jeep and the men are waiting outside, but I feel I don't want to part with you. So I'm not—come, join me.

(To Bruria)

Child of mine,

That's what you are now—a child. Both a child, and very much mine. And I want to take you in my arms and soothe you, and tell you that everything will be all right, and that there will be endless moments of happiness, and each moment will be full of interest and excitement, and that it'll all be idyllic or stormy, with lightning and fire; that everything will be like the burning bush, going up in fire and not consumed.

But I can't say that that's how it will be, or promise things that are beyond my control. Promises can be made in play, or in fantasy, and sometimes out of a faith that needs no basis in reality; because that's the nature of faith. But we are human, some of us good, some bad, and generally both good and bad; some happy with our lot and in tune with the world, some searching and searching. I don't know which category I belong to, because I've never bothered to think about it much—and you no doubt think that's wrong, and perhaps you're right (but I don't think about it because there are other things that are on my mind).

So I can't promise that there won't be any more days like the ones last week; and I don't pretend, because I'm too busy with the life I'm passing through, and I don't need any other place. And you know as well as I do that there can be good days and bad, full or empty, and the only thing that can change our momentary state of mind is our *general* state of mind, which guides us through life.

Perhaps I am partly to blame for the dark moods that come over you. I don't think my share is very large. Maybe it is, but I don't think so. Maybe it's your work, or perhaps your leaving home, and all your expectations not coming true as you had imagined and dreamed and prayed for. Enthusiasm and imagination soaring to the skies are the gods of youth, and I want to believe that in you they are eternal. I want to believe it, first, because youth becomes you; and second, because if you should ever lose them, your sense of loss will be unbearable, and I, who love you so, will grieve with you.

We are made differently, you and I. I live my life intensely, and most of the time I'm happy in this world of ours. There are many things I would like to do, but I'm so absorbed in whatever I *am* doing that I generally forget to think of the other things.

I don't regret the crossroads I've passed. Once past the crossing, I'm on my own way. And if there is more beauty, more flowers along the road I didn't take, I still don't regret it, because it wasn't my road. My path will pass through fertile fields and lovely gardens, and over mountains and rocks and even deserts, but in all its twists it will be the one path—known and yet mysterious. Our life is a world unto itself within many others— for the roads are numberless. Some intersect while others pass through planes that will never touch. And all the roads are traveled by people, and sometimes they meet at the crossroads, and sometimes continue together, and sometimes part again and sometimes not. And it isn't just a matter of direction, but of time as well. And why be so interested in other planes, when we can hardly master our own?

I'm happy, then, and unhappy, like everybody else, but more happy than unhappy. Because I don't care so much "where I stand"—except where it concerns my current work. And I don't care whether I can count on a future assignment (by way of a "safe job"), and it doesn't bother me whether I have money or not, or how much I'll need to save, and there are still other things that I don't care about either.

I feel I'm beginning to lose the thread; well, I won't explain myself, I'll leave what I've written as it stands.

My company commanders have just returned from a reconnaissance patrol and I've debriefed them one by one, and everything's okay.

I've also reread what I wrote and realized that this is a confused letter, skipping from one subject to another and not explaining properly what I meant to say, and not very characteristic of me either.

(To Bruria)

I told you that I had lost my innocence and my blind faith in the eternity of love. And that's a pity—truly a pity, because I *want* to believe in it with my whole being. If I'm skeptical, it's not about now, but about the distant future. We are separated for too long at a time for us to be bound together forever. There's something hopeless and very sad about this feeling. You asked me about a child, and I said what I did because I'm not thinking that far ahead—because a child is the most wonderful creation and the final bond between a man and a woman (at least, that's how I see it, or let's say, that's how it should be and how I'd want it to be). And I'm not thinking that far ahead because I'm not convinced it's eternal. I only wish I *could* free myself of this doubt.

It's dark already, and I have to strain my eyes to see; there's no electricity, and I have to hold the page to what little light comes in through the window.

There, I lit the candles.

When we were talking yesterday, I said it bothers me that other people are with you—and I'm not. I'm not "jealous" of those others, because they can't take you away from me—not in the usual sense, as between man and woman. But I *am* jealous that they can be with you for hours on end. Because what can separate us is not this or that friend of yours, but all of them together, and the life that flows and renews itself around you, and the changes in yourself—and all at a distance from me, without me taking any active part in it.

Work in the army has one single purpose and it leads in one single direction, but outside the army the range of possibilities is vast—which is as it should be. There's always the chance that you might take a direction that I wouldn't be able to take with you (not that I can picture it, but anything can happen), and if that should happen, what then . . . ? (What really? At least it's certain that we'll go on living our lives, each at his own inner pace.)

And maybe none of this will happen. I imagine you starting to tell me that the world around you won't part us and that I've no cause to worry about it, and I want to believe—believe with all my heart—that that's how it will be; but—as I've said before—I've lost that wonderful innocence and blind faith, and doubt has crept in—the feeling that anything's possible, nothing's forever. My God, how I wish I was free of it!

December 19, 1974

(To Bruria)

I told you once that perhaps the most wonderful period of my life (that's how I remember it) was my childhood—when I lived in Talpiot and wandered through fields with anemones and turtles and ladybirds, with an ancient grove of woods and a tumbledown synagogue, with endless inner joy and with wide-open eyes, believing in everything, with a faith that all was perfect.

There have been other wonderful, exciting, intense and enchanted times in my life. The war, for instance, or the time after the Six-Day War when I was in the hospital, or the summer of '73 when I was studying in the States, or border crossings and various operations, or a woman's love —and I love you so very much.

And generally I am happy, or at least not unhappy (not always), I get on well with myself and with the world I happen to live in (though that isn't always the case).

January 8, 1975

Brur mine,

I'm not removing your flowers from my desk, because they belong to us, because they came from you, because I see them and remember. Remember and feel a lump in my throat—because you're not here. I love you so.

I believe that one of the differences between us, between our ways of loving, is that your love depends on events and has ups and downs—steep ones, sometimes—whereas mine doesn't have any downs. My love ascends the slopes of a mountain range (long, with intermediate peaks).

What I write is true, except that it suddenly occurred to me that while I generally don't have downs—perhaps because I don't let myself slip downhill when love declines—I do sometimes have a sudden break—a sort of drastic fall. And then, as a rule, I don't let it last.

I don't know why I'm writing this to you, as you may misinterpret it.

I'm writing it because that is what's on my mind at this moment, and it may not even be right or accurate—but no matter. I don't believe it will happen to me either. I have a feeling that if we should part, it'll be because your strength will fail, because you'll feel yourself constrained because of me (not *by* me—because of me), because you'll start loving from afar. But I also have a feeling that we won't part (at least, not for the next twenty years, as you said when you were here on Saturday—Up! —but you spoke differently yesterday on the phone—Down!). The answer is in God's hands. Actually, to a large extent, in our hands too.

I've just reread what I wrote, and I noticed something. I wrote "no matter" about something that may possibly matter very much. And I wrote this because, besides everything else, I believe in words and clarifications only up to a certain point. In the sphere of emotions—when inner awareness, feelings and senses are there in all their certainty—there's no need to try to put them into words. It nearly always diminishes their intensity. That's why I wrote "no matter." Because the sentence didn't convey what I feel and what is beyond words.

Real love doesn't end, it always remains—a sea. Calm or rough, rippling or rolling, heaving or warming in the sun—but always a sea. Why then did I write that I sometimes reach a break, a drastic fall? Apparently I didn't really love on any of the occasions I remember now. I thought I was in a sea, but actually I was in a lake, or a pool, and sometimes maybe just a puddle.

When I wrote that love is infinite, I didn't forget that in a way it is finite and ends in death. But I still wrote "infinite" because in another way it doesn't end in death. It exists as an absolute value, and the moment it appears a new spirit is born, hovering somewhere in the universe.

And sometimes, as years pass and circumstances change, new real loves appear, and when that happens, there are bodies that can contain two such love-spirits, and there are others that are completely filled with the newborn entity. Such bodies have no room for two or three or more love-spirits, and then the old ones hover, peerless, in infinite space—but still continue to exist.

January 12, 1975

Dear and beloved Mother and Father,

Another year has come. Day follows day, and every day I miss you more, and we remain scattered and divided by a great ocean. And every day brings its own demands of work and effort, and there's no relief, no brief respite to write and put into words what is clear above all—that we are together in spite of everything.

Nearly eleven years have passed since I left home for the army, and I am seized by a longing for family togetherness. How little all of us—sons and parents—have managed to be together during those years. Changing circumstances drag each of us along the swift-moving current of life, and the result is a longing for tranquil moments, for moments of "before it all started," unburdened moments, free of the strains and stresses of every day. It seems that moments like these wouldn't stand the test of reality, because even as children we were busy with the endless game of surmounting the various stages of growing up, and you parents with the many problems of parents in the adult world.

I feel overcome by a very real nostalgia this drizzly morning. I look back in longing on breakfasts in the kitchen with you and Bibi and Iddo when we were in our teens, or—plunging even deeper into the past—on Passover nights with old Klausner in Talpiot, or the lighting of the Hanukkah candelabra and the singing of *Maoz Zur,* or Friday night dinners with the candles and Kiddush blessing in the house on Haportzim Street (how I used to love that, and what a pity we didn't go on with it through the years), or . . . and the images flit and pass before my eyes, pass one after another and are stored up in my mind.

At this moment I halt the frantic rush forward, the need to get work finished in time, stop thinking of the situation the country's in, all that still needs to be accomplished, the mad race to be doing and doing, the time "running out," everything. I stop and admit openly—at this moment I want my life in Talpiot again, the fields with the ladybirds, the anemones, the house with the barred windows and the mysterious courtyard with the shed at the corner, and Berkowitz's chicken coop next door, and mad Joshua's yard.

It's a world of its own—full and complete—the world of an enchanted child.

And look, even this plunge into the past, into the warmth of a loving family, into the enchantment of youth, isn't possible today except for one brief moment.

It's morning now, and time is pressing as ever, and the road is long.

Don't worry about me. I often see Iddo and Daphna, and I'm well. It's all right.

Your very loving
Yoni

January 15, 1975

Brur mine,

I forgot to tell you that yesterday, in the early hours of a cold morning, I was driving fast across the terrain and all the fields were covered with the glittering white of frost, and all the puddles by the roadside bore a thin coating of ice, and the rising sun cast its light over it all, and it reflected a cool, yellow radiance—and I was in the fairy tale of reality.

I'm finding it almost impossible to stop thinking of you, and not just in those hours when I'm not under pressure. You are constantly with me.

I remember that what I was about to write next was something like: it's midday now, and I want to talk to you—well then, I'm going to phone you.

Instead I gave an alert exercise to one of the companies and made them sweat a bit. It went fairly well. I had some doubts about the ability of *all* the tanks to move *instantly* on getting the order—and I feel easier about that now. Everything's okay.

Yes, and phoning you now is out, too, because according to the time table I've set, I must go to Z. to check if they've corrected the faults I found at my inspection there yesterday.

And so into the night, out of afternoon minutes.

Yours,
Yoni

January 25, 1975

(To his parents)

Hallo!

I'm in high spirits. Nothing special has happened—just a Saturday in Jerusalem, and I'm happy. I was surprised to hear that you're "worried," Mother, that your eldest isn't married yet. In the first place, it doesn't suit you to worry about things like that; in the second, I've had one go at it, and I'm in no hurry now (not putting it off either, just not rushing headlong into anything). Besides, I have a nice girl friend who lives in Petah-Tikva, and as I'm weak on relating anything that concerns personal subjects, I know I won't manage to enlarge on it, but really, everything's fine and there's nothing to worry about.

My work, as usual, is plentiful and leaves me very little free time, but it absorbs me, and as I'm aware of its importance, it satisfies me as well. As for what will follow—I haven't made up my mind definitely yet, but as I still have a few months to go in my present job, I can afford not to worry about it now.

January 25, 1975

(To Benjamin and Micki)

Hi, folks!

I finally got to Jerusalem ("after two thousand years of exile") and found a pile of letters—even one from you. Now, that's something. So I settle behind the desk (Father's desk that used to be in his study at Haportzim Street) and write. What about, though? Politics? The army? Don't feel like it . . . so I'll write a bit about myself beyond the usual accepted pattern.

I was a bit concerned to learn today from one of Mother's letters that she's worried about her eldest not being married yet. A tough situation. Actually I've no definite or concrete plans on the subject; but everything is okay. In general, if there were no wars, and there was no need to do so much work in so little time—the world would be a much nicer place to live in.

I'm delighted to hear that you two are hitting it off; very glad you're moving along in your studies, and most important, trying to do your share to save the country.* A pity I'm not with you—I suppose it'd have thawed out my usual restraint with people and made me try to do something, too, in that direction.

All's well in the army—the work's going well and the battalion is ready for war. Not that there's an end to it—it's a bottomless pit, and you never know where the blow will come from (in military terms, of course). So you stay on your toes, and that's that.

Yours,

Yoni

P.S. Last time I was in Jerusalem a month ago, Iddo had a mustache. Now it's gone. Apart from that there's nothing new with the young couple —an ideal model of marital bliss.

*The reference is to an informational campaign carried on by Benjamin and his friends in Boston, and to conversations with key public figures in America, in which Professor Netanyahu was also involved.

February 1, 1975

(To Bruria)

It's five hours since we talked this morning, and the dust carried by the wind drifts grey in the thin drizzle that disappears and comes back in sprays with every returning gust.

I was sad when I talked to you. Now the sadness has faded a little, and it's remote—hovering, touching but not quite touching. I feel a special sort of sadness when I'm with you, yet not entirely with you; for instance, when we're talking on the phone.

After a while I rang up Tutti and told her I was in the army and was sad—because I wanted to be with you. And she was very surprised, because I'd never told her that there were times when I had found it hard in the army. Perhaps I didn't have it so hard in the past, because by now I've been in the army for so many years, and lately I've begun to miss the tension and the interest that I used to feel in the earlier period. Still, I sometimes had bad stretches even then, but I never told her anything about them.

I remember a few years ago, there was a whole month of nothing but border crossings, and on three consecutive occasions I had encounters with Arabs (very deep inside their territory), and on one of them I killed a man, for the first time at such close range—about two feet—and I emptied an entire clip of bullets into him till he stopped twitching and died. And each time, when I came home, I wouldn't tell her about it, just hold her tighter each time. It was hard then.

To kill at such very close range isn't like aiming a gun from a hundred yards away and pulling the trigger—that's something I had already done when I was young. I've learned since how to kill at close range too—to the point of pressing the muzzle against the flesh and pulling the trigger for a single bullet to be released and kill accurately, the body muffling the sound of the shot. It adds a whole dimension of sadness to a man's being. Not a momentary, transient sadness, but something that sinks in and is forgotten, yet is there and endures.

At one of our first meetings I said to you that I am not shy or afraid of revealing myself; and this is so because I'm not bothered by what people will think of me—except that I never felt the need to do it. And you have awakened that need. Not the need to *express*, but the need to *share*, the need for *you* to know how things are with me, the need to reveal my inner being to you so that you can feel me—and with me.

I've read over what I've written up to here, and I want to go on to another subject.

It's not that I'm "fed up" with my army work; it isn't that at all. I'm working in the same manner and at the same pace and with the same standards as always, yet I find that my interest is diminishing. There's no novelty, no suspense, nor the sense of adventure that comes with danger. There's a system here that requires a tremendous investment of work, in order to preserve what we've achieved so far and to improve it further in order to win the war, in order to prevent the world from annihilating us. That's important, in that I believe. Yet personally the job holds no more novelties for me, and I'm already starting my tenth month as a battalion C.O. and could carry on with it for a long time still, but . . . and there is a but. And one of the "buts" is that I miss you.

The sun has come out now and the wind has scattered the clouds.

February 3, 1975

(To Benjamin and Micki)

My dear family,

Bibi, how did you guess what I had in mind when you sent me that Harvard catalogue? There's a chance I may get to the U.S. for the *summer course* plus *one term*. Here's how it'll work out: I may get the command of the unit next winter instead of this summer. I haven't yet given a positive reply on my candidacy for next winter (around January), but I haven't rejected it either. If I do take it, I could study this summer and fall, and push on to my B.A. As a matter of fact, that's what appeals to me most in this whole switchover.

Armor is an interesting area. Infantry has nothing to match it in sheer power, and its maneuvering ability is impressive. It's good to be familiar with both—the two elements making up today's land warfare.

My battalion is considered Number 1 in the division—and that's not my invention. In all modesty, it really is a fine battalion. As usual, I hasten to add that there's still much to improve, and that the job never ends. But I've been a battalion C.O. for ten months now (time flies), and my term will soon be over. I may carry on a bit beyond the usual year, but not too long. I still don't know what lies ahead for me in armor, but I assume it will be second-in-command of a brigade or some corresponding position. If I only get to the unit by winter, it'll take some three years before I come back to armor. That's a long time, and if I spent it in armor I'd manage to advance quite a bit.

Still, I'm not after promotion. If I don't stay on in armor, I can manage both to study and to be in the unit, and the unit still interests me in spite of everything. It's still an open question, but the ray of light in the whole thing is the chance to study and to rest.

No need for me to write in detail about what's going on in the country. It's common knowledge. We're being sold out. See you in the next war.

Maybe there won't be a war so soon: why should the Arabs fight if they're going to get it all for nothing?

We're all delighted to hear that you are working so hard for our common cause—our survival. I was pleased to learn of your successes. I'd like to hear more about your public activity, which is very important.

I got a letter from Father about a week ago, written in reply to a nostalgic letter I wrote to them. I was merely raking up childhood memories and they started to come in a flood. As a result, Father apparently got the idea that he'd neglected us, as it were. I'll write and try to explain to him that no harm's been done, the three of us turned out okay, sound as a bell and well brought up. Try to set their minds at rest, because it seems that, without meaning to, I wrote things that upset them, whereas actually I was just being nostalgic for days gone by.

A sign I'm growing old.

I was at Haportzim Street a few days ago, wandering about the yard. I told Bruria this was where I used to play tag, and I suddenly realized —and added—that this was twenty years ago. What do you know!

We move through time at a frantic pace, and we imagine it's time that's running away from us. It amazes me—the time dimension in its bearing upon our life's purpose.

Iddo and Daphna are, as ever, a wonderful couple. Iddo is studying rather hard (as far as I can see), is doing well at his studies and—I'm glad to say—is enjoying them too. Daphna is as delightful as ever. Seeing these two makes you smile with pleasure.

February 25, 1975

Brur mine,

It's evening now, and there's no electricity, and I'm "a worried commander." I discovered today that I have one platoon commander who isn't doing his job properly, and I'm beginning to have doubts about him.

You have no idea how much this troubles me. Every officer is absolutely precious, and I wonder how this one happened to slip through my fingers. Some extenuating circumstances exist that may explain his shocking unfamiliarity with the terrain (quite a few circumstances, in fact), and yet . . . I'm uneasy.

The fault can be corrected, of course, and fairly easily too, but once again I realize that I must attend to these things personally and constantly keep up the pressure, that it's not enough to keep control from above and hand out detailed instructions. There's no way of verifying things all the way except by personal intervention. And as that's no news to me, I'm all the more troubled that I didn't deal with this officer before.

I'm writing by candlelight. Romantic but not practical.

Tonight I was giving a topography lesson to all the tank commanders, and the light kept going out every fifteen minutes, till finally it went out for good. Afterwards the entire camp was in darkness, and now I've a whole battery of Hanukkah candles of various heights here, their light reflected in the glass-topped table.

I miss you, but right now I can't keep my thoughts of you separate from the problems of my job. It's always the same when I'm troubled: I won't manage to free myself of the problem until I've solved it, and till then I'll keep coming back to it again and again.

Just now, for instance, I want it to be tomorrow, to be daylight, so I can continue to put pressure on the system and get it to cope with the issue.

I'm telling you all this because I want to share with you some of the things that are on my mind. I'm telling you what's wrong, not what's right. Because right is the general state of things.

Yet even in this general state of "rightness," I always find things that need correcting, so as to keep me from resting on my laurels.

March 25, 1975

Bruria mine,

Tomorrow is Passover.

I've always thought it the most wonderful of all our holidays. It's an ancient celebration of freedom—a thousands-of-years-old liberty. When I sail back over the seas of our history, I pass through long years of suffering, of oppression, of massacres, of ghettos, of banishments, of humiliation; many years that, in a historical perspective, seem devoid of any ray of light—yet it isn't so. For the fact that the idea of freedom remained, that the hope persisted, that the flame of liberty continued to burn through the observance of this ancient festival, is to me testimony of the eternity of the striving for freedom and the idea of freedom in Israel.

In this search through our past we come upon other periods—of tranquillity and liberty, when we were the People of the Land as well as the People of the Book. Yet even then Passover was celebrated with the same ardor, for freedom is precious and its remembrance, long.

And there were other periods—of transition from bondage to liberty, periods of rising and revolt—and it is of those that Passover reminds me most of all. When I say Passover—the Feast of Freedom—I think at once of the Hasmonaeans and the Bar-Kokhba Revolt and the Exodus and Joshua's conquest of the Land.

Of course then, too—as in our times—there were many shameful periods in our history, for which we can only blame ourselves, but that's beside the point.

I also have a special feeling about Passover because of the Seder, which for me, as for all of us, stirs up personal memories of the past. I clearly remember one Seder in Talpiot, in Jerusalem, when I was six. Among the guests were white-bearded old men like Rabbi Binyamin and Professor Klausner, and my father was there too, and others I don't remember, and there was a big table and much light, and I was in a completely perfect world, and I kept absorbing it and absorbing it. Storing up impressions of a great and beautiful world with myself in it—taking it in, as it were, to sort it all out in adulthood—yet today I know it wasn't in order to sort it out, but to treasure it that I took it all in.

Last year I celebrated Seder with my men in a big tent near a tel in the Syrian enclave that was being shelled, and that too was a wonderful Seder in its way.

My yearning for the past mingles with my longing for you, and because of you I find myself in my past, and find the time and the desire to reminisce in order to share my life with you. Yet by "past" I mean not only my own past, but the way in which I see myself as an inseparable part, a link in the chain of our existence and Israel's independence.

(March 1975)

My Bruria,

We had a fine Seder at the battalion. I talked about the uniqueness of the Feast of Freedom and its significance, and after the Seder the religious soldiers danced with much stamping of feet, while many of the others, who hadn't slept for some forty hours, went to bed. Oh yes—the mess hall looked wonderful, and there were lots of wild flowers, which the girls had picked after some urging on my part, and afterwards the company C.O.'s organized a sort of party in my office with some of the office girls —and it was fun; and Z. got a bit drunk in an endearing way. And the girl officers turned up at the end of the Seder to "say hello to our girls," as they put it, and I had to make an effort to get them off my hands and see to it that one of the company C.O.'s took them under his wing and finally drove them safely back. I'm amused by this sort of thing, but I don't really feel up to it—I must be getting old.

Suddenly I begin to feel very lonely. To be alone all day and in the evening to sit by myself in the room and share my solitude with you— it's a bit lonely. I'm alone all day because even when I'm working with other people, I'm always by myself. On the other hand, when I'm with you—I'm with you.

April 15, 1975

(To Benjamin)

Hi!

Independence Day!

I'm at the Hadera post office and at last have the chance to tell you that I'm alive and that I read every word you write to your poor family in Jerusalem with great interest and pleasure.

Well, today I got my promotion to Lieutenant Colonel, though I wasn't in line for it yet by any sort of reckoning. The C.O. Northern Command and the Armor Corps C.O. recommended a "special promotion," and after a brief delay at Personnel Administration ("no such precedents today," etc.), confirmation came through.

On top of that it's fairly certain I'll get command of the unit and start the "overlap" quite soon. The Corps has given its consent, and so apparently has the Chief of Staff. The official reply should come in a few days, and it doesn't look as if there'll be any surprises.

What else?

I've been recommended for a D.C.C. (Distinguished Conduct Citation) for my actions in the war, and though I frankly told the C.O. Training Command (who's chairman of the awards committee) not to bother me with that sort of nonsense, it probably won't stop them, and it seems that when they finally get through with the paperwork (after the next war, no doubt), I'll even get a medal.

April 24, 1975

Brurimine,

I love you very much!
I say it with a cry, and with somberness, and with longing.
I also love with grief.
And I love with almost unbearable restraint—hence the
    cry.
            That's how it is now.
But I also love you with a kiss and a caress
And with a smile
And with tenderness and strength.

As I love—so I love you.
And in other words, I'd say you're the axis
    round which I turn.
Sometimes I circle round very close, and sometimes
    the circle is very wide—
But always round and round
You—the hub.

May 8, 1975

Dearest Mother and Father,

I was so pleased reading your letter today, Mother. It'll be wonderful if Father comes here soon for a while and even more wonderful if you both come. I like your ideas about Europe; a pity I can't join you.

Today there was a ceremony awarding medals of valor for those who fought in the Yom Kippur War. I took Bruria and Iddo and Daphna along, and as it was held at the National Auditorium in Jerusalem, I got a day's leave out of it too, and the chance to get a bit of rest. There were some 220 D.C.C. recipients (many of them, sadly, among the fallen, whose families received the medal for them), and the ceremony was relatively okay. I and a few others received the award after the official ceremony was over—and that for field security reasons (i.e., not to be photographed, not to be seen on TV, etc.)—which suited me.

Next week I'll take a long leave from armor and go back to the unit. As far as I can see, I'm going to have some time for rest during the next few months, before I get up to my neck in work again.

We hear only rarely from Bibi and Micki—which is a pity. Maybe you could fill us in on what's happening with them.

Just now I'm sitting at Iddo's flat, and it's nice and cool and quiet here. Incidentally, a terrorist bomb exploded recently in the high-rise across the street, and the results were fairly nasty; but not to worry—it can't happen at their place.

Write often, because a day with a letter from you is a red-letter day for me.

(To Bruria)

The gap between our daily life and our political life is astounding. We are facing a series of wars (which we shall win), yet we spend our time on arguments about religious laws in the Knesset, on airline strikes, on buying fabrics and antique furniture, and on "when shall we get married." Maybe it's just as well, but there is something comic and pathetic about it. There are also in this some little crumbs of what is eternally human.

May 11, 1975

(To Benjamin)

Hello!

In another four days I'm winding up my armor assignment and returning to my place of origin.* I must admit that I'm a little sorry to leave. I've built up something of value here, and as there's still a lot of work to be done, I feel as if I'm leaving an unfinished job. For all that, I like the idea of returning to the unit, and I'm anxious to get there as soon as possible.

No big news on the political scene. Everything's as usual—i.e., pretty miserable and crying out for improvement. You hear the news as I do, or maybe more—and it'd therefore be a waste of time to write two lines about it. Sad! I'm beginning to feel like a little Vietnamese. What's needed is wisdom to fight the process of isolation that's closing in on us; but there are no wise men in Israel.

*Yoni's old unit.

Thirteen months ago, during the War of Attrition, I received the command of this battalion. At that time it was a battalion in the making. Four months earlier it did not exist; and it was under gun and shell fire that it started to come into being.

A battalion isn't built in a day, nor by the work of one man. A battalion is the sum of all the hundreds of men who make it up; and the degree of their dedication and perseverance, their systematic training, their understanding of the priorities of the tasks at hand, their steadfastness in fulfilling those tasks, and above all their awareness of our mission as soldiers of Zahal, and of the importance of our stand here in the face of so many enemies—these are the factors that distinguish one unit from another.

In the short time since the war we have managed to do much. You have all had a part in building the battalion—you have created something out of nothing. But this isn't the end of the road, only the beginning. We have fashioned the framework—and it is strong. It's up to you now to erect the entire structure upon it—and much work is still needed.

The basic assumption in all our work and the principal task of this battalion has been to prepare for war in the best way possible, so that we may stand calmly on the day of judgment, when it comes, secure in the knowledge that we did all we could in the time we had.

I believe in a number of things that I consider essential for maintaining any organization, of whatever size—and these I'd like to leave with you:

1. I believe first of all in common sense, which should guide all of our actions.

2. I also believe in the responsibility of commanders. A good commander—whether in charge of a tank, a platoon, a company, transport or supply—is one who feels absolutely responsible for anything connected, even indirectly, with his command.

3. I believe that the buck should not be passed to anyone else —that it should stop here, with us.

4. I believe in getting down to the smallest details. Anyone who fails to do that and tries to spare himself the effort is doing a disservice to our goal, which is preparing the unit for war.

*Yoni's parting address to the tank battalion he commanded.

5. I believe that there can be no compromise with results. Never accept results that are less than the best possible, and even then look for ways to improve and perfect them.
6. I believe that the greatest danger in the life of a unit is to lapse into self-satisfaction. I would like the men of this battalion always to be a bit worried—perhaps there is something else we might have done, something we might have improved and didn't.
7. I believe that all the battalion's efforts must be subordinated to the main aim—victory in war. Let us therefore never confuse our priorities.
8. I believe with all my heart in our ability to carry out any military mission entrusted to us, and I believe in you—the battalion.
9. And I believe in Israel and in the sense of responsibility that must accompany every man who fights for the fate of his homeland.

For the period of over a year during which I have had the command of the battalion, I have seen you grow and mature; I have seen with pleasure the forging of a sound framework of regular servicemen in the battalion—N.C.O.'s and officers. I have seen the battalion making progress week by week, never resting on its oars. I have seen you, officers and men, achieve good results and always press onward.

I feel confident that you will continue on the course we have taken, and strive to do still better.

I leave with the feeling that much remains to be done, and I admit that I find it hard to leave. But I also know that I am leaving the battalion in the hands of good people, who know what must be done, and how.

I also want you to know that I believe in you—the officers and men of this battalion. With a battalion like this, one can go into battle with a calm heart.

In conclusion, I want to thank you for the pleasure, and privilege, of being your commander over the long months we have worked together.

SELF-PORTRAIT OF A HERO

September 19, 1975

My dear Mother and Father,

I'm writing this in flight on a small plane bound for Tel Aviv from the south. Beneath me lies the sea in all its shades of green, and to the right the sandy coastal strip, and a bit farther away the massed buildings of Tel Aviv rising out of the wasteland around them.

It's been a long time since we wrote to each other. I got a letter from you, Mother, two days ago, and a little while before a post-card from Iddo and Daphna, all of which made me very happy. I live in a cycle of work and activity from which it's hard to emerge even for the briefest of moments. And so it happens that the days follow one another, and every so often I tell myself that now I'm going to sit down and write, and nothing comes of it. In fact, I hardly even manage to glance at the headlines in the newspaper.

All the same, I managed to "steal" a brief hour at the close of Yom Kippur, and we went to the Carmelis to break the fast with them. They are good, warmhearted people, and as always I enjoyed being with them. I saw a snapshot of myself as a child there and couldn't help smiling. In so many ways I haven't changed outwardly since I was a baby!

The plane is landing and the wheels are touching down. Now I'm already driving through town, and on my way to the base I'll drop in at home for a few minutes.

My flat is finished and in two weeks I'll move in. I picked up some furniture from our storeroom in Jerusalem—things that were on the point of ruin: two armchairs, a couch, the chess table and a stool. I gave them to a carpenter to be rubbed down and got some new upholstery for them, so that now, with the table and chairs, I have a reasonable minimum of furnishings. After buying a few more necessities, my money will run out, and I must say there's room for some further items (such as wardrobes, of which I have none). But this problem, too, will be solved in due time.

There's so much work to do that I find it hard to free myself for anything else. I do believe that, barring unforeseen circumstances (such as another war), I shall finally take up my studies as soon as I'm through with my present job.* Incidentally, I received a very nice reply from Harvard, saying I could come back any time I wished at only six weeks' notice.

---

*As commander of an elite unit.

Lieutenant Colonel Jonathan Netanyahu reading the names of the fallen on Israel's Memorial Day, 1976

December 2, 1975

Dear Father,

For a start, I want to thank you for the money you sent me to buy furniture for my flat. It was timely and will certainly help. My main problem, now as always, will be to find time for taking care of all the little things that still have to be seen to.

Mother has been here now for several weeks and it's wonderful to see her and be with her. Unfortunately, I couldn't get as much time off as I would have liked (just as I couldn't get away from work completely when you were last here). The result is that Mother spends most of her time at Iddo and Daphna's, at her sisters', or at the Carmelis'. Maybe I'll have more time to spare during the last part of her stay.

I won't bore you with a lecture about our gloomy political situation. Events are moving just as you predicted a very long time ago—and there's no one to hold them back. Every now and then I ask myself whether I'm personally contributing anything to Israel's defense besides words, and my answer (and it's small comfort) is that in my own way I'm doing a great deal. It's not the mere fact that I'm serving in Israel's army, but the specific task I'm fulfilling, and the positive results accompanying it. The trouble is that it's not much in face of the political and economic swamp we're sinking in. I feel the noose tightening around us—slowly but unceasingly. But enough of that. I really didn't mean to get into this depressing subject.

I think you were right to refuse the university's offer.* I think it would have been a waste of your talents and your precious time, and it's more important for you to finish the vast project you've been working on all these years. I hope you'll manage to take some time off for a visit to Israel —to rest, and not necessarily to work.

Much love,
Yoni

Bruria mine,

It's 09:00 in the morning and I'm off and I've just seen your note.

The Town Beyond the Wall† is a marvellous book, one of the few that held me spellbound. I got it one day in June 1967, when I was lying

*An invitation to teach at one of Israel's universities.
†By Elie Wiesel.

wounded in the hospital in Safed (the hospital people were distributing books to the wounded, and by a stroke of good fortune I got *The Town Beyond the Wall*). It's fortunate to be fortunate. We are. I lose myself in *The Town Beyond the Wall*. But no, not lose myself, just the opposite —I find myself richer, cleaner, stronger. I gather all my wandering thoughts into me and become more complete, more unified, and I say soberly—more purified as well. The sensitivity in me rises to the surface and finds a hold on my exterior—my face, fingertips, everything—and somehow it turns out I'm more concentrated too. There are some other books that have done this for me, or maybe have done different things, but with a similar intensity. A few events in my life affected me in a similar manner—the necessity to break away once more from everything and go to the U.S. when I was sixteen and a half, the Six-Day War in particular, my divorce, and maybe others.

Now I'm off—

That's what I said at the start, and meanwhile a lot of time has gone by.

Yours,
Yoni

(To Bruria)
My beloved woman,

We're in for a bit of a hard stretch, because I've got to stay on the job all this week.

I know the house is like a railway station where you and I pass through at different hours and never meet.

It's not at all like that in my own feelings. The situation hurts and troubles me. It's hard not to be with you, and even harder to upset you and impose on you a burden of loneliness.

I've been thinking of how to change my way of life so that we could live together like a normal couple, and as yet haven't found a solution. Maybe I will.

But for the present, however hard it is for me (and even more so for you), I see no concrete, immediate solution. I'm thinking of the future —maybe there, in the future, the real key lies.

February 15, 1976

(To Bruria)

Woman,

Being what we are, we must take life as it comes—at least, in the framework of our present existence. If we want to live differently, we shall have to take a big step outward. It's not enough that, potentially, I could live in a horse-drawn wagon (I could all right!), because in actual practice we live differently. I don't know if I will always live this way—at least, as a soldier. It seems I will. At present I'm still young enough to start all over again, but I plan to see my present job through at least, and after that—I don't know if I'll have the strength. I think I will, but it's just as likely all the same that I won't stay in the army after all.

But the problem isn't just our outer way of life, but our inner one—the sharing and the bond. These things have been bruised a little, and we'll have to invest a lot of thought and energy to get us into a life pattern in which these things endure. I don't lack the enthusiasm that you say you miss in me, or the renewal of love. What I lack is the bond between us. We are withdrawing farther and farther into ourselves (in one of Shakespeare's plays an actor explains: "A dialogue—a monologue between two people"), and more than anything else, I feel lonely. Maybe it's my concern about the work and being restless that affect my inner feelings. And as they're the kind of difficulties I can't share with you (I can share happy things, of course), the gap between us only grows.

For your part, you must take on yourself more than is usually expected in a two-way relationship. Since you're more sensitive than I am to things and events, do stay one step ahead of me and try to be a screen between the weary life and the two of us.

I need a full month of Sabbaths—three to rest and the others to do all sorts of things. As I never have time enough to rest, I find myself together with you in a rather vicious circle. If I went in for lyricism I'd picture the two of us inside that circle, moonstruck, trying to grasp its rim to steady ourselves—only it has no rim.

You can set your imagination free and let it soar—but we are still here.

June 12, 1976

(To Benjamin and Miriam)
Dear Bibon and Micki,

I have recently decided to return to Harvard next year. What gave me the push was a meeting I had with Professor Schelling of Harvard. Here's what happened.

Two weeks ago Michael Handel phoned to say that Schelling was in the country and would like to tour the Golan Heights. I arranged things with Schelling, and last Sunday I took D.'s Plymouth and picked up Schelling and Michael in Jerusalem at 08:00 in the morning. We came back to Jerusalem at midnight, by which time Schelling and I had found a common language. Schelling took down my address and said he'd be very glad to help me at Harvard. Later he told Michael privately that he'd been very impressed by his meeting with me and hinted he'd be glad to help me obtain a scholarship. At any rate, I explained Israel's position to him better than it's generally done by our representatives, and also the problem of withdrawal from the territories. I'd say he understood very well. He impressed me as a thorough, pragmatic person who asks shrewd and probing questions. He's going back to Harvard in two weeks, and I'll be glad if you make his acquaintance.

My decision to return to Harvard at this stage is quite firm. I don't suppose the army will underwrite my undergraduate studies, and even if it wanted to, I wouldn't agree. I'll take a leave of absence from Zahal and make up my mind afterwards whether to go back to the army or stay out. If everything works out, I may arrive in June for the summer course; if not, in September. Find out for me if this involves any problems.

Though I'm using the second person masculine singular, this letter is addressed to you both (how are things, Micki?). I'll give it to Yosi so he'll have something to bring you from Israel. I liked him very much.

June 12, 1976

Dear Mother and Father,

I've just written a letter to Bibi which I'll send with Yosi, who's going back to Boston next week. Just now we're at Iddo and Daphna's in Jerusalem.

The other day I met Professor Schelling of Harvard, who's here on a few months' visit (he returns to the U.S. in two weeks). I gave him a private tour of the Golan Heights, which lasted a full sixteen hours. We met through Michael Handel, whom I met at Harvard. I explained a number of things to him that he had not fully realized before. For details, see my letter to Bibi and Micki—so I won't repeat myself.

This letter is mainly to tell you that if nothing unexpected happens, I'll resume my studies at Harvard next year—possibly as early as next June, when the summer course begins. Money will be a problem of course, because I don't want to study at the army's expense and tie myself down to more years of service. I assume I'll be able to get a partial scholarship (Schelling told Michael after we had parted that he'd be happy to help me at Harvard).

On the personal plane—I'm growing fond of my flat. It's attractive and comfortable and nearby. The army burdens me with an enormous load of work and doesn't allow me a minute for my private affairs. There is real satisfaction in this kind of work, but it's immensely tiring, gradually leading to physical and mental exhaustion. It's very important for me, therefore, to get out of this round of work and explore new fields.

I have no plans to marry for the moment—at least not before I get out of the vicious circle of my current work and can measure my life with other yardsticks.

I'm impressed with Yosi, Bibi's friend, and look forward to meeting the fine group that's now in Boston.

Yours, missing you badly,
Yoni

June 19, 1976

Dear Father and Mother,

I have already told you about my touring the Golan Heights with Professor Schelling of Harvard and Dr. Michael Handel (whom I met when I was a student in Boston). A short while ago I attended some lectures in Jerusalem on "Termination of Wars," and one of the lectures was given by Schelling. I was pleased to hear him talk about the situation on the northern front as follows (I quote from the *Ma'ariv* evening paper): "If I were a Syrian, I would realize there is no chance whatever of stabilizing the Middle East situation without territorial concessions, however much I might hesitate to give up the Golan to Israel. No one can guarantee that making such a concession would bring about a political settlement, and anyone bold enough to make it would be committing political suicide; but it is vital that a 'dove' should appear who could rise to such an act of courage and self-sacrifice, without which wars cannot be terminated."

The quotation isn't exact, but this is the first time we've heard an influential American argue that for the sake of a settlement the *Syrians* should withdraw and give up territory, not Israel. This is definitely an achievement I'm taking credit for.

My plans to return to Harvard still stand, and I intend to carry them out (if no surprises take place). I guess I'll reopen my dialogue with the university soon. Meanwhile I've asked Bibi to look into the situation at Harvard for me.

Iddo and Daphna tell me that your project, Father, is making headway, and that's cheering news. It's good to hear of progress, not of marching in place.

I'm writing this letter at Michael's home (in Jerusalem, on Mount Scopus), and don't want to make it too long.

Yours with much love,

Yoni

(June 29, 1976)

(To Bruria)

I find myself at a critical stage in my life, facing a profound inner crisis that has been disturbing my whole frame of reference for a long time.

What's so sad and ridiculous about it is that the only solution my way of life until now suggests is just to go on ploughing the same deep furrow in the same laborious field.

I am tired most of the time, but that's only part of the problem—I have lost the spark that is so vital for any achievement, the spark of creative joy, of self-renewal, of reawakening.

I keep asking myself: Why? Why now of all times? Is it that my work doesn't absorb, doesn't hold me? Wrong! On the contrary, it possesses me and I don't want it to. I do things because they have to be done, and not because I want to. And the same haunting question returns—can I let myself live like this, work like this and wear myself out? And the answer is always that I must persevere and finish what I have begun—that I have an obligation not only to the job, but to myself as well—but how do I know if I can hold out for another ten months?

There, most of what I've written comes with a question mark. If I knew

The last photograph taken of Yoni,
a few weeks before the Entebbe raid

the answers, I wouldn't be so harassed by doubt, I wouldn't torment myself so.

I don't even have the time to do the little necessary things—replace a filling that's come out of a tooth, fix a torn lamp fixture, buy a length of electric cable for the record player, and rest, rest, rest, do nothing obligatory—come to a stop.

Yes, I'm having a hard time as seldom before in my life, and what troubles me is that even the alternatives outside the army have lost much of their luster. Perhaps they always attracted me more because I didn't think they were real, and now that I'm trying to picture them to myself, I'm having some doubts. Will I have the energy to start everything from scratch? And I don't want to burn any bridges behind me either (something I've always done in my strange life—strange as the life of any man). Because I may yet want to return to the army, in which I've been involved all my young manhood. But I've got to stop and get off now, at once, or very soon—and I shall, but in a while.

I recall the mad, miserable cry in a play I saw long ago: "Stop the world, I want to get off!"

But it isn't possible to stop the mad globe we're moving on, and the force of gravity won't let us escape its pull, and so, willy-nilly, alive or dead (alive, of course, and as long as possible), you're in.

Good that I have you, my Brur, and good that I have somewhere to lay my weary head.

I know I'm not with you enough, and that it's hard for you to be alone so much, but I trust you, me, both of us, to succeed in living our youth to the fullest—you to live your youth and your life, and I—my life and the flicker of my youth.

It'll be okay.

Afterword

Yoni's Final Days

Y ONI'S LAST LETTER WAS PROBABLY
written either on Monday or Tuesday. The raid occurred several days
later, just past midnight on Saturday July 4. Yoni does not explain in his
letter the nature of the crisis he was undergoing, but some of the causes
no doubt had to do with what he had seen and encountered around
him—both inside and outside the armed forces—things that caused him
great concern, especially as they related to the state of the country.

In the brief few days left, Yoni's mood changed dramatically. Once he
was ordered to prepare for the raid, Yoni mustered all his strength and will
to get ready to lead his men to Entebbe. Numerous accounts by his soldiers
and other officers attest that Yoni was in high spirits during those days.
These accounts would eventually cause us to believe that by the end of the
week, certainly while flying to Entebbe, Yoni had overcome his personal
state of dejection. One may also assume that, had Yoni returned to Israel
alive, following the enormous success of the raid, his frame of mind would
have been quite different from the one reflected in his last letter.

In the early part of that critical week beginning Sunday June 27, Yoni
was engaged in a military operation which is still to this day classified,
shuttling repeatedly from Sinai to central Israel. Late Sunday night he
spent a few hours with his troops at Lod airport. A hijacked Air France
plane, with scores of Israelis on board, had just taken off from Libya after
a brief stopover there, and it was assumed that the hijackers might land
the plane in Israel. The plane, however, did not proceed to Israel but
turned southeast, in the direction of East Africa, and landed on Monday
morning at Entebbe airport in Uganda.

There, the four terrorists who had hijacked the plane, two Germans and two Arabs, were met by several other Arab terrorists. The hostages were taken to the airport's old terminal building. There they were held under guard by the army of Uganda, whose head, the notorious Idi Amin, colluded with the Arab terrorist organizations. The terrorists demanded the release from jail of over fifty of their colleagues, most of whom were behind bars in Israel, a few in other countries. The deadline for their release was set for Thursday afternoon. Israel was warned that if by that date the jailed terrorists were not released, the hostages would be killed.

Late Tuesday and Wednesday, some low-key discussions took place among Israeli army strategists about the possibility of rescuing the hostages. Yoni was kept informed of these discussions, although he was still tied up with other operations of his Unit (the Sayeret Matkal). For the time being, the discussions led nowhere. But on Wednesday night Yoni received word that the talks seemed to have taken on a more meaningful tone.

"On Wednesday evening the phone calls began to come in," recalls Avi, the Unit's head of intelligence, who was with Yoni in Sinai, "informing us that a directive had been issued for the unit to start planning [a rescue operation]. During the night there were quite a few calls . . . mostly from Muki [an officer of the Unit who was to be Yoni's number-two man in the raid]. Muki was pressing us to return to Israel, because he was repeatedly asked: 'When can Yoni get here?' . . . With every phone call you said to yourself, 'Maybe there's a chance that something will happen after all.' The pressure was pretty serious, and we understood that by the next day, first thing, we'd have to fly back."

Yoni did indeed fly north early on Thursday. That morning, however, with the ultimatum nearing its deadline and with no acceptable rescue plan available, the government of Israel decided to negotiate with the terrorists, stating its willingness to release terrorists for hostages. By then, most of the non-Israeli hostages had been released and flown from Entebbe to Paris. Of the 106 hostages remaining in Entebbe, most were Israelis. "My intention was not to use a ruse or a tactical ploy to gain time," Prime Minister Rabin wrote of his government's decision, "but to enter into serious negotiations, with Israel fulfilling whatever commitments it made."

With the release of the non-Israeli hostages, important information started to come in on the state of affairs in the old terminal at Entebbe. Such information was crucial for planning any rescue, and so the military option had acquired momentum. By late afternoon, Yoni received the formal order to start planning and preparing the Unit for a possible raid on Entebbe.

Landing C-130 transports directly at the airport of Entebbe was considered a feasible way of bringing in the rescue force. Sayeret Matkal, the Unit that Yoni commanded, was given the brunt of the job. It had been ordered to take control of the old terminal building, where the hostages were being held and where the terrorists and the Ugandan troops were positioned, and was also to seal off the whole area from any possible counterattack by the Ugandan army until the planes could take off.

"The instructions were extremely general," says Biran, the intelligence officer of Dan Shomron, the man who was given overall command of the ground operation. "Yoni had logistical questions . . . for which we as yet had no answers. Everything was still up in the air." In the meeting between Yoni and Shomron and their staffs, "we still did not go into specifics about who, how many, how, and what. It was obvious that all this would have to be studied and developed. As for the Unit's plan of action, Shomron did not get involved. He said: 'These are men who know their job. There's no point for me to interfere.'"

Yoni returned to his Unit, gathered a few of his officers in his office, and started formulating with them the Unit's plan of action for the rescue at Entebbe. All the while, intelligence information concerning the hostages and terrorists, as well as about the layout of the old terminal building, was filtering in. After several hours of brain-storming, the Unit's plan of action was formed. Although certain revisions would be made by Yoni during the following day and a half, the plan for the most part remained unchanged. In fact, it was carried out almost to the letter.

The plan called for the Unit's initial force of some thirty men to be flown to Entebbe and to land at night near the new terminal. From there the men were to proceed to the old terminal, arriving in a Mercedes and two Land Rover jeeps, the kind of vehicles frequently used by the Ugandan army. It was hoped that the Ugandan guards surrounding the building would assume that this was a force of their own, perhaps the one that accompanied President Idi Amin on his occasional visit to the hostages. In this manner, it was hoped that the Unit's men would be able to approach the Ugandan guards without first being fired upon.

"According to the intelligence we had at the time, there were dozens of Ugandan guards," explains Avi. "Yoni was adamant that we had to find some sort of solution to the problem concerning the Ugandan security belt." Thus they came upon the idea of the Mercedes and jeeps, which was meant to "delay opening of fire by the Ugandans as long as possible."

Ideally, the guards might even wave the vehicles through. However, should they want to check the vehicles and their passengers, "our men would have to open fire," continues Avi. "They would be at the point of no return anyway."

The remainder of the plan was as follows. After the possible encounter with the guards, the force would proceed rapidly to the building, get out of the vehicles, and run to the various entrances, the squads entering their assigned entrances simultaneously. Several squads were assigned to the two main halls on the ground floor where the hostages were thought to be held; other squads were assigned to the top floor, where Ugandan soldiers were stationed; while some commandos were to clear the other rooms on the ground floor that were occupied by terrorists. Yoni and his command team would position themselves outside the main entrance in order to be able to control the flow of men and, in case of a hitch, go in. At the second stage of the mission, a second force of the Unit, driving in four APC's, would land and quickly proceed to the old terminal, cordoning its environs from any possible counterattack by the Ugandan army. Besides the large Ugandan force believed to be stationed in the old terminal, there was an Ugandan regimental air force base some 200 yards from the building.

The Unit's officers convened around midnight to receive an initial briefing from Yoni and instructions on preparations. "Yoni was very tired," recalls Muki. "You could see it by looking at him. Actually we were all tired from the whole week we had just finished, the officers in particular. So at a certain point I suggested that we stop and get some sleep. This was around 2 or 3 A.M. on Friday morning. Yoni agreed, and the small planning team went to sleep, but it turned out later that Yoni remained alone at his office and continued to work on the plan. And in fact, when he presented the plan at 7 A.M. the following morning, after sleeping at most one or two hours, I saw how far he had carried the work from where we left off. There were many points in the plan that we had not considered, which Yoni had thought through to the end. That morning he presented the plan complete, perfect, down to the last detail."

As more information came in, however, Yoni changed certain points in the plan. He gave briefings to the soldiers and officers, supervised some of the rehearsals, took care of numerous matters that cropped up, held a meeting in his office with the commander of the C-130 transport squadron, and went over to the Kirya, the military headquarters of the IDF, several times for meetings and briefings.

His most important meeting at the Kirya was, without a doubt, the one he had with Defense Minister Shimon Peres.

"I asked somebody what the meeting was about," says Rachel, the secretary to Motta Gur, the chief of staff. When she saw Yoni waiting to go into Peres's office, she "was told that Shimon had asked Yoni to come so that he could look him in the eyes and ask him straight, 'Yoni, can it be done?' That was the whole purpose of the meeting. Yoni stood there [outside Peres's door] with maps in his hands, very preoccupied. . . . He was pressed for time and said that he was in a terrible hurry and they should let him in already."

"He presented the plan to me in detail," recalls Peres, "and I liked it very much. The two of us sat alone. . . . My impression was one of exactingness and imagination . . . and complete self-confidence . . . which without a doubt influenced me. We had a problem with lack of intelligence. But Yoni said: 'Do you know of any operation that wasn't carried out half blind? Every operation is half blind.' But Yoni was well aware of the problem, and he told me that the operation was absolutely doable. And as to the cost, he said we had every chance of coming out of it with almost no losses."

That night, with Chief of Staff Motta Gur looking on, the various forces, including that of the Unit, conducted a full model exercise. "We practiced according to the plan," says Muki. "We placed two soldiers who acted as 'guards' on the runway. They ordered us to stop. We did, and Yoni 'shot' at them with a silencer. We then continued toward the terminal." Several years later Muki also explained: "During the preparations for the raid Yoni foresaw a situation whereby we encountered two Ugandan guards . . . and our response in such a case was to take out the two guards with silencers."

This encounter with the guards was followed by a dash to the old terminal building and a rapid run from the vehicles to the entrances. Speed was now considered critical. The purpose was to reach the entrances before the terrorists realized what was going on and started to kill off the hostages with automatic-weapons fire and grenades.

Following the exercise, the chief of staff met with the various commanders and wanted to know their opinion about the chances of success. He spent the longest amount of time with Yoni.

"Yoni said to Motta that he had every reason to believe that if the hostages were in fact still there, the Unit, with the methods and men at its disposal, could pull it off," recalls Muki. "It was fairly natural for Yoni to think so, but he [also] had good reason [for saying that]. The bottom line of what he said was: 'It can be done.' I saw Motta's reaction, and I'm convinced that Yoni's words gave Motta . . . the required confidence to push on and get the go-ahead from the cabinet."

In fact, following his discussion with Yoni, Dan Shomron, and other officers, Motta Gur said that he had reached a decision in favor of the operation and was going to recommend it to Prime Minister Yitzhak Rabin and Defense Minister Peres.

A few hours later Yoni went home for a brief nap. Early the following morning, Saturday July 3, he said goodbye to Bruria and rushed back to the Unit. He held one last inspection of the men, then conducted an hour-long tactics session with the officers.

"It was a productive hour," says Giora, one of the leading officers. "There was a lot of discussion about how things would be done under that kind of pressure. Different questions came up. . . . [We considered] what would happen if a team was knocked out, who would replace it, and so on. We raised these questions, and Yoni answered them on the spot: 'We'll do it this way or that.' It was an excellent meeting."

Yoni then left his men and went with some of his officers to Lod airport for the final general briefing, headed by Deputy Chief of Staff Yekutiel Adam, who during the last two days had been pushing indefatigably for the execution of the raid.

There, in the squadron briefing room at Lod, Yoni met again with Joshua Shani, the lead pilot and commander of the Hercules transport squadron. He spent some time with him going over the joint plan of action. Yoni also took aside Amnon Halivni, the pilot of the hostage evacuation plane, who had spent some time in Uganda and was acquainted with the old terminal and the Ugandan army. "Yoni wanted to know details about the building, from the shed for firefighting equipment on the right end to the control tower on the left," Halivni says. "He wanted to know where the stairs were, what kind of windows there were, what the approach to the entrances was like and more. . . . He asked me one more thing: 'How do you think the Ugandan sentries will react to the Mercedes and jeeps?' I told him: They'll yell 'Stop!' or something like that, and they'll point their bayoneted rifles at you. And if you don't stop, they'll shoot."

By the time the general briefing with Adam was over, Yoni's men had arrived at the airport with their vehicles. At noon four planes took off for Sharm-el-Sheikh, at the southern tip of the Sinai desert. There they would await word as to whether the government had given them the go-ahead to continue on to Entebbe.

The flight to Sharm-el-Sheikh was rocky, causing much discomfort among the men. After landing at Sharm, the men got off, refreshed themselves a bit, and then gathered to hear Yoni's final briefing.

"It was a speech I'll never forget," says Alex, one of the assault soldiers. "He gave us confidence that we could do it. His leadership and his ability to affect us were simply above and beyond anything."

The government was still in session and had not yet decided whether to approve the operation. But if the raid was to be executed at all, the planes would now have to take off for their destination, since Entebbe was eight hours away, and the plan called for landing at what was considered the optimal hour: midnight Ugandan time. Thus, with the understanding that if the government did not approve the operation the planes would turn around midway and head back to Israel, the force was instructed to take off.

"Yoni told the men to get on board the plane, and they were surprised to hear they were actually going," says Shlomo. "Not that he was raring to fight, but he didn't look at all worried by the go-ahead either. You could see that he felt very comfortable, that he was finally starting to breathe easily."

The lead plane was crowded. It carried Yoni's assault party with its three vehicles and a paratooper force. They were flying over the Red Sea, just a few yards above water to avoid radar detection by Egypt and Saudi Arabia. Yoni and Muki sat down with Amos, a soldier of the Unit who had been transferred at the last moment from the peripheral APC force to the assault force. Amos had replaced a soldier who had become ill on the flight to Sharm and couldn't participate in the raid. Yoni sketched for him (on the back of an air sickness bag) the plan of the terminal and the assault routes, indicating to him the various entrances and the task of each squad, including that of Amos.

"While Yoni was explaining all this to me," says Amos, "we were informed that the government had given us the green light to carry on to Entebbe, that we were going to do it. . . . Yet he stayed completely calm . . . and went on explaining to me my job as though we were going to perform an exercise."

On the way some of the men slept while sitting in their seats in the vehicles. Some were sprawled over the car hoods or lying on the floor beneath the jeeps. For a while Yoni sat next to Muki in the Mercedes, reading a book. Yoni too was exhausted after a week during which he had hardly slept a wink. At a certain stage he went to the cockpit, where some of the officers were gathered, and lay down on the bunk bed. A little while later the lead pilot wanted to grab a nap as well.

"I looked back and saw Yoni sleeping in that bed," says Shani. "Under normal conditions, if some battalion commander is resting there, I tell him politely but firmly to go rest in the rear of the plane. This time I couldn't bring myself to do it, because my theory was that the chances of the first group that would storm that building to stay alive were fifty-fifty. I said to myself: 'He's taking a huge personal risk in this, that's for sure. He's grabbing some sleep here. So am I going to wake him up?' On the other hand, I also wanted to lie down. He was curled up on the edge. I lay down next to him, getting closer little by little till I was a few millimeters away from him. I myself was afraid of a failure on a national level . . . that we simply wouldn't succeed, that we'd cause a disaster. I looked at Yoni from about an inch away, nose to nose, and he was sleeping like a baby, utterly at peace. I asked Tzvika, the navigator, when Yoni had gone to sleep, and he said, 'He went to sleep [a while ago] and asked me to wake him up a little while before the landing.' And the thought flitted through my mind: Where does this calmness of his come from? Soon you're going into battle, and here you are, sleeping as if nothing is happening! I myself couldn't fall asleep. I got up and went back to my seat."

By this time the planes were already flying high over the skies of Africa, first over Ethiopia, then over Kenya. Finally they reached Lake Victoria, on whose shores lay Entebbe airport. A tremendous lightning storm caught them as they entered the lake.

Yoni got up. He went back to the hold, where his men were about to get ready, and woke up some of those who were still asleep. The men put on their ammo vests. Each took his place in his vehicle.

Yoni then proceeded to move among his men.

"There was this reddish light, and I remember that we saw his face," relates Shlomo, one of the soldiers. "He wasn't wearing his beret, or his ammo vest or gun. . . . He spoke to the men, smiled at us, said a few words of encouragement to each one. It was as though he were leaving us, as though he knew what was going to happen to him. He didn't issue any orders but just tried to instill confidence. I remember that he shook hands with the youngest guy on the force. . . . He acted more like a friend. . . . I sensed that he felt that from here on everything, or at least nearly everything, depended on us. He'd seen a lot of combat, and quite a few of the soldiers there had seen none at all, or a lot less than he had. And I remember him going by, joking a little, exchanging a few words, easing the men's tension before battle."

They had already reached a small island in the lake, just south of Entebbe. The other three planes of the convoy now stayed behind, flying in circles, while the lead plane shut its running lights and headed north. The storm was behind them. All of a sudden the airport could be seen at a distance, with its runway lights fully lit. Yoni proceeded to get into the passenger seat of the Mercedes. The back ramp was being lowered as the plane was descending toward the runway, and Yoni told Amitsur, the driver, to start the car's engine.

As the plane landed on the tarmac, the Ugandans in the main control tower probably did not understand what was going on. Some paratroop soldiers jumped off while the plane was taxiing, placing lighted markers on the runway, so that the other three planes would be able to land in case the runway lights were switched off by the men in the control tower. The Hercules transport came to a halt at the designated point.

The vehicles got out quickly. Yoni turned around to verify that the two jeeps were behind him and told Amitsur to head along the diagonal runway. After a mile or so, the three vehicles turned left onto the approach runway. This runway led directly to the old terminal building, where the hostages were being held. However, they now saw two Ugandan guards— at exactly the spot that had been envisaged during the rehearsal in Israel. One of the guards shouted at them to stop. "When I saw those two guards waiting for us, like the guards that Yoni had placed in the rehearsal, I knew that this operation would succeed," says Bukhris, the youngest soldier on the force.

"We were sitting in the jeep," recalls Amir. "We saw it as if in a movie. The Mercedes was advancing, and at a certain point we were approaching the terminal. . . . We saw a Ugandan soldier to the right and another one to the left. The runway lights were on either side . . . and we were driving in the middle. This was about 200 meters from the building. . . . The guard on the left disappeared from view. Suddenly the one from the right came toward us. He approached the Mercedes and made a threatening movement with his weapon. . . . He cocked his rifle. . . . It was obvious to me that the guard had to be taken out."

"The guard shouted something," relates Rani, one of the officers who sat in the first jeep. "He then moved into a shooting position, raised the rifle to his shoulder. I was sure he was about to fire—no 'ifs' about it."

"If the guard had fired first, the whole operation might have sunk," explains Amitsur, one of the Unit's officers and the man who was driving the Mercedes. "Yoni told me: 'Slow down a little, we'll approach them.' He told me to slow down so that we wouldn't frighten them, as if we're about to identify ourselves. . . . Yoni was quite calm."

Yoni and Giora, another officer of the Unit who sat behind him, had their silenced pistols ready in hand. When the Ugandan soldier who was aiming his rifle at them was only several yards away, they both fired. The

Ugandan recoiled and wobbled. He was probably hit but was not totally incapacitated. It was then that loud shots were heard. It is impossible to say what the origin of these shots was. Some claim it came from one of the two Ugandan guards. Some men in the Mercedes say that it came from the jeeps, while one or two men in the jeeps thought it came from the Mercedes. In any case, once the loud shots were heard, the men in the Land Rovers fired freely on the two Ugandan guards (the one on the left had reappeared), knocking them out. "One does not leave behind an armed soldier . . . who would use his weapon once he realized what you were going to do," explains Yiftach, the deputy commander of the Unit.

"We could not have approached the terminal building silently any closer than we did," sums up Amir. "We started shooting heavy fire, and had we not done that, I'm sure they would have fired on us."

"Yoni told me now to speed up," recalls Amitsur. "We went at full speed . . . for about 200 meters or so. . . . He instructed me to stop in front of the control tower. . . . It was a spot that was relatively sheltered and that is why he chose it. He then gave an order to get out of the car and start running, and they all started running toward the terminal."

The jeeps were right on the heels of the Mercedes. They too had stopped and the men got out quickly, the first ones running on the heels of those who had gotten out of the Mercedes.

"When I got out of the jeep, I saw Yoni out of the corner of my eye going a bit sideways, slightly at an angle . . . so that he could be in a position of control. . . . We ran to the near corner of the terminal building," relates Rani.

"I saw the lead man running and shooting, I don't know at what, and then he pulled to the left, to the building, and stopped," recalls Amos. "Yoni was then a little bit behind him. The men didn't understand what was going on, why the lead man had stopped. Most of the men congregated and stopped behind him. So Yoni shouted to run forward. . . . All of us understood that it was a matter of seconds before the terrorists came to their senses."

"Yoni stood apart from us . . . and kept shouting: 'Forward! Come on!' calling the lead man by his name," recalls Alex.

The pause in the assault could have had disastrous consequences had it continued longer than it did. Every second's delay increased the chances that the terrorists would begin to kill the hostages. When Yoni saw that the lead man did not respond to his commands, he lurched ahead, thereby signaling the men to follow him.

"Yoni shouted to run forward," explains Amos, "and I remember him running forward himself. . . . He passed the [lead man who had stopped]. . . . The one who was first out of the corner of the building was Yoni. . . . He then ran a bit to the right, to let the men [who were meant to go inside the building] pass him. . . . Right afterward Amnon and Amir passed Yoni. . . . The pause in the assault had lasted a few seconds."

Amir by then had come from behind, after having gotten out of the jeep relatively late. He kept on running forward, passing Yoni and thus becoming the first in line of the assault force. The men were running now exposed in front of the mostly glass wall of the terminal building, with the terrorists positioned inside behind that wall.

"At some point [as we were running in front of the entrances]," continues Amos, "I think I caught up with Yoni, so that Yoni was just to my right. . . . At this stage, while running to the entrance, I saw Yoni fall. This was while Amir was at his entrance, about to burst in. I think that this was the point in time when Yoni was hit. . . . At that stage there was already shooting, some shots were fired into the building [through the glass wall], and we had just fired on a Ugandan soldier outside it."

"I looked to my left," says Shlomo, "because I wanted to see where I was supposed to go in. At that stage I saw Yoni, and I think that that's when he got hit, because I saw him make half a turn, with his face contorted . . . sinking down a little bit, with his knees bent."

Someone had shouted that Yoni was hit, but the men of the force continued in their tasks, following Yoni's orders not to take care of the wounded until the hostages were freed. Each of them realized that time was of the essence, as it would have taken only seconds for the terrorists, once they fully realized what was going on, to have sprayed automatic fire on the huddled hostages.

"When I was about ten yards from the door I saw the glass break and understood that someone was shooting at me," says Amir. "Without thinking twice I shot him through the glass and saw that he was hit."

After shooting at the terrorist in the building who had fired more than half a magazine at the force, Amir entered the main hall, where the hostages were being held. He discovered that he was the first soldier inside. Immediately upon his footsteps came his commander Amnon, who, once he entered the room, saw two terrorists crouching, a man and a woman, aiming their Kalashnikovs at Amir. He quickly fired at them and killed them. Next Muki and Amos entered, apparently together. Amos was scanning the room, looking for more terrorists. "First thing I saw Amnon," says Amos. "Then I looked to my left and saw the two terrorists who were shot. I also saw the fully lit room with all the hostages lying on the floor. And after a short time, from the left, a terrorist suddenly leaped up, holding a weapon. I shot him. The first bullet hit his Kalashnikov, went through his weapon, and entered his chest. It shot three bullets that hit him and finished him off."

With that, the four terrorists who were inside the main hall and posed the most immediate threat to the hostages were killed. The hostages were still in a daze, flattened out on the floor. Almost all of them were unhurt; three of them, however, were hit by the gunfire and would later die of their wounds.

Simultaneously, other teams from the Unit entered the rest of the building, killing three more terrorists and encountering several dozen Ugandan soldiers, most of whom were killed in the ensuing gunfire. Some of the Ugandan soldiers who were stationed on the upper floor had quickly scuttled from the building and fled.

Yoni was lying on the tarmac. He was still alive but rapidly losing blood. He had been hit by a burst from a Kalashnikov in his arm and, more seriously, in his chest. The bullet had entered the front of the chest and exited from the back. "At the end of the fighting," says the Unit's doctor, "somebody came to help me place him on a stretcher. It was then that some consciousness returned to him. . . . He was perhaps roused by a soldierly instinct. There was a lot of shooting toward the control tower, which made a lot of noise, and he tried to get up."

Yoni was transferred by jeep to the evacuation plane, which was positioned close to the old terminal. There a team of doctors tried to resuscitate him, but their lengthy attempts were of no avail. Yoni was pronounced dead.

Shortly thereafter, the evacuation plane, loaded with the hostages and Yoni's body, took off from Entebbe. Half an hour later it landed at Nairobi, Kenya, Uganda's neighbor. Kenya had earlier agreed to let the Israeli planes refuel on their way back.

The other three planes carrying the soldiers landed one by one. The Unit's soldiers, who knew that Yoni was hurt, did not yet know of his death. They were instructed to remain inside their plane while it was refueling.

"On our plane there had been endless chatter," recalls Shlomo, "everyone telling what happened to him. It seemed that everything was going great, that we'd succeeded. And then someone came in and said that Yoni had died, and all at once, it seemed as if someone had turned off the entire plane. Everybody was silent. . . . We were hit hard, and each of us withdrew into himself."

Matan Vilnai, the head of the paratrooper contingent in the raid, went over to the hostages' plane. "I saw Yoni's body lying in the plane, wrapped in one of those awful aluminum blankets the doctors use," says Matan. "I saw the hostages completely stunned, shadows of men. They were very depressed. And what hit me then was a kind of feeling that was, for an army man like myself, totally illogical: that if Yoni was dead, then the whole thing wasn't worth it."

When the planes left Kenya a short time later, no report had yet arrived in Israel of any dead among the force. "When the last plane took off from Nairobi," says Rachel, Gur's secretary, "there was a wave of rejoicing [at the Kirya headquarters]. The chief of staff's driver brought in a few bottles of champagne, and everyone celebrated. In the end, they left. It got quiet, and Motta was left alone in the room with his aide Hagai Regev. I went to the kitchen to make some coffee. Suddenly the other secretaries came over, grabbed me, and said: 'Yoni was killed.' I dropped everything and went to the chief of staff's office. I opened the door of the room I'd left two minutes before, when it had been full of happiness over the success . . . and I saw the chief of staff sitting, face fallen, terribly sad. Not to mention Hagai, who was just crushed. In one minute, all the joy had been erased. . . . It was as though nothing else mattered. Everything took on a different meaning."

Gur went over to Peres's office, where the defense minister had laid down to rest, to inform him of Yoni's death. "He got up to open the door," says Gur. "When he heard of Yoni's death, he was clearly shocked. I could see he was taking it personally. He said, 'My God,' or something like that. He took it very hard—not like a defense minister hearing about an officer who had been hit."

Peres wrote in his diary the following lines: "At four in the morning, Motta Gur came into my office, and I could tell he was very upset. 'Shimon, Yoni's gone. A bullet hit him in the heart. Apparently, it came from the control tower. . . .'

"This is the first time this whole crazy week," Peres wrote, "that I cannot hold back the tears."

The planes carrying the soldiers landed in Israel in the morning, at the military base at Tel Nof. Rabin and Peres were there to greet them. When Muki came out of the plane, Peres turned to him and asked: "How was Yoni killed?"

"He went first, he fell first," Muki answered.

* * *

Two days later Yoni was brought to burial at Mount Herzl, at Jerusalem's military cemetery. Thousands attended his funeral. Peres delivered the eulogy. Yoni, who was unknown to the public because of the secret nature of his work, overnight became known throughout Israel. His loss was widely felt as a bitter blow to the nation, injecting a lasting note of tragedy into the great achievement at Entebbe.

—Iddo Netanyahu

Statement by
General Shlomo Gazit,
Chief of Israeli
Military Intelligence

Tel Aviv, July 13, 1976

THE DECISION TO INVADE ENTEBBE with units of the Israel Defense Force (IDF), to take control of the airport and free the hostages, the Air France passengers, was one of the most difficult decisions ever taken by the General Staff of the Government of Israel.

On Saturday, July 3, I accompanied the Chief of Staff when he presented the plan of the operation to the Minister of Defense, the Prime Minister and the entire Cabinet. The anxiety concerning the question whether this would be a "clean" action weighed most heavily on all of them. The decision to undertake the operation was determined in a large measure by the statement of the Chief of Staff, reporting in whose hands the proposed mission would be entrusted—Yoni's. He spoke of the unit and its commander and related how impressed he personally had been when he inspected the preparatory exercise Yoni had conducted the previous night and described the great confidence Yoni inspired in all in his ability to achieve the goal.

Yoni had a complex personality. On the one hand, a warrior and commander among the most superb, most thorough, bravest and most devoted that the Israel Defense Force ever had. On the other hand, a man blessed with many talents, of broad horizons, with a rich and fertile imagination and an exceptional analytical mind.

Yoni returned to his unit as its commander a year ago. He regarded it as a high point of his military career. In this unit he was called on to tackle and resolve problems that were above and beyond the responsibility of any other commander in the army. Yoni found in this task a challenge and an intellectual satisfaction, which he unequivocally preferred to promotion in rank or to "making a career." Here, in this post, he found a broad field for his imagination . . . here he was required to probe and analyze, with exact scientific discipline, the task before him; above all, here he found himself as the commander heading a military unit comprised of the finest of Israel's youth . . .

The IDF operation at Entebbe was a brilliant military victory, reflecting imagination, daring, courage and professional skill of the highest quality anywhere in the world. The success of the *main* objective of the mission—storming the terminal building, wiping out the captors and guards and speedily liberating the hostages so that nearly all of them remained unharmed—this success must be credited in decisive measure to the commander of the force who planned, prepared and rehearsed the breakthrough—that is, to the credit of Yoni. Perhaps it may be said paradoxically that precisely the success of the operation after Yoni himself was hit and did not live to see its extraordinary conclusion testifies, more than anything else, to the extent to which he prepared the force for its mission, to its precise and meticulous execution, so that it could be completed flawlessly even without its commander.

It is, of course, difficult to know how Yoni would have continued and what heights he would have reached in whatever course he would have followed—military or academic. But whatever that course might have been, we have all lost one of the most wonderful, promising and outstanding young men of Israel.

Eulogy for Lt. Col. Jonathan Netanyahu, Delivered by Shimon Peres, Israel's Defense Minister

July 6, 1976

O PERATION ENTEBBE IS UNIQUE IN military history. It proved that Israel is capable of maintaining not only defensible frontiers but also a defensibly erect stature. Against a peak of terror, which was assisted by the army and president of Uganda, at a distance of over four thousand kilometers from home, in one short hour, the posture of the entire Jewish people—in fact, the posture of free and responsible men all over the world—was straightened.

This operation necessitated the taking of an enormous risk, but a risk that seemed to be more justifiable than the other one that was involved —the risk of surrender to terrorists and blackmailers, the risk that is inherent in submission and capitulation.

The most difficult moment of this night of heroism occurred when the bitter news arrived that a bullet had torn the young heart of one of the finest sons of Israel, one of the most courageous warriors of Israel, one of the most promising among the commanders of the Israel Defense Force —the magnificent Jonathan Netanyahu.

I saw him several nights earlier, when he stood at the head of his men somewhere in the country, his entire being taut in preparation for another possible battle. He stood there with his characteristic calm, the natural commander in the field.

When this handsome man assumed the leadership of his unit, we already regarded him as an unusually gifted commander, growing and rising to the highest ranks of a unit that worked tirelessly and incessantly to bring deliverance to his people.

What burdens did we not place on the shoulders of Jonathan and his comrades? The most difficult tasks of the Israel Defense Force, the most audacious of its operations. Missions far from home and close to the enemy, the darkness of the night, and the solitude of the warrior, the grappling with the unknown, and the hazards that recur in peace as in war.

There are times when the fate of an entire people rests on a handful of fighters and volunteers. They must secure the uprightness of our world in one short hour. In such moments, they have no one to ask, no one to turn to. The commanders on the spot determine the fate of the battle.

The essential goal of the Entebbe Operation was to rescue by the force of Israel, by an Israeli force, the passengers the Arabs and Germans had marked down as ultimate hostages simply because they were Israelis.

Yoni was the commander of the force to whom the task of rescue and salvation was entrusted.

It was not by chance that he was chosen for this mission. He had already been known as a daring and relentless liberator. In the document that accompanied the Medal of Heroism, which was conferred on him (after the Yom Kippur War), it was stated:

"When a senior officer was wounded at Tel Shams, Major Jonathan Netanyahu volunteered to head the rescue squad, after a previous rescue attempt had failed, and he succeeded in this task. By his bravery, the swiftness of his actions and insistence in carrying out the mission, he served as an inspiring model to his men."

Jonathan was an exemplary commander. With the boldness of his spirit he overcame his enemies, with his wisdom he won the hearts of his comrades. Danger did not deter him, and triumphs did not swell his heart. Of himself he demanded much, while to the army he gave the sharpness of his intellect, his competence of action and his skill in combat.

In the university he studied philosophy. In the army he taught self-sacrifice. To his soldiers he gave his human warmth, and in battle he imbued them with coolness of judgment.

This young man was among those who commanded an operation that was flawless. But to our deep sorrow this operation entailed a sacrifice of incomparable pain—the first among the storming party, the first to fall. And by virtue of the few, the many were saved, and by virtue of the one who fell, a stature bent under a heavy burden rose again to its full height.

And of him, of them, one may say in the words of David:

> "They were swifter than eagles,
> they were stronger than lions . . .
> O Jonathan, thou wast slain in thine high places.
> I am distressed for thee, my brother Jonathan . . .
> Very pleasant hast thou been unto me,
> thy love to me was wonderful . . . "

The distance in space between Entebbe and Jerusalem has of a sudden shortened the distance in time between Jonathan the son of Saul and Jonathan the son of Benzion.

The same heroism in the man. The same lamentation in the heart of the people.

Index

INDEX

4: 3/99
7: 4/05